WAN Technologies
CCNA 4 Companion Guide

Allan Reid

Cisco Press

800 East 96th Street

Indianapolis, Indiana 46240 USA

WAN Technologies CCNA 4 Companion Guide

Allan Reid

Copyright© 2007 Cisco Systems, Inc.

Published by:
Cisco Press
800 East 96th Street
Indianapolis, IN 46240 USA

Printed in the United States of America 1 2 3 4 5 6 7 8 9 0

First Printing August 2006

Library of Congress Cataloging-in-Publication Number: 2005934968

ISBN: 1-58713-172-2

Trademark Acknowledgments

All terms mentioned in this book that are known to be trademarks or service marks have been appropriately capitalized. Cisco Press or Cisco Systems, Inc. cannot attest to the accuracy of this information. Use of a term in this book should not be regarded as affecting the validity of any trademark or service mark.

Warning and Disclaimer

This book is designed to provide information about CCNA 4: WAN Technologies of the Cisco Networking Academy Program CCNA curriculum. Every effort has been made to make this book as complete and accurate as possible, but no warranty or fitness is implied.

The information is provided on an "as is" basis. The author, Cisco Press, and Cisco Systems, Inc., shall have neither liability nor responsibility to any person or entity with respect to any loss or damages arising from the information contained in this book or from the use of the discs or programs that may accompany it.

The opinions expressed in this book belong to the author and are not necessarily those of Cisco Systems, Inc.

This book is part of the Cisco Networking Academy® Program series from Cisco Press. The products in this series support and complement the Cisco Networking Academy Program curriculum. If you are using this book outside the Networking Academy program, then you are not preparing with a Cisco trained and authorized Networking Academy provider.

For information on the Cisco Networking Academy Program or to locate a Networking Academy, please visit www.cisco.com/edu.

Publisher
Paul Boger

Cisco Representative
Anthony Wolfenden

Cisco Press Program Manager
Jeff Brady

Executive Editor
Mary Beth Ray

Managing Editor
Patrick Kanouse

Senior Development Editor
Christopher Cleveland

Senior Project Editor
San Dee Phillips

Copy Editor
Gayle Johnson

Technical Editors
Mark Newcomb
Robert Rummel

Book and Cover Designer
Louisa Adair

Composition
Mark Shirar

Indexer
Tim Wright

Feedback Information

At Cisco Press, our goal is to create in-depth technical books of the highest quality and value. Each book is crafted with care and precision, undergoing rigorous development that involves the unique expertise of members of the professional technical community.

Reader feedback is a natural continuation of this process. If you have any comments about how we could improve the quality of this book, or otherwise alter it to better suit your needs, you can contact us through e-mail at feedback@ciscopress.com. Please be sure to include the book title and ISBN in your message.

We greatly appreciate your assistance.

Corporate and Government Sales

Cisco Press offers excellent discounts on this book when ordered in quantity for bulk purchases or special sales. For more information, please contact:

U.S. Corporate and Government Sales 1-800-382-3419 corpsales@pearsontechgroup.com

For sales outside of the U.S. please contact: International Sales international@pearsoned.com

CISCO SYSTEMS

Corporate Headquarters
Cisco Systems, Inc.
170 West Tasman Drive
San Jose, CA 95134-1706
USA
www.cisco.com
Tel: 408 526-4000
800 553-NETS (6387)
Fax: 408 526-4100

European Headquarters
Cisco Systems International BV
Haarlerbergpark
Haarlerbergweg 13-19
1101 CH Amsterdam
The Netherlands
www-europe.cisco.com
Tel: 31 0 20 357 1000
Fax: 31 0 20 357 1100

Americas Headquarters
Cisco Systems, Inc.
170 West Tasman Drive
San Jose, CA 95134-1706
USA
www.cisco.com
Tel: 408 526-7660
Fax: 408 527-0883

Asia Pacific Headquarters
Cisco Systems, Inc.
Capital Tower
168 Robinson Road
#22-01 to #29-01
Singapore 068912
www.cisco.com
Tel: +65 6317 7777
Fax: +65 6317 7799

Cisco Systems has more than 200 offices in the following countries and regions. Addresses, phone numbers, and fax numbers are listed on the
Cisco.com Web site at www.cisco.com/go/offices.

Argentina • Australia • Austria • Belgium • Brazil • Bulgaria • Canada • Chile • China PRC • Colombia • Costa Rica • Croatia • Czech Republic
Denmark • Dubai, UAE • Finland • France • Germany • Greece • Hong Kong SAR • Hungary • India • Indonesia • Ireland • Israel • Italy
Japan • Korea • Luxembourg • Malaysia • Mexico • The Netherlands • New Zealand • Norway • Peru • Philippines • Poland • Portugal
Puerto Rico • Romania • Russia • Saudi Arabia • Scotland • Singapore • Slovakia • Slovenia • South Africa • Spain • Sweden
Switzerland • Taiwan • Thailand • Turkey • Ukraine • United Kingdom • United States • Venezuela • Vietnam • Zimbabwe

About the Author

Allan Reid is the Cisco Academy Main Contact and Curriculum Lead for the Centennial College CATC in Toronto, Ontario, Canada. He has taught cabling, routing and switching, remote access, troubleshooting, wireless networking, and IT essentials to instructors from universities, colleges, and high schools throughout Canada. He has been working in the IT industry for more than 20 years and is currently a principal in a company specializing in network design, management, and security. He is a professor and program supervisor at Centennial College, teaching students in various areas of networking and IT. He is responsible for the college's CE offerings in IT. In addition, he works as a contractor for Cisco Systems, working on curriculum development and the creation of assessment questions for the Cisco Networking Academy Program courses. He has also served as a technical reviewer for other Cisco Press publications.

About the Technical Reviewers

Mark Newcomb, CCNP, CCDP, is a retired network security engineer. He has more than 20 years of experience in the networking industry, focusing on the financial and medical industries. He is a frequent contributor to and reviewer for Cisco Press books.

Robert Rummel, CCIE No. 9012, is a systems engineer for Cisco Systems on the Federal Navy-Marine team. He has more than 16 years of networking and telecommunications experience. He has a diverse background, ranging from serving eight active-duty years in the Navy to operating a satellite teleport. He currently resides in San Diego with his wife, Vivian, and children, Brittany and Jordan.

Dedication

This book is dedicated to my children: Andrew, Philip, Amanda, Christopher, and Shaun. You are my inspiration, and you make it all worthwhile.

Acknowledgments

I would like to thank the entire "e-wing" team for providing me with the motivation to complete this work. You set the standard high, and I hope I have lived up to it and continue to do so.

Special thanks go to the Cisco Press team—especially Mary Beth Ray and Christopher Cleveland, whose guidance and patience made this a very enlightening and rewarding experience.

Last, but definitely not least, I would like to express my appreciation to the technical editors of this book, Mark Newcomb and Robert Rummel, for their excellent comments and suggestions. Your contributions have definitely made this book much better than I could have created alone.

Contents at a Glance

Contents

Icons Used in This Book

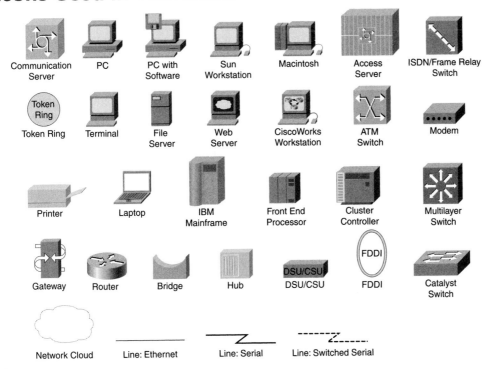

Command Syntax Conventions

The conventions used to present command syntax in this book are the same conventions used in the IOS Command Reference. The Command Reference describes these conventions as follows:

- **Bold** indicates commands and keywords that are entered literally as shown. In actual configuration examples and output (not general command syntax), bold indicates commands that the user inputs manually (such as a **show** command).

- *Italic* indicates an argument for which you supply an actual value.

- Vertical bars (|) separate alternative, mutually exclusive elements.

- Square brackets ([ ]) indicate an optional element.

- Braces ({ }) indicate a required choice.

- Braces within brackets ([{ }]) indicate a required choice within an optional element.

Introduction

The Cisco Networking Academy Program is a comprehensive e-learning program that provides students with Internet technology skills. A Networking Academy delivers web-based content, online assessment, student performance tracking, and hands-on labs to prepare students for industry-standard certifications. The CCNA curriculum includes four courses oriented around the topics on the Cisco Certified Network Associate (CCNA) certification.

This book is the official supplemental textbook to be used with v3.1.1 of the CCNA 4 online curriculum of the Cisco Networking Academy Program. As a textbook, this book provides a ready reference to explain the same networking concepts, technologies, protocols, and devices covered in the online curriculum.

This book goes beyond earlier editions of the Cisco Press *Companion Guides* by providing many alternative explanations and examples as compared with the course. You can use the online curriculum as normal and use this *Companion Guide* to help solidify your understanding of all the topics through the alternative examples.

Goals of This Book

First and foremost, by providing a fresh, complementary perspective on the content, this book is intended to help you learn all the required materials of the fourth course in the Networking Academy CCNA curriculum. As a secondary goal, the text is intended as a mobile replacement for the online curriculum for those who do not always have Internet access. In those cases, you can instead read the appropriate sections of the book, as directed by your instructor, and learn the same material that is covered in the online curriculum. Another secondary goal is to serve as your offline study material to prepare for the CCNA exam.

The Audience for This Book

This book's main audience is anyone taking the fourth CCNA course of the Cisco Networking Academy Program curriculum. Many Academies use this textbook as a required tool in the course, and other Academies recommend the *Companion Guides* as an additional source of study and practice materials.

The secondary audience for this book includes people taking CCNA-related classes from professional training organizations, as well as anyone wanting to read and learn about the basics of computer networking.

Book Features

All the features of this book are either new or improved to facilitate your full understanding of the material covered in the course. The educational features focus on supporting topic coverage, readability, and practice of the course material.

Topic Coverage

The following features give you a thorough overview of the topics covered in each chapter so that you can make constructive use of your study time:

- **Objectives**—The objectives at the beginning of each chapter list the *core* concepts covered in the chapter. The objectives match the objectives stated in the corresponding modules in the online curriculum; however, the question format in the *Companion Guide* encourages you to think about finding the answers as you read the chapter content.

- *New* **Additional Topics of Interest**—Chapter 6 contains topics that cover more details about previous topics or related topics that are less important to the chapter's primary focus. The list at the beginning of the chapter lets you know that additional coverage can be found in the "Additional Topics of Interest" section.

- **Notes, Tips, Cautions, and Warnings** are short sidebars listed in the margins.

- **Chapter Summaries**—At the end of each chapter is a summary of the concepts covered in the chapter. It provides a synopsis of the chapter and serves as a study aid.

Readability

The material has been completely rewritten in a more conversational tone, adhering to a consistent, accessible reading level. In addition, the following features have been updated to assist your understanding of the networking vocabulary:

- *New* **Key Terms**—Each chapter begins with a list of key terms, along with the page number on which the term appears. The terms are listed in the order in which they are explained in the chapter. This handy reference allows you to find a term, flip to the appropriate page, and see the term used in context. The Glossary at the end of the book defines all the key terms.

- *New* **Glossary**—This book contains an all-new glossary with more than 320 terms. The Glossary defines not only the key terms from the chapters but also terms you may find helpful in working toward your CCNA certification.

Practice

Practice makes perfect. This new *Companion Guide* offers you ample opportunities to put what you've learned into practice. You will find the following features valuable and effective in reinforcing the instruction you are receiving:

- *New* **Check Your Understanding Questions and Answer Key**—Updated review questions are presented at the end of each chapter as a self-assessment tool. These questions match the style of questions that you see on the online course assessments. Appendix A, "Answers to Check Your Understanding and Challenge Questions and Activities," provides an answer key for all the questions and includes an explanation of each answer.

- *New* **Challenge Questions**—Additional, more challenging, review questions are presented at the end of the chapters. These questions are purposefully designed to be similar to the more complex styles of questions you might expect to see on the CCNA exam. Appendix A provides the answers.

- **Lab References**—The book uses the lab icon to note good places for you to stop and perform the related labs from the online curriculum. The supplementary book *WAN Technologies CCNA 4 Labs and Study Guide* by Cisco Press contains all the labs from the curriculum plus additional challenge labs and study guide material.

How This Book Is Organized

The book covers the major topics in the same sequence as the online curriculum for the CCNA 4 Cisco Networking Academy Program course. The online curriculum has six modules for CCNA 4, so this book has six chapters with the same numbers and similar names as the online course modules.

To make it easier for you to use this book as a companion to the course, in each chapter, the major headings match the major sections of the online course modules.

However, this *Companion Guide* presents many topics in slightly different ways than the online curriculum. As a result, you get more detailed explanations, and different sequences of individual topics, to aid your learning process. This new design, based on research into the needs of the Cisco Networking Academies, should help you lock in your understanding of all the topics in the course.

If you're reading this book without being in the CCNA 4 class, or if you're just using this book for self-study, the sequence of topics in each chapter provides a logical sequence for learning the material presented.

Chapter Descriptions

The book has six chapters and an appendix. The chapters match the six modules of the online curriculum in number and topics covered:

- **Chapter 1, "Scaling IP Addresses,"** introduces methods currently deployed to help conserve the available IPv4 address space. Private addresses are reviewed, and the concepts of NAT/PAT and DHCP are introduced.

- **Chapter 2, "WAN Technologies Overview,"** takes a survey approach to the technologies currently deployed on a WAN. This chapter introduces much of the terminology and general concepts encountered in a wide-area network. It lays the groundwork to help you understand some of the more advanced concepts presented in later chapters.

- **Chapter 3, "PPP,"** examines Point-to-Point Protocol and its use and configuration. This standards-based protocol provides a mechanism to interconnect equipment from multiple vendors, as well as many advanced features, such as link-quality determination, authentication, compression, and multilink.

- **Chapter 4, "ISDN and DDR,"** discusses the benefits and applications of Integrated Services Digital Network. It examines both legacy applications and the application of dialer profiles.

- **Chapter 5, "Frame Relay,"** describes the application and configuration of Frame Relay technology in point-to-point and multipoint modes. In addition, it examines the methods Frame Relay uses to deal with network congestion and bandwidth constraints.

- **Chapter 6, "Introduction to Network Administration,"** introduces network administration and management. It examines the roles of servers and clients, as well as the basic purpose and functionality of operating systems and network operating systems. Methods used to monitor and control network resources are discussed, with emphasis on CMIP and SNMP.

- **Appendix A, "Answers to Check Your Understanding and Challenge Questions,"** provides the answers to the Check Your Understanding questions that you find at the end of each chapter. It also includes answers to the Challenge Questions and Activities.

- The **Glossary** lists all the key terms that appear throughout this book.

About the CD-ROM

The CD-ROM included with this book provides many useful tools:

- **Interactive Media Activities**—The interactive media activities from the online course demonstrate visually some of the topics in the course. These tools can be particularly useful when your Academy does not have the same cables or hardware, or when you use this book for self-study.

- **Packet Tracer v3.2**—Included on the CD-ROM is the full version of Packet Tracer v3.2. Configuration files can be found at http://www.ciscopress.com/title/1587131722. These files cover v3.2 and will cover any subsequent releases of Packet Tracer. You can load the configuration and watch the flow of packets, or you can configure options to alter the type and frequency of packet flow.

About the Cisco Press Website for This Book

Cisco Press provides additional content that you can access by registering your book at the ciscopress.com website. Becoming a member and registering is free, and you then gain access to exclusive deals on other resources from Cisco Press.

To register this book, go to http://www.ciscopress.com/bookstore/register.asp and enter this book's ISBN, located on the back cover. You're then prompted to log in or join ciscopress.com to continue registration.

After you register your book, a link to the supplemental content is listed on your My Registered Books page.

About the CCNA Exam

The computing world has many different certifications available. Some of these certifications are sponsored by vendors, and others by consortiums of different vendors. Regardless of the sponsor of the certifications, most IT professionals today recognize the need to become certified to prove their skills, prepare for new job searches, and learn new skills while at their existing job.

Over the years, the Cisco certification program has had a tremendous amount of success. The CCNA certification has become the most popular networking certification. Also, the CCIE certification has won numerous awards as the most prestigious certification in the computing industry. Cisco has more than 70 percent of the market share in the enterprise router and switch marketplace. Having Cisco-specific certifications on your resume is a great way to increase your chances of landing a new job, getting a promotion, or looking more qualified when representing your company on a consulting job.

How to Obtain Your CCNA Certification

Cisco Systems requires that you take one of two paths to get your CCNA certification. You can take a single comprehensive exam, or you can take two exams in which each exam covers a subset of the CCNA exam topics. Table I-1 lists these exams.

Table I-1 CCNA Exam Names and Numbers

Name	Exam	Description
INTRO exam	640-821	Maps to Cisco Networking Academy Program CCNA 1 and 2
ICND exam	640-811	Maps to Cisco Networking Academy Program CCNA 3 and 4
CCNA exam	640-801	Covers all four courses

So, you could take the first two courses, do some extra preparation for the exam, and take the INTRO exam. Then, you could take courses 3 and 4, prepare for the ICND exam, and break up your study. Alternatively, you could take the CCNA exam at the end of all four courses.

How to Prepare to Pass the CCNA Exam(s)

The Cisco Networking Academy Program CCNA curriculum helps prepare you for CCNA certification by covering a superset of the topics on the CCNA exam. The four courses of the online curriculum, and the corresponding Cisco Press *Companion Guides*, cover many more introductory topics than the topics required for CCNA. The reason is that the curriculum is intended as a very first course in computing, not just networking. So, if you successfully complete all four courses in the CCNA curriculum, you will learn the topics covered on the CCNA exam.

However, taking the CCNA curriculum does not mean that you will automatically pass the CCNA exam. In fact, Cisco purposefully attempts to make the CCNA exam questions prove that you know the material well by making you apply the concepts. The CCNA exam questions tend to be more involved than the Cisco Networking Academy Program CCNA assessment questions. (For a deeper perspective on this point, refer to http://www.ciscopress.com/articles/article.asp?p=393075.) So, if you know all the concepts from the CCNA curriculum and *Companion Guides*, you have most of the factual knowledge you need for the exam. However, the exam requires that you apply that knowledge to different scenarios. So, many CCNA students need to study further to pass the exam(s).

Many resources exist to help you in your exam preparation. Some of these resources are books from Cisco Press, and some are other online resources. The following list details some of the key tools:

- *CCNA Certification Library (CCNA Self-Study, Exam 640-801)* **by Wendell Odom**— This book covers the CCNA materials in more depth, with a large (more than 300) question bank of exam-realistic questions and many other tools to help in your study.

- *Cisco CCNA Network Simulator (CCNA Self-Study, 640-801)* **by Boson Software, Inc.**—This software tool is a router/switch/network simulator that you can use to practice hands-on skills on Cisco routers and switches without having to use a real lab.

- **Cisco CCNA Prep Center (http://www.cisco.com/go/prepcenter)**—This is a free online resource from Cisco Systems. (You need a Cisco.com account to access this site, but registration is free.) It has discussion boards, interviews with experts, sample questions, and other resources to aid in your CCNA exam preparation.

What's on the CCNA Exams

As with any test, everyone wants to know what's on the exam. Thankfully, Cisco Systems publishes a list of exam topics for each exam to give candidates a better idea of what's on the exam. Unfortunately, those exam topics do not provide as much detail as most people want to see. However, the exam topics are a good starting point. To see the exam topics for the CCNA exams, follow these steps:

Step 1. Go to http://www.cisco.com/go/ccna.

Step 2. Click the text for the exam about which you want more information.

Step 3. In the next window, click the **Exam Topics** link.

Beyond that, the CCNA curriculum covers a superset of the CCNA exam topics. For example, the CCNA 4 curriculum covers managing network resources. None of the CCNA exam topics covers this material to the same extent. However, the CCNA exams do cover the vast majority of the topics in the CCNA *Companion Guides*.

Some topics are certainly more important than others for the exams—topics that many people already know are more important. Network Address Translation and DHCP are extremely important topics because of their widespread usage. Frame Relay is still widely deployed around the world. Even though ISDN is losing ground to some of the newer technologies such as DSL and cable, it still has a large user base. Any hands-on skills covered in the curriculum are also important topics to know about.

Ironically, some of the topics that seem too basic to be on the exam just happen to be required for you to understand the more advanced topics. So, other than some of the extra details in the curriculum, you might see most of the rest of the topics in the curriculum and *Companion Guides* on the CCNA exam(s).

Because a typical CCNA exam has only 45 to 55 questions, your individual exam cannot possibly cover all the topics in the CCNA curriculum. The comments listed here refer to the possible topics for the exams.

CHAPTER 1

Scaling IP Addresses

Objectives

Upon completion of this chapter, you should be able to answer the following questions:

- What methods are currently available to overcome the depletion of IPv4 address space?

- How can RFC 1918 address space be used to help conserve IP addresses?

- What types of NAT are currently available, and in which situations should they be deployed?

- What are the relative advantages of each type of NAT?

- What commands are used to configure, verify, and troubleshoot NAT operation?

- What is DHCP, and how does it differ from its predecessor, BOOTP?

- What commands are used to configure, verify, and troubleshoot DHCP operation?

- What is a helper address, and why is it required?

Key Terms

This chapter uses the following key terms. You can find the definitions in the glossary at the end of the book.

continues

continued

When the current *IPv4* addressing scheme was developed, nobody anticipated the explosive growth that networking would undergo and the impact that this would have on the available IP address space. IPv4 was first standardized in 1981 by *ARPANET*. The decision to use 32-bit addresses and to assign them in large blocks resulted in a rapidly diminishing supply of available addresses. In addition, the recent incorporation of IP addresses into many aspects of everyday life, such as cell phones, has greatly contributed to this address space exhaustion.

Original expectations were that the IPv4 address space would be completely exhausted during the 1990s. This prompted the development of many different techniques to help alleviate the problem. The most ambitious endeavor to date has been the development of an entirely new addressing scheme known as *IPv6*. The development of IPv6 started in 1992. It increased the number of bits used to assign an address from the 32 used by IPv4 to 128. This change greatly increased the number of addresses available for allocation. The downside of IPv6 is that it requires additional equipment and configurations to fully implement. To date it has not been widely deployed.

Recent announcements by the U.S. government will compel all U.S. federal agencies to upgrade their network backbones by 2008. With these agencies forced to upgrade, government contractors, hardware and software vendors, and service providers will need to make certain that their offerings are also updated. This is expected to be the catalyst that will spark adoption of IPv6 in the commercial world.

The slow acceptance of IPv6 is partly due to the development of techniques to conserve the current IPv4 address space that have reduced the necessity for a rapid migration to the new system. One technique that has contributed greatly to the conservation of IPv4 addresses is the change from the *classful* system of addressing to the *classless* system. The wasteful assignment of equal-sized subnets encountered in the classful system is eliminated in the classless system, where the assignment of addresses can be more closely structured to the requirements of the individual network segment. This is accomplished through the use of a *Variable-Length Subnet Mask (VLSM)*, which essentially allows a subnet to be subnetted even further. The migration to the classless system has allowed many large pools of addresses to be returned for reallocation and has decreased the urgency of migrating to IPv6.

Other techniques for address conservation have also been developed:

- RFC 1918 address space
- Network Address Translation (NAT)
- Dynamic Host Configuration Protocol (DHCP)

These techniques can be deployed either independently or in combination and are discussed in this chapter.

Scaling Networks with NAT and PAT

In most current network installations, Network Address Translation (NAT) is deployed along with private address space to allow the network administrator to efficiently and securely manage the corporate IP resources. This combination not only offers flexibility in the distribution of internal address space, but also contributes to the preservation of the current IPv4 address space.

Private Address Space (RFC 1918)

IETF RFC 1918 sets aside three blocks of IP addresses that are reserved for private use only and will not be assigned to any one individual or organization. Table 1-1 summarizes the RFC 1918 address space. Because these address blocks will remain unregistered, any organization is free to use them on its internal networks. Properly configured routers will not advertise this address space to the Internet, and packets that contain these addresses will be dropped as soon as they hit the Internet. The use of this address space on an organization's internal network eliminates the waste and expense of maintaining large pools of routable addresses and allows the network administrator to design an IP addressing scheme that reflects the organization's structure.

Table 1-1   RFC 1918 Address Space

Class	Range	CIDR Notation
A	10.0.0.0 to 10.255.255.255	10.0.0.0/8
B	172.16.0.0 to 172.31.255.255	172.16.0.0/12
C	192.168.0.0 to 192.168.255.255	192.168.0.0/16

Network Address Translation (NAT)

Deploying RFC 1918 addresses within an organization presents an interesting challenge. Because these addresses cannot be routed on the Internet, any packets that leave the internal network must have their source address replaced by one that is routable. Replies addressed to this routable address must then have the destination address translated back into the original private address before being placed on the internal network. This process of rewriting the Layer 3 information as a packet moves between the internal and external networks is known as *Network Address Translation (NAT)*. NAT, as discussed in IETF RFC 1631, allows an organization to present itself to the Internet with fewer IP addresses than there are nodes on the internal network. NAT usually maps an unregistered address used on an internal network to a registered address for use on the Internet, but it can also map between networks deploying routable or nonroutable addresses for certain applications. This chapter covers three forms of NAT:

- Static NAT

- Dynamic NAT

- Overloaded NAT or Port Address Translation (PAT)

NAT Terminology

Understanding the process of NAT and being able to troubleshoot it as issues arise requires a detailed understanding of the terminology used. NAT divides the network into two areas: inside and outside. The *inside network* is usually an organization's internal LAN, and the *outside network* is usually the Internet, although it could be any other network. *Local addresses* refer to a node on the network as seen by another node on the same network. *Global addresses* are how a node on one network is seen by a node on another network. For example, how a machine on the LAN appears to another machine on the same LAN is an *inside local address*, whereas that same machine would be seen by the *inside global address* from the outside world. A *translation* is the rewriting of information in the packet header from one IP address to another as the packet passes between the internal and external networks. The IOS maintains a *translation table* in RAM that tracks current translations. NAT simply changes the source IP address or port numbers on outbound traffic and the destination IP address or port number on inbound traffic. Figure 1-1 shows the inside local address being replaced with the inside global address on packets leaving the internal network. Then the inside global address is translated back to the inside local address in the replies before they are placed on the internal network.

Figure 1-1   NAT Translation

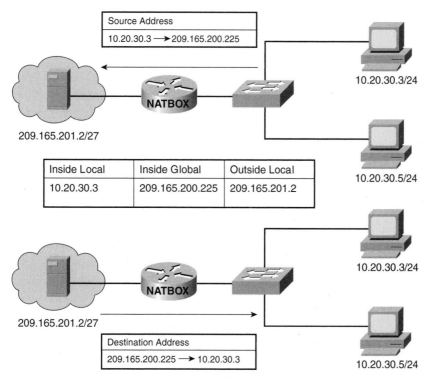

Understanding and Configuring Static NAT

One form of NAT that is commonly implemented is known as *static NAT*. In this scenario, the network administrator manually configures a predefined one-to-one mapping of addresses between the internal and external networks. Static NAT has no conservation of IP address space, because each internal IP address must be mapped to a unique, routable external address. This mapping of addresses, illustrated in Figure 1-2, ensures that no packets are dropped due to lack of available address space. It also minimizes the delay introduced by building a dynamic translation.

Figure 1-2   Static NAT

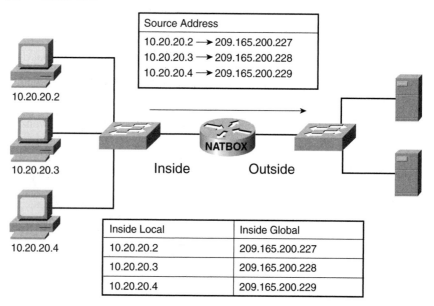

Source Address
10.20.20.2 → 209.165.200.227
10.20.20.3 → 209.165.200.228
10.20.20.4 → 209.165.200.229

Inside Local	Inside Global
10.20.20.2	209.165.200.227
10.20.20.3	209.165.200.228
10.20.20.4	209.165.200.229

Static NAT is often deployed together with dynamic NAT, which is discussed in the next section. Static NAT is usually deployed to allow access to internal servers from the outside world. Servers that must be accessed from the outside are assigned an IP address consistent with that deployed on the internal network. Then a *static map* is created that maps a routable IP address to the internal address. This allows the server to be accessed using the inside local address from within the organization and also from outside the LAN using the inside global address. If the location of the internal server is changed, a new static map is created, making the change transparent to external users. In all forms of NAT, the hiding of internal address space from the external world provides a limited level of security in that no direct access to the internal network from the outside world is possible.

To configure static NAT, the inside and outside interfaces must be identified. Usually the
Ethernet or LAN port is the *inside interface* and the serial or WAN port is the *outside interface*.
This must be clearly stated, because all translations are done in the specified direction only.
Figure 1-3 shows a typical assignment of inside and outside interfaces, and Example 1-1
provides the corresponding configuration. Inside and outside interfaces are defined using the
ip nat inside and **ip nat outside** commands at the appropriate interface configuration prompt.

Figure 1-3   Multiple Inside Interfaces with NAT

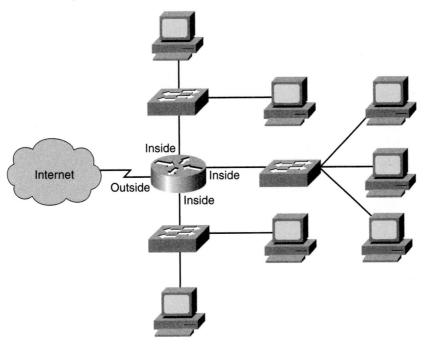

Example 1-1   Configuring Inside and Outside Interfaces

```
interface FastEthernet0
 ip address 10.20.20.1 255.255.255.0
 ip nat inside
 speed auto
!
interface FastEthernet1
 ip address 10.20.30.1 255.255.255.0
 ip nat inside
 speed auto
!
interface FastEthernet2
 ip address 10.20.40.1 255.255.255.0
 ip nat inside
 speed auto
!
interface Serial0
 ip address 209.165.200.226 255.255.255.224
 ip nat outside
 no fair-queue
!
```

As soon as the inside and outside interfaces are established, the direction of translation and the actual translation are defined. The translation is an inside local address to an inside global address, as shown in the following syntax:

```
Router(config)#ip nat inside source static inside_local inside_global
```

For example, if you wanted to create three static translations to internal servers, as illustrated in Figure 1-2, you would issue the following commands:

```
Toronto(config)#ip nat inside source static 10.20.20.2 209.165.200.227
Toronto(config)#ip nat inside source static 10.20.20.3 209.165.200.228
Toronto(config)#ip nat inside source static 10.20.20.4 209.165.200.229
```

The NAT table in Example 1-2 clearly shows the mapping of the inside local address to the inside global address.

Example 1-2   Viewing the NAT Translation Table

```
Toronto#show ip nat translation
Pro Inside global      Inside local      Outside local      Outside global
-- 209.165.200.227     10.20.20.2         --                 --
-- 209.165.200.228     10.20.20.3         --                 --
-- 209.165.200.229     10.20.20.4         --                 --
```

Depending on the deployment scenario, it may be desirable to NAT the inside source, outside source, or inside destination addresses. This may be accomplished by modifying the commands shown in Table 1-2.

Table 1-2 Selection of Address to NAT

Command	Description
ip nat inside source	Enables NAT of the inside source addresses
ip nat outside source	Enables NAT of the outside source addresses
ip nat inside destination	Enables NAT of the inside destination addresses

 Lab 1-3   Configuring Static NAT Addresses (1.4.1c)

In this lab, you configure a router to use NAT to convert internal IP addresses, typically private addresses, into outside public addresses. You configure static mapping to allow outside access to an internal host.

Understanding and Configuring Dynamic NAT

Dynamic NAT eliminates the requirement for equal numbers of internal and external addresses by creating a pool of IP addresses that can be used for translation. Dynamic NAT does not allow for the assignment of a predefined address between the internal and external networks. Therefore, it is of little use for mapping internal servers to the outside world. This is why it is often deployed together with static NAT. Dynamic NAT does not guarantee that a translation will be successful if the pool of addresses is exhausted. Therefore, you must take care to provide an address pool of sufficient size to handle all possible simultaneous translations.

The most common use of dynamic NAT is to provide Internet connectivity to the employees in an organization that deploys RFC 1918 address space on the internal network. Because not all employees will require Internet access simultaneously, a pool of registered addresses smaller than the number of internal addresses can be configured. This reduces the expense of maintaining registered addresses for all employees, as would be required in a purely static NAT deployment.

Addresses are translated as packets leave the internal network. Translations are active only for the duration of the conversation or a configurable time period, whichever occurs first, as illustrated in Figure 1-4. After the reply is received, the translation is dissolved, and the address is returned to the NAT pool for reuse. The router maintains a record of active translations in the form of a translation table. Each *active translation* consumes approximately 160 bytes of DRAM. This translates to approximately 1.6 MB of DRAM for 10,000 active translations. Modern routers have more than enough memory to support thousands of NAT translations.

Figure 1-4   Dynamic NAT Translation

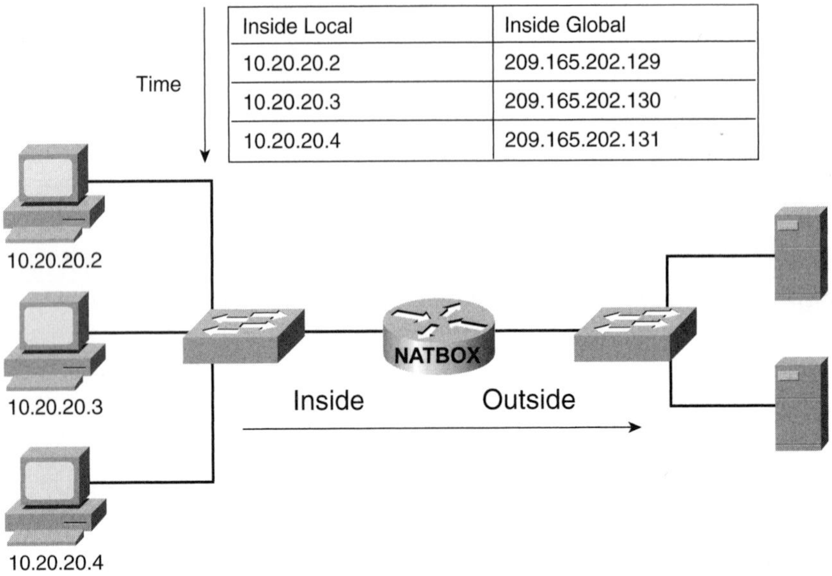

To create the pool of addresses used in dynamic NAT, use the following global configuration command:

```
ip nat pool name start-ip-address end-ip-address {netmask netmask | prefix-length
   prefix-length} {type rotary}
```

Giving the *NAT pool* a name that describes the location or task makes troubleshooting easier if multiple pools are to be configured.

In the example pictured in Figure 1-4, if you wanted to use the 209.165.202.129/27 subnet as a pool of addresses for dynamic NAT on the Toronto router, you would issue the following command:

```
Toronto(config)#ip nat pool border 209.165.202.129 209.165.202.158 netmask
   255.255.255.224
```

It is neither necessary nor advisable to translate all traffic found on the network, because this would waste valuable router resources. Traffic that should be translated is termed *interesting traffic* and is selected with the aid of an *access control list (ACL)*. NAT does not translate traffic not considered interesting as defined by the ACL.

If you wanted to allow only traffic originating on the 10.20.20.0/24 subnet of the Toronto network, you could use the following ACL to select the interesting traffic:

```
Toronto(config)#access-list 7 permit 10.20.20.0 0.0.0.255
```

The ACL is then tied to the NAT pool. The direction of translation is defined by the following global configuration command:

```
ip nat inside source {list {access-list-number | name} pool name [overload] |
    static local-ip-address global-ip-address]
```

Continuing with our example, you would tie the ACL to the NAT pool using the following command:

```
Toronto(config)#ip nat inside source list 7 pool border
```

This command checks the source address on packets entering an interface that has been defined as an inside interface. If the source address matches the specified ACL, the traffic is identified as interesting, and the address is translated to an address found in the NAT pool before the traffic is moved out through the outside interface. If the source address does not match the ACL, the packet is not translated. A record of the translation is maintained in the NAT table. The router uses it to translate the IP address of replies before they are placed on the internal network.

> **Note**
>
> It is also possible to specify **outside** or the destination in the command to have complete control over the direction of translation. Although it's beyond the scope of this book, this material will be discussed in future CCNP-level courses.

Lab 1-1   Configuring NAT (1.1.4a)

In this lab, you configure a router to use NAT to convert internal IP addresses into outside public addresses.

Understanding and Configuring Overloaded NAT

A modified form of dynamic NAT is *overloaded NAT*, which is also known as *Port Address Translation (PAT)*. With overloaded NAT, many addresses can be mapped to a single IP address using port numbers. This further reduces the number of addresses required by an organization to provide Internet connectivity to its users. Most large organizations now deploy PAT with a pool of IP addresses.

PAT divides the available ports per global IP address into three ranges of 0–511, 512–1023, and 1024–65535. When a translation is requested, PAT tries to preserve the *source port* on the global IP address. If the source port is unavailable, PAT begins searching from the beginning of the particular port range to find the first available port. If no ports are available in the selected range, the packet is dropped.

PAT can also be supplied with a pool of addresses to use. If PAT is requested and a pool of IP addresses has been configured, PAT first attempts to maintain the original source port on the first available global IP address. If this port is unavailable, PAT starts searching from the beginning of the relevant port range for an available port. If no ports are available in the relevant port range, PAT checks the second global IP address, trying to maintain the original source port. If the original port is unavailable, PAT again searches from the beginning of the relevant port range for an available port. This process is repeated until a new source port-IP address can be assigned or until PAT runs out of IP addresses to search. If PAT cannot find an available IP address-source port, it drops the packet. Figure 1-5 shows how PAT works.

Figure 1-5   Overloaded NAT or PAT

Inside Local	Inside Global
10.20.20.2:2345	209.165.201.2:2345
10.20.20.3:1765	209.165.201.2:1765
10.20.20.4:2345	209.165.201.2:2816

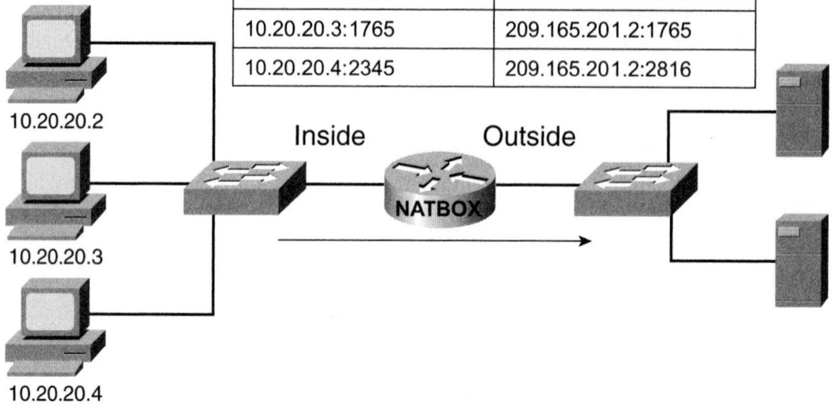

The configuration of PAT is nearly identical to the configuration of dynamic NAT, except that the keyword **overload** must be specified when setting up the translation. This keyword allows NAT to reassign ports on the source address while preserving the original IP address. It is also possible to overload an interface's IP address, commonly the WAN interface, instead of supplying a separate pool of addresses. Because the WAN port of most border routers is configured with an IP address that has been supplied by the ISP, using this address eliminates the requirement of obtaining a new IP address. The problem with this approach is that only one IP address is available, so if many translations must be made, one address may not suffice. To overload either a pool of addresses or the address assigned to an interface, use one of the following global commands:

```
ip nat inside source list acl_list_number pool pool_name overload

ip nat inside source list acl_list_number interface interface_name overload
```

Assume that you want to use the single address 209.165.201.2 to provide connectivity to the Internet. To accomplish this, you would need to define both the inside and outside interfaces, create an ACL to select interesting traffic, create a pool of addresses, and then apply the translation. It is possible to create an address pool that contains only one address by specifying the same address for both the beginning and ending address in the pool. Here are the final two steps:

```
Toronto(config)#ip nat pool border2 209.165.201.2 209.165.201.2 netmask
  255.255.255.224
Toronto(config)#ip nat inside source list 7 pool border2 overload
```

If you decided to overload the IP address associated with the outside interface instead of creating a separate pool, the command would simply be as follows:

```
Toronto(config)#ip nat inside source list 7 interface serial 0 overload
```

Lab 1-2   Configuring PAT (1.1.4b)

In this lab, you configure a router to use PAT to convert internal IP addresses into outside public addresses.

Verifying NAT/PAT Functionality

A good place to start to verify NAT functionality or to troubleshoot a problematic implementation is with the **show ip nat statistics** command. This command provides information such as the number of packets that matched the ACL and were translated versus those that did not match the ACL, the location of the inside and outside interfaces, and the number of currently active translations. Quite often, this points to a problem with either the ACL or the assignment of interfaces. Example 1-3 provides sample output from the **show ip nat statistics** command.

```
Example 1-3    Viewing NAT Statistics
Toronto#show ip nat statistics
Total active translations: 0 (0 static, 0 dynamic; 0 extended)
Outside interfaces:
  Serial 0
Inside interfaces:
  FastEthernet0
Hits: 47  Misses: 3
Expired translations: 50
Dynamic mappings:
-- Inside Source
[Id: 1] access-list 7 pool toronto2 refcount 0
 pool toronto2: netmask 255.255.255.224
      start 209.165.201.2 end 209.165.201.2
      type generic, total addresses 1, allocated 0 (0%), misses 0
```

To view translations that are currently active, use the **show ip nat translations** command. This displays the contents of the translation table, allowing you to determine the correctness of the translations that are occurring. An improperly configured address pool could be handing out addresses outside of the desired range and impacting network accessibility. The addition of the keyword **verbose** to this command provides additional information such as how long the translation has been active. This can help diagnose issues related to network connectivity and improperly configured timeout values. Remember that NAT relies on an ACL to select traffic that is to be translated. By checking to see which packets matched the ACL, you can determine if any problems encountered are with the NAT translation process or merely the selection of interesting traffic by an improperly configured ACL. Example 1-4 provides sample output from the **show ip nat translations** command.

```
Example 1-4     The NAT Translation Table
Toronto#show ip nat translations
Pro Inside global       Inside local       Outside local     Outside global
icmp 209.165.201.2:7972 10.20.20.1:7972    209.165.200.225:7972 209.165.200.225:7972
icmp 209.165.201.2:7973 10.20.20.1:7973    209.165.200.225:7973 209.165.200.225:7973
icmp 209.165.201.2:7974 10.20.20.1:7974    209.165.200.225:7974 209.165.200.225:7974
icmp 209.165.201.2:7975 10.20.20.1:7975    209.165.200.225:7975 209.165.200.225:7975
icmp 209.165.201.2:7976 10.20.20.1:7976    209.165.200.225:7976 209.165.200.225:7976
```

You can configure the length of time a translation remains active and stays in the translation table. Normally the translation is released when a reply is received, at which time the IP address is returned to the NAT pool. If a reply is not received, the entry stays in the table until it is removed by the *timeout value* or is manually removed by the network administrator. By default this timeout is set to 24 hours for TCP and 5 minutes for UDP. During the time that a translation remains in the NAT table, no other translation can use the IP address. If network delays or other issues arise that prevent the NAT process from receiving the reply, it is quite possible to run out of IP addresses that can be used for translations. This prevents users from accessing the Internet. Careful consideration of the timeout value is most important in dynamic NAT, which has a limited number of addresses available. In static NAT the mapping is predetermined, and PAT usually has large numbers of potential translations available.

You can configure a number of different timeout values in global mode to affect how NAT functions. Table 1-3 provides the commands necessary to set these timeout values along with the default values.

Table 1-3   Setting NAT Timeout Values

Command	Default Value
ip nat translation timeout *time*	**24-hours**
ip nat translation tcp-timeout *time*	**24-hours**
ip nat translation udp-timeout *time*	**5-minutes**
ip nat translation finrst-timeout *time*	**60-seconds**
ip nat translation dns-timeout *time*	**60-seconds**

To remove a translation that is currently active, you must clear it from the NAT table. The command used to remove an active translation from the NAT table depends on the type of translation that has occurred:

- **clear ip nat translation *** clears all dynamic NAT translations.

- **clear ip nat translation inside** *global_ip local_ip* {**outside** *local_ip global_ip*} removes a single dynamic translation entry.

- **clear ip nat translation** *protocol* **inside** *global_ip global_port local_ip local_port*
  {**outside** *local_ip local_port global_ip global_port*} removes the extended dynamic entry.

To verify that the correct translations are occurring, use the **debug ip nat** [**detailed**] command. The output from this command, as shown in Example 1-5, provides information detailing the translation of packets as they occur. In this output the source address is specified by an s, and d identifies the destination IP address. An arrow (->) indicates a translation that has occurred.

Example 1-5   Debugging NAT Translations

```
Toronto#debug ip nat
*Mar  1 14:01:01.620: NAT: s=10.20.20.1->209.165.201.2, d=209.165.202.130 [107]
*Mar  1 14:01:01.620: NAT*: s=209.165.202.130, d=209.165.201.2->10.20.20.1 [3926]
*Mar  1 14:01:01.624: NAT: s=10.20.20.1->209.165.201.2, d=209.165.202.130 [108]
*Mar  1 14:01:01.624: NAT*: s=209.165.202.130, d=209.165.201.2->10.20.20.1 [3927]
*Mar  1 14:01:01.628: NAT: s=10.20.20.1->209.165.201.2, d=209.165.202.130 [109]
*Mar  1 14:01:01.628: NAT*: s=209.165.202.130, d=209.165.201.2->10.20.20.1 [3928]
*Mar  1 14:01:01.628: NAT: s=10.20.20.1->209.165.201.2, d=209.165.202.130 [110]
*Mar  1 14:01:01.632: NAT*: s=209.165.202.130, d=209.165.201.2->10.20.20.1 [3929]
*Mar  1 14:01:01.632: NAT: s=10.20.20.1->209.165.201.2, d=209.165.202.130 [111]
*Mar  1 14:01:01.632: NAT*: s=209.165.202.130, d=209.165.201.2->10.20.20.1 [3930]
```

The first packet in any conversation must be *process-switched*, which establishes the translation entry. As soon as an entry exists in cache, any remaining packets in the conversation may take the *fast-switched* path. Packets that have taken the fast-switched path are flagged with an asterisk in the debug output.

NAT has contributed greatly to the conservation of existing address space by allowing the privatization of internal networks. It also allows an organization's internal network configuration to remain unchanged when moving from one service provider to another. Furthermore, it provides limited security by hiding the internal address space from the outside world. Unfortunately, applications that rely on end-to-end IP addressing for their functionality do not work across a NAT router. If the remote IP address is contained in a packet's data portion instead of the header, NAT cannot occur. This is because NAT/PAT examines only the header. Any application that uses physical addresses instead of a qualified domain name will not reach destinations across a NAT router. This problem can sometimes be overcome using static mappings. The following applications do not always function across a NAT router, although methods exist to allow them to function:

- Routing table updates

- DNS zone transfers

- BOOTP

- Talk, ntalk

- Simple Network Management Protocol (SNMP)
- VoIP

Lab 1-4   Verifying NAT and PAT Configuration (1.1.5)

In this lab, you configure a router for NAT and PAT, test the configuration, and verify NAT/PAT statistics.

Lab 1-5   Troubleshooting NAT and PAT (1.1.6)

In this lab, you configure and troubleshoot a router for NAT and PAT.

Dynamic Host Configuration Protocol (DHCP)

Before the advent of *Dynamic Host Configuration Protocol (DHCP)*, all hosts on a network had to be manually configured with a separate, unique IP address before they could use network resources. Because of the static nature of the assignments, it was not possible to reuse any addresses, and any changes in network configuration required the network administrator to manually reconfigure each device. DHCP allows the automatic assignment of network configuration information to hosts on a network. With DHCP, addresses are assigned when required and are returned to a common pool when not in use. The DHCP protocol is described in RFC 2131 and is a successor to BOOTP.

BOOTP, as explained in RFC 951 and RFC 1542, was designed to enable diskless workstations to boot and request a minimal network configuration based on their MAC address. A BOOTP server is configured with a table of MAC addresses and the corresponding IP address that the administrator wants to assign. The server matches the Layer 2 address in the request to the Layer 3 address, and then this is sent back to the client in a reply. With BOOTP the same IP address is always handed to a workstation. This permanent assignment of IP addresses, static mappings, and a limit of four configuration parameters restricted BOOTP's usefulness and paved the way for a more versatile technique to dynamically configure network parameters.

DHCP reduces Internet access costs when NAT/PAT is not deployed by allowing address space to be dynamically assigned and reused. It also minimizes the time and expense of client configuration and provides a means for centralized management of IP information. There are many reasons why a network administrator may decide to run DHCP on a router rather than on a server-based system. Running DHCP on a router eliminates the need for extra hardware and allows DHCP to be run locally even if WAN connectivity is lost. On the downside, this decentralized method of running DHCP can complicate management and troubleshooting. Running a

DHCP server on a router forces a network administrator to use the Cisco IOS commands instead of a graphical configuration tool such as that provided by Windows. It also adds another service on a device that may at times already be overburdened.

DHCP provides a mechanism by which a client can be assigned an IP address for a limited amount of time known as the *lease* period. This allows a client to be assigned another address when it moves to a different subnet. It also lets the DHCP server assign the address to another client when the first client no longer requires it. This address reuse is a major factor in the conservation of IP addresses. If, at the end of the lease period, the client still requires the use of the same networking information, it may request a renewal of the lease from the DHCP server. DHCP additionally provides a method by which a client can gather other IP configuration information, such as the location of WINS and DNS servers, along with a domain name. The Cisco IOS implementation of DHCP supports more than 30 configuration parameters.

DHCP is not always possible or desirable. Servers on a network often require a static address, and some network administrators still prefer to statically assign network addresses to simplify management and security. In addition, the DHCP server must be available whenever an address is required, and end users must be prevented from manually configuring their network settings and potentially generating a conflict with dynamically assigned addresses.

DHCP supports three mechanisms for address allocation:

- **Automatic allocation** assigns a permanent address to the client.

- **Dynamic allocation** assigns an IP address for a fixed period of time or until the client relinquishes the address.

- With **manual allocation**, the administrator assigns an IP address to the client, and DHCP is used to convey the assigned address to the client.

DHCP, like its predecessor, BOOTP, uses UDP port 67 for requests and UDP port 68 for replies. The DHCP request is sent out as both a Layer 2 and Layer 3 broadcast for the destination but contains the client's MAC address as the source. The request asks the server to supply a client IP address and mask. The server responds to the request with a unicast message supplying the requested information. If the client is on the same segment as the DHCP server, the gateway IP address field is set to 0, and the IP address of the receiving interface is used to determine the pool of addresses that will be used. If the gateway IP address field is not 0, it is used to determine the subnet of the pool of addresses that should be distributed. In the reply, the destination MAC is the client's MAC address, and the destination IP address is one that has been supplied by the DHCP server. The Layer 2 and Layer 3 source address for the reply is that of the DHCP server. The client accepts this information and configures its network settings accordingly, as shown in Figure 1-6.

Figure 1-6   DHCP Requests and Replies

DHCP Request

MAC	IP	UDP	DHCP Request
SRC: Client DST: FF:FF:FF:FF:FF:FF	SRC: ? DST: 255.255.255.255	67	CIADDR:? GIADDR: ? Mask: ? CHADDR: A

DHCP Reply

MAC	IP	UDP	DHCP Reply
SRC: Server DST: Client	SRC: 209.165.200.254 DST: 209.165.200.227	68	CIADDR: 209.165.200.227 GIADDR: ? Mask: 255.255.255.224 CHADDR: Client

CIADDR: Client IP Address, GIADDR: Gateway IP Address, CHADDR: Client Hardware Address

The DHCP Process

Properly troubleshooting the DHCP process requires a deeper understanding of how DHCP works. Figure 1-7 shows the complete process by which a DHCP configuration is requested:

1. The first step in the process is when the client machine issues a broadcast *DHCPDISCOVER* message to locate a DHCP server on the network.

2. Any DHCP servers that hear the message generate a unicast *DHCPOFFER* that contains configuration information such as an IP address, lease period, and domain name. If multiple DHCP servers are available on the network, the client may receive more than one DHCPOFFER. The client evaluates the offer and decides which one to accept. Usually the client accepts the first offer it receives. This is only an offer of configuration information at this point; the server has not assigned the information to the client.

3. The server usually reserves the information for the client until it has a chance to receive a *DHCPREQUEST* broadcast message from the client or it learns that the client has accepted configuration information from another server. The DHCPREQUEST is sent as a broadcast so that other DHCP servers on the network will not wait to hear from the client and will reclaim the addresses they had offered.

4. The server confirms that the offered information is still available and has been allocated to the client by issuing a *DHCPACK* unicast message to the client.

Figure 1-7   DHCP Process

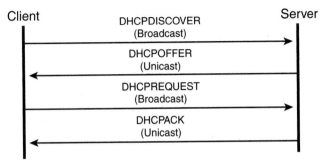

If the DHCPOFFER is seen as invalid, the client refuses the offer by issuing a *DHCPDECLINE* broadcast message. If the client is slow in responding to the server, or an error occurs in the negotiation of parameters, the server issues a broadcast *DHCPNAK*. When the client no longer requires the IP address, it issues a *DHCPRELEASE* message telling the server that it may return the address to the pool for reassignment.

Configuring DHCP

By default the IOS DHCP service is enabled on routers. To enable the service if it has been disabled, use the global configuration command **service dhcp**. On larger networks, DHCP services are usually handled by one or more dedicated servers that provide a more robust solution than can be implemented on a single router. For security reasons, it's a good idea to disable all services on a network device except those required for network operability. Use the global command **no service dhcp** to disable the DHCP service on a router.

After the service is enabled on a router, you must create a pool or pools of addresses using the following command:

```
Router(config)#ip dhcp pool name
```

Troubleshooting is much easier if the name chosen for the *DHCP pool* is meaningful within the context of the network or organization.

After the address pool is defined, you must specify the addresses it contains. You can specify the network or subnet range available for the address pool by a network subnet address followed by either a valid subnet mask or the prefix length, as shown here:

```
Router(dhcp-config)#network network-number [mask | /prefix-length]
```

From this point, you can specify a number of optional configuration parameters, including the domain name, the location of the DNS and NetBIOS name servers, the default gateway (default-router), and the lease's duration. For the location of the DNS server, NetBIOS name server, and default gateway, you can specify up to eight addresses, but only one is required. The default lease period is 24 hours. These parameters are configured in DHCP configuration mode, as shown here:

```
Router(dhcp-config)#domain-name domain
Router(dhcp-config)#dns-server address [address2 ... address8]
Router(dhcp-config)#netbios-name-server address [address2 ... address8]
Router(dhcp-config)#netbios-node-type type
Router(dhcp-config)#default-router address [address2 ... address8]
Router(dhcp-config)#lease {days [hours][minutes] | infinite}
```

One last step in DHCP configuration is the removal of addresses from the DHCP pool that have been used on the network or that should be reserved for other uses. This includes addresses assigned to servers and the default gateway, along with any static pools that are required. You can remove IP addresses from the DHCP pool using the following global configuration command:

```
Router(config)#ip dhcp excluded-address low-address [high-address]
```

Example 1-6 provides a sample DHCP configuration for the network illustrated in Figure 1-8. The configuration gives the DHCP clients connected to the LAN segment of the border router an IP address from the 10.20.30.0/24 subnet. It also sets the domain name to cisco.com and the default gateway to 10.20.30.1. The first ten addresses of this subnet are excluded and are not assigned to any clients.

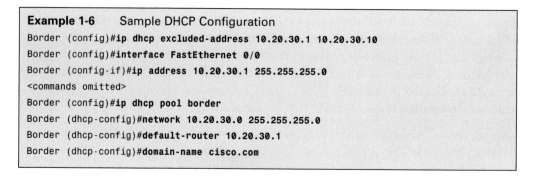

Example 1-6   Sample DHCP Configuration
```
Border (config)#ip dhcp excluded-address 10.20.30.1 10.20.30.10
Border (config)#interface FastEthernet 0/0
Border (config-if)#ip address 10.20.30.1 255.255.255.0
<commands omitted>
Border (config)#ip dhcp pool border
Border (dhcp-config)#network 10.20.30.0 255.255.255.0
Border (dhcp-config)#default-router 10.20.30.1
Border (dhcp-config)#domain-name cisco.com
```

Figure 1-8   DHCP Implementation

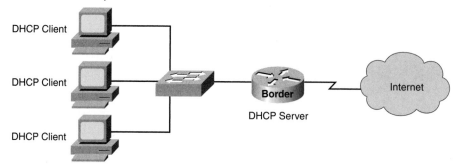

Lab 1-6   Configuring DHCP (1.2.6)

In this lab, you configure a router for DHCP to dynamically assign addresses to attached hosts.

DHCP Verification and Troubleshooting

DHCP binds an IP address to a MAC address. You can obtain information on the *binding* using the following command:

```
Router#show ip dhcp binding [address]
```

Example 1-7 shows a sample binding of MAC to IP addresses. This output also shows how the addresses were assigned and when the lease expires.

Example 1-7   Viewing DHCP Bindings

```
Toronto#show ip dhcp binding
Bindings from all pools not associated with VRF:
IP address          Hardware address        Lease expiration        Type
10.20.20.7          0100.e098.97d9.e7        Mar 02 1993 07:09 PM    Automatic
10.20.20.8          0100.10a4.e411.6f        Mar 02 1993 07:09 PM    Automatic
```

Bindings normally are removed at the end of the lease period unless the client renews the lease. To remove bindings before the lease expires, use the following command:

```
Router#clear ip dhcp binding {address | *}
```

To view the binding process in real time, use the following command:

```
Router#debug ip dhcp server {events | packets | linkage}
```

Example 1-8 shows sample output for a debugging session in which two hosts have been assigned IP addresses.

Example 1-8   Debugging DHCP

```
Toronto#debug ip dhcp server events
*Mar  1 19:14:26.299: DHCPD: assigned IP address 10.20.20.7 to client
   0100.e098.97d9.e7.
*Mar  1 19:14:28.615: DHCPD: checking for expired leases.
*Mar  1 19:14:36.815: DHCPD: assigned IP address 10.20.20.8 to client
   0100.10a4.e411.6f.
*Mar  1 19:16:28.615: DHCPD: checking for expired leases
```

Detailed information on the DHCP messages that the DHCP server has seen and replied to can point to improperly configured clients or loss of network connectivity. If the server is not seeing the DHCPREQUEST message, it cannot respond. If DHCPREQUEST messages are being seen, but the server is not responding, this indicates that the service is not properly configured. This information can be obtained from the command **show ip dhcp server statistics**, as shown in Example 1-9.

Example 1-9   Viewing DHCP Server Statistics

```
Toronto#show ip dhcp server statistics
Memory usage          14468
Address pools         1
Database agents        0
Automatic bindings     2
Manual bindings        0
Expired bindings       0
Malformed messages     0

Message               Received
BOOTREQUEST           0
DHCPDISCOVER          18
DHCPREQUEST           23
DHCPDECLINE           0
DHCPRELEASE           16
DHCPINFORM            6

Message               Sent
BOOTREPLY             0
DHCPOFFER             18
DHCPACK               26
DHCPNAK              0
```

DHCP Relay

In an enterprise environment, it is not uncommon to place all servers on one segment of the network and have users on other segments. Figure 1-9 shows an enterprise network that has collected all servers on one segment to form a *server farm*. Even if DHCP is running on a router, the network administrator may choose to use only one router in the organization as a DHCP server to simplify management. Because routers normally block broadcasts, they must be told to allow the DHCP request to come through and reach the DHCP server. This *DHCP Relay* is accomplished by implementing a *helper address*.

Figure 1-9   DHCP Relay

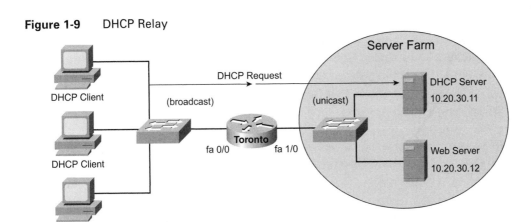

A helper address accepts the broadcast on one interface and turns it into a unicast. The **ip helper-address** command must be applied on the interface on which the broadcast would be received. The IP address specified is that of the server that the broadcast should be able to reach. The syntax of this command is as follows:

```
ip helper-address address
```

Specifically, in Figure 1-9, the command would be applied to the FastEthernet 0/0 interface of the Toronto router as follows:

```
Toronto(config-if)#ip helper-address 10.20.30.11
```

This forwards the DHCP broadcasts originating on the FastEthernet 0/0 segment of the network to the DHCP server located at 10.20.30.11.

By default, this command forwards eight UDP services. If this is not the desired result, these services must be disabled individually. Table 1-4 lists the services forwarded by helper addresses.

Table 1-4   Default UDP Services Forwarded by a Helper Address

Service	Port
Time	37
TACACS	49
DNS	53
BOOTP/DHCP server	67
BOOTP/DHCP client	68
TFTP	69
NetBIOS name service	137
NetBIOS datagram service	138

If it is desirable to forward additional ports, you can use the global **ip forward-protocol** command. To minimize the impact of unnecessary traffic on a segment, it might be desirable to disable forwarding of certain ports. This can be accomplished using the global **no ip forward-protocol** command. The following shows the syntax for both commands:

```
ip forward-protocol {udp [port] | nd | sdns}
```

```
no ip forward-protocol {udp [port | nd | sdns}
```

The **ip forward-protocol** command allows the forwarding of UDP ports, the Network Disk (**nd**) protocol used by some older diskless Sun workstations, and Secure Data Network Service (**sdns**).

Although security best practices do not recommend doing so, it is possible to use a logical broadcast address as the destination address in the **helper-address** command. To do so, you must enable *directed broadcasts* on the exit interface using the **ip directed-broadcast** command:

```
ip directed-broadcast [access-list-number] | [extended access-list-number]
```

When this command is used, the router converts the Layer 3 *logical broadcast* address into a Layer 2 *physical broadcast* with an address of FF-FF-FF-FF-FF-FF. This combination of **helper-address** and **directed-broadcast** commands lets the router accept a broadcast on one segment and send it to another segment as a directed broadcast. This allows all machines on the destination segment to hear and respond to the request as appropriate.

DHCP is an extremely valuable tool in a network environment that may be run on either an IOS router or a server, depending on the organization's needs. It is easy to implement and troubleshoot and greatly simplifies the job of maintaining up-to-date network configurations on networked machines.

 Lab 1-7   Configuring DHCP Relay (1.2.8)

In this lab, you configure a router for DHCP, add the ability for workstations to remotely obtain DHCP addresses, and dynamically assign addresses to the attached hosts.

Summary

Many techniques have been developed to help conserve the diminishing supply of IPv4 addresses. The most notable change has been the adoption of the classless system of IP addressing and the implementation of VLSM to minimize waste in the allocation of address space that was generated by the classful system.

Within individual organizations, the implementation of private address space on the internal network and the use of NAT to allow packets to travel to the Internet have reduced the requirements of maintaining large pools of registered addresses. Of the many different forms of NAT available, most enterprise network managers deploy PAT to give internal users access to the Internet in combination with static NAT to give outside users access to internal resources. In addition, the implementation of DHCP on internal networks allows the dynamic allocation of network resources and minimizes the amount of time required to configure hosts. These techniques allow network administrators to make more efficient use of the available IP address space. Their implementation has extended the lifetime of the current IPv4 addressing scheme and has reduced the necessity for a rapid migration to IPv6.

The next chapter examines the equipment and technologies used in a WAN environment. We consider both circuit-switched and packet-switched technologies, looking briefly at such things as dialup, ISDN, Frame Relay, cable, and DSL. WAN design and current standards also are introduced.

Check Your Understanding

Complete all the review questions listed here to test your understanding of the topics and concepts in this chapter. Answers are listed in Appendix A, "Answers to Check Your Understanding and Challenge Questions."

1. Which type of NAT is usually configured to provide Internet connectivity to corporate users in a large organization?

   A. Dynamic

   B. Static

   C. Overloaded

   D. Manual

2. Through which kind of address does a machine on the external network see another machine on the same external network?

   A. Inside local

   B. Inside global

   C. Outside local

   D. Outside global

3. What does PAT do first if the source port is in use on the first available inside global address and a pool of addresses has been configured?

   A. PAT moves to the next available address and checks for source port availability.

   B. PAT checks for an available port in the same range as the source port on the first available global address.

   C. PAT randomly picks a source port on the first global address for the translation.

   D. PAT randomly picks a source port-global address combination from the available resources.

   E. PAT does not translate the packet.

4. Which port does DHCP uses for a DHCPREQUEST?

   A. TCP 67

   B. TCP 68

   C. UDP 67

   D. UDP 68

5. Which message does the DHCP server issue if the client takes too long to accept the DHCPOFFER?

   A. DHCPACK

B. DHCPDECLINE

C. DHCPNAK

D. DHCPOFFER

E. DHCPREQUEST

6. Which DHCP message informs the client that it can use the supplied network configuration?

A. DHCPREQUEST

B. DHCPOFFER

C. DHCPDISCOVER

D. DHCPACK

E. DHCPNAK

7. Which DHCP messages are sent as a broadcast?

A. DHCPDISCOVER

B. DHCPOFFER

C. DHCPREQUEST

D. DHCPACK

E. DHCPDECLINE

F. DHCPNAK

8. Which command provides detailed information about the DHCP messages seen by and replied to by the IOS DHCP service?

A. **show ip dhcp services**

B. **debug ip dhcp events**

C. **show ip dhcp server statistics**

D. **debug ip dhcp**

9. Which command allows the network administrator to exclude the first ten addresses in the 10.20.30.0/24 DHCP subnet pool for use by devices requiring static IP addresses?

A. Router(config-dhcp)#**exclude 10.20.30.1 10.20.30.10**

B. Router(config-dhcp)#**exclude first 10**

C. Router(config-dhcp)#**ip dhcp excluded-address 10.20.30.1 10.20.30.10**

D. Router(config)#**ip dhcp excluded-address 10.20.20.1 10.20.30.10**

10. Why is a helper address required in an environment where the DHCP server is on a different segment of the network than the hosts?

    A. The helper address forwards all DHCP messages from the client to the server.

    B. The helper address forwards all DHCP messages from the server to the client.

    C. The helper address forwards all broadcast DHCP messages from the client to the server.

    D. The helper address forwards all broadcast DHCP messages from the server to the client.

11. What technology is described by each of the following IETF RFCs?

    RFC 951

    RFC 1542

    RFC 1631

    RFC 1918

    RFC 2131

12. What are the three mechanisms by which DHCP can assign an IP address?

13. How does the classless system help conserve the existing IPv4 address space?

14. Why might a network administrator want to run DHCP on a router instead of a server?

15. Why is it important to adjust the timeout value for dynamic NAT?

16. By default, which UDP ports are forwarded by a helper address?

Challenge Questions and Activities

Complete the following questions as well. These questions are purposefully designed to be similar to the more complex styles of questions you might expect to see on the CCNA exam. This section may also list activities that will help you prepare for the exams.

Activity 1

Using Packet Tracer, load the NAT_preconfigs.pkt configuration file that can be downloaded from www.ciscopress.com/1587131722. This configuration matches Figure 1-10. Complete all exercises using this as a starting file.

Figure 1-10   Sample Network Diagram

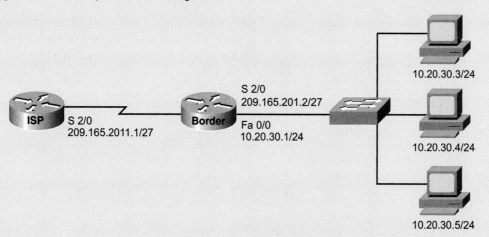

ABC Inc. has decided to reduce its network expenses by implementing NAT on the border router. Different scenarios are currently being investigated, and you have been asked to implement appropriate solutions for each scenario. Figure 1-10 diagrams the network. The starting configurations can be found in the file NAT_preconfigs.pkt.

After much discussion, it was decided to evaluate three different scenarios for possible implementation. The first scenario evaluates static NAT, the second dynamic NAT, and the third PAT. Each of these is to be evaluated independently for possible inclusion in the final solution.

Scenario A

Two machines belong to the network administration team and require static addresses to be used for translation. The machines have the internal addresses 10.20.30.3 and 10.20.30.4. These must be translated to the addresses 209.165.200.225 and 209.165.200.226, respectively, before leaving the internal network.

Scenario B

All IP traffic originating on the 10.20.30.0/24 network must be assigned an address from the address pool 209.165.200.225 to 209.165.200.230 before leaving the internal network.

Scenario C

IP traffic originating from the 10.20.30.0/24 network should use the address of the exit interface (serial 2/0) when leaving the internal network.

Final Implementation

After careful consideration of the benefits of each of the different types of NAT that were evaluated, it was decided that a solution combining the technologies was the most appropriate for the company. Implement the solution documented next using the NAT_preconfigs.pkt file as a starting point.

Static maps must be created for the machines in the IT department. These machines have IP addresses ranging from 10.20.30.11 to 10.20.30.15 and must be mapped to the addresses 209.165.200.231 to 209.165.200.235.

All other IP traffic originating from the 10.20.30.0/25 subnet should use the addresses 209.165.200.225/27 to 209.165.200.229/27 for translation.

IP traffic originating from the 10.20.30.128/25 subnet must use the address 209.165.200.230/27 when exiting the network.

Activity 2

As a network administrator, you have decided to rearrange the network to create a server farm that will house all servers, including those that support DHCP, NetBIOS, and TFTP. Figure 1-11 shows both the old and new networks. Part (a) of Figure 1-11 diagrams the initial network, and part (b) diagrams the new network. What changes will have to be made in the router configuration to give clients on the fastethernet 0/0 and fastethernet 0/1 segments access to the server farm resources?

Figure 1-11   DHCP Network Redesign

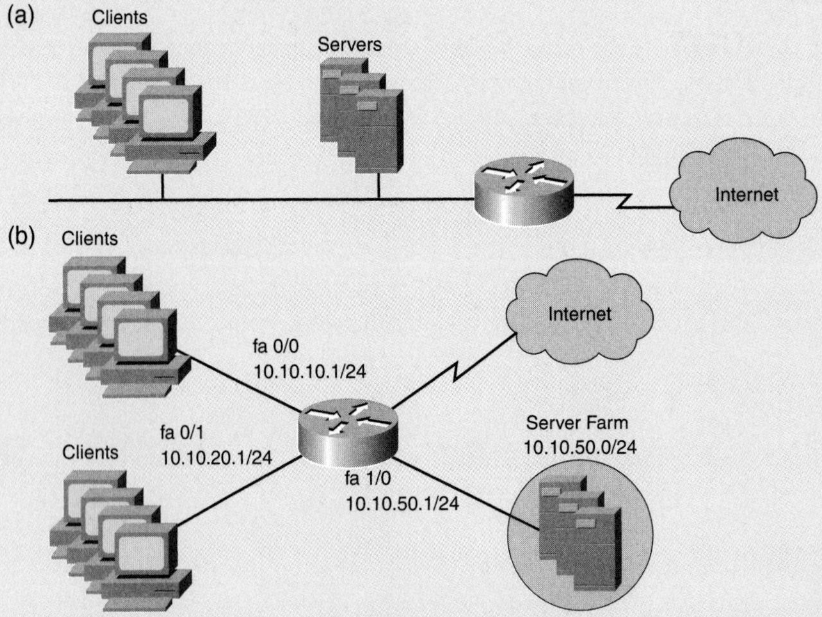

CHAPTER 2

WAN Technologies Overview

Objectives

Upon completion of this chapter, you should be able to answer the following questions:

- What differentiates a WAN from a LAN?

- What are some common WAN devices, and what is their purpose?

- Which organizations produce WAN standards, and what do they standardize?

- What is the structure of the standard HDLC frame?

- What are the available WAN technologies, and when is it appropriate to use each?

- What are the available WAN link options, and when is it appropriate to deploy each?

- How do cable and DSL technologies provide broadband connectivity, and what are their limitations?

- Which topologies are commonly deployed in a WAN, and what are the advantages and limitations of each?

- What steps should be followed whenever a new WAN is being designed or an existing one is modified?

- What is the goal of WAN design?

- What is a hierarchical WAN design, and when is it appropriate to deploy a one-layer, two-layer, or three-layer design model?

Key Terms

This chapter uses the following key terms. You can find the definitions in the glossary at the end of the book.

continues

continued

Modern society has become increasingly dependent on the ability to communicate seamlessly, regardless of the physical location of both the sender and the receiver. There is an increased tendency to eliminate different networks for the movement of voice, video, and data. They are all incorporated into a single IP-based network that can efficiently move all data formats over vast distances. Individual departments within an organization connect primarily through high-speed data links deploying Ethernet technology. The speed of these links is typically 100 Mbps, with gigabit and 10-gigabit technology not uncommon. These individual segments are then interconnected using Layer 2 technology to form a switched network that is known as a *local-area network (LAN)*. LANs that are in close proximity can be interconnected through high-speed data links to form a *campus LAN*, but those that are separated geographically must deploy different technologies to communicate. The interconnection of geographically separate LANs is known as a *wide-area network (WAN)*. This chapter introduces some of the technologies, standards, and equipment deployed in a modern WAN.

WAN Technologies Overview

A number of different technologies may be encountered in a WAN environment. These technologies generally function at Layers 1 and 2 of the OSI model and are primarily concerned with the movement of data between LANs. WANs use leased-line, circuit-switched, and packet-switched technology and must often be capable of handling voice, video, and data traffic simultaneously.

WAN Versus LAN

In most situations, an organization must subscribe to an outside provider to gain access to WAN carrier services. Organizations use these services to connect branches and also to access the services of other networks and provide access to remote users. A WAN typically carries voice, video, and data traffic between multiple sites. Although some larger organizations have their own WANs, most small- to medium-sized organizations have neither the technological nor financial resources to build and maintain a private WAN.

LANs generally offer high-speed connections and span a limited geographic area, whereas WAN bandwidths are usually less than that encountered on a LAN and span larger geographic areas. The administrative control of a LAN often resides with a single administrator or administrative body, whereas WANs might be controlled by multiple organizations. Although generally true, these characteristics do not specifically differentiate between a LAN and a WAN. The distinction between a LAN and a WAN is generally based on the technology deployed and is addressed in this and subsequent chapters.

Equipment located at a subscriber's site is known as *customer premises equipment (CPE)*. The CPE connects to the service provider at the *central office (CO)* through a copper or fiber cable known as the *local loop* or "*last mile*." Figure 2-1 illustrates this equipment setup.

Figure 2-1   WAN

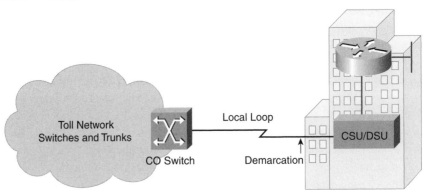

The point at which the customer turns over control to the WAN service provider is known as the *demarcation point* or simply the *demarc*. *Data terminal equipment (DTE)* at the subscriber's site passes the data to a device known as *data circuit-terminating equipment* or *data communications equipment (DCE)*, which prepares the data and places it on the local loop for transmission to the *service provider*. Various physical layer protocols establish the code and electrical parameters that the DTE and DCE devices use to communicate. Figure 2-2 illustrates the protocols used for communication between DTE and DCE devices.

Figure 2-2   Physical Layer LAN Protocols

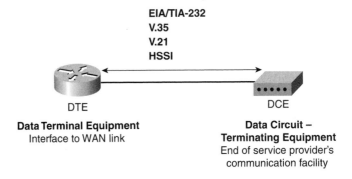

The local loop's data-carrying capacity can vary from approximately 56 kbps to several gigabits per second, as indicated in Table 2-1. In North America the T1 line is common. Many other countries, especially those of the European Union (EU), deploy E1 lines. Depending on the technology deployed, the available bandwidth can be used either partially or in its entirety.

Table 2-1 Bit Rates of Various Lines

Line Type	Signal Standard	Bit Rate
56	DS0	56 kbps
64	DS0	64 kbps
T1	DS1	1.544 Mbps
E1	ZM	2.048 Mbps
E3	M3	34.064 Mbps
J1	Y1	2.048 Mbps
T3	DS3	44.736 Mbps
OC-1	SONET	51.84 Mbps
OC-3	SONET	155.54 Mbps
OC-9	SONET	466.56 Mbps
OC-12	SONET	622.08 Mbps
OC-18	SONET	933.12 Mbps
OC-24	SONET	1244.16 Mbps
OC-36	SONET	1866.24 Mbps
OC-48	SONET	2488.32 Mbps

The communications link to the service provider requires signals to be in a specific format. For example, if the link is designed to carry analog signals such as those encountered on the *Public Switched Telephone Network (PSTN)*, a *modem* is required. The word modem comes from the terms modulator and demodulator, which describes its functionality. This device modulates or superimposes the digital data on an analog carrier signal for transmission across the network. As soon as the signals arrive at their destination, they are demodulated, and the data is extracted. Modems come in many varieties, depending on their intended use. Figure 2-3 shows a modem's functionality.

Figure 2-3   Data Transmission on the PSTN

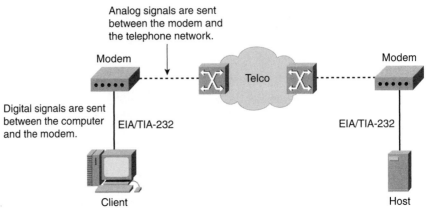

On a purely digital network, there is no need for the data to be converted from digital to analog and vice versa. The signal does, however, need to be modified to a format compatible with the technology deployed. Devices known as a *channel service unit (CSU)* and a *data service unit (DSU)* are needed to put the signal in the required format. These devices are usually combined into one box called a *CSU/DSU*. They can either be supplied by the service provider or be purchased by the end user, depending on the technology and country. The CSU/DSU functionality is often incorporated into the router interface.

WAN Protocols

WANs primarily function at Layers 1 and 2 of the OSI model. WAN standards describe both the physical and data link layer characteristics and can include physical addressing, flow control, and encapsulation. Many different organizations issue WAN standards, as shown in Table 2-2.

Table 2-2   WAN Standards Organizations

Acronym	Organization
ITU-T	International Telecommunication Union Telecommunication Standardization Section
ISO	International Organization for Standardization
IETF	Internet Engineering Task Force
EIA	Electronic Industries Appliance
TIA	Telecommunications Industries Association

Physical layer protocols specify the electrical, mechanical, operational, and functional connections to the WAN services. Table 2-3 lists these standards.

Table 2-3   Common Layer 1 WAN Standards

Standard	Description
EIA/TIA-232	Formerly known as RS-232, this standard allows connection speeds up to 64 Kbps. Uses a 25-pin D connector.
EIA/TIA-449/530	A faster (up to 2 Mbps) version of EIA/TIA-232. Uses a 36-pin D connector and is capable of longer cable runs. Also known as RS-422 and RS-433.
EIA/TIA-612/613	The High Speed Serial Interface (HSSI), which provides access to services at speeds up to 52 Mbps. Uses a 60-pin D connector.
V.35	An ITU-T standard for synchronous communications between a network access device and a packet network at speeds up to 48 Kbps. Uses a 34-pin rectangular connector.
X.21	An ITU-T standard for synchronous digital communications. Uses a 15-pin D connector.

Data link layer protocols define how the data is encapsulated, as well as how it is transported between sites. A number of technologies exist at this layer, including ISDN, Frame Relay, and ATM. Figure 2-4 illustrates these technologies, which are discussed in more detail later in this and subsequent chapters.

Figure 2-4   WAN Data Link Layer

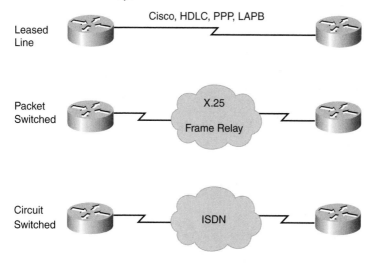

Network layer data is encapsulated into frames at the data link layer. The specific type of *encapsulation* depends on the type of technology being deployed on the link and must be configured on the serial interface. Most Layer 2 encapsulations use either the ISO standard *High-level Data Link Control (HDLC)* framing mechanism or a modification of it. Table 2-4 lists some of the common data link layer protocols found in WANs.

Table 2-4   Common Layer 2 WAN Protocols

Protocol	Usage
Link Access Procedure, Balanced (LAPB)	X.25
Link Access Procedure on the D channel (LAPD)	ISDN D channel
Link Access Procedure for Frame Relay (LAPF)	Frame Relay
High-level Data Link Control (HDLC)	Cisco default
Point-to-Point Protocol (PPP)	Dialup connections

Figure 2-5 shows the HDLC frame format. The opening and closing *Flag fields* indicate the start and end of each frame. In an HDLC frame, this 8-bit flag is set to 01111110. To prevent this from being confused with normal data streams, HDLC inserts a 0 after every five 1s, thus making this sequence impossible in any location other than the Flag field. The redundant 0s are removed at the receiving end of the transmission.

Figure 2-5   HDLC Frame Format

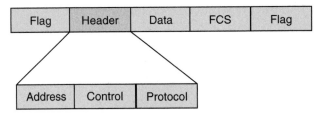

The *Address field* is either 1 or 2 bytes in size, depending on the frame's origin. Because most WAN links are *point-to-point* in nature, the Address field is not required. The *Control field* is normally 1 byte long, but it can be 2 bytes in extended sliding windows systems. The Control field indicates the type of frame:

- *Unnumbered frames* carry line setup information.

- *Information frames* carry network layer data.

- *Supervisory frames* control the flow of information frames and also request data retransmission in case of an error.

Generally the Address and Control fields form the frame header, but both *PPP* and the Cisco version of HDLC have an extra field in the header to identify the Layer 3 protocol of the encapsulated data. The encapsulated data follows the frame header, which is followed by the *frame check sequence (FCS)*. The FCS uses the *cyclic redundancy check (CRC)* to generate a 2- or 4-byte field used to verify the frame's integrity.

Leased Line, Circuit Switching, and Packet Switching

Figure 2-6 illustrates the different WAN link options. These links can use dedicated lines to carry data to the service provider or can use switched technology. Switched networks can be circuit-switched, packet-switched, or cell-switched. Technologies can also be either connection-oriented or connectionless. If a network path is not predetermined and relies on each switch in the path to make a decision for each packet, the network is termed connectionless.

Figure 2-6   WAN Link Options

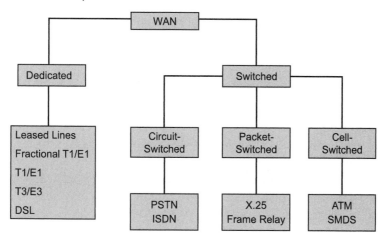

Each of these technologies handles data differently and introduces different amounts of delay and jitter. *Delay* or *latency* is caused when a device must process some part of the frame as it enters before moving on to the next part of its journey. *Jitter* is defined as the variation in delay of received packets. At the sending side of a connection, packets are placed on the medium in a steady stream and are spaced evenly. Because of congestion, improper queuing, or configuration errors, the delay between packets can vary at the receiving end of the connection. Some traffic types, notably voice, are extremely sensitive to delay and jitter. A good understanding of the various network technologies therefore is imperative for proper WAN design.

Circuit-Switched Networks

Perhaps the most common network in existence is the public switched telephone network (PSTN). This is an example of a *circuit-switched* network, as shown in Figure 2-7, which is used to place voice calls between sites around the world. When a call is placed, it signals the switches in the service provider's network to create a continuous path from the calling party to the called party. If the telephones are replaced with modems, this network gains the ability to carry data. An Integrated Services Digital Network (ISDN) network is another common type of circuit-switched network. ISDN technology is digital end-to-end, whereas the *Plain Old Telephone Service (POTS)* requires a modem to modulate the digital signal so that it can be placed on the analog PSTN.

Figure 2-7   Circuit-Switched Network

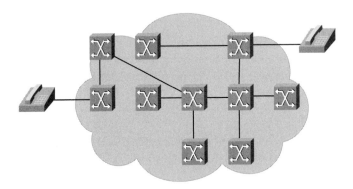

Leased-Line Networks

If the delay associated with building the switched circuit is unacceptable, it is possible to lease a dedicated connection from the service provider. *Leased lines* are acquired to provide a dedicated amount of bandwidth to an organization. In North America, leased lines are commonly T1 (1.544 Mbps) or T3 (44.736 Mbps) bandwidth, whereas in the EU E1 (2.048 Mbps) and E3 (34.064 Mbps) lines are common. Leased lines are usually deployed to connect the subscriber to the service provider. The cost of a leased line is based on the connection's bandwidth and length. This makes the construction of a long-haul network from leased-line technology cost-prohibitive.

Circuit-switched networks are extremely inefficient when carrying bursty traffic, as is common on the Internet. The purchased bandwidth must be determined based on the maximum amount that the link will be expected to carry at any one time. This produces periods in which the line is underused but must still be paid for. If a lower-bandwidth line is leased, it cannot carry the peak loads, resulting in congestion and potential data loss, requiring retransmission. *Time-division multiplexing (TDM)* can divide the circuit into multiple time slices and allocate different slices to different conversations. However, slices assigned to conversations that have no data to transfer go unused and contribute to the technology's inefficiency.

Packet-Switched Networks

An alternative to circuit-switched technology is packet switching. In *packet-switched* technology, the individual bits are collected into packets, frames, or cells. The path that these packets take through the network is determined by addressing information included in each packet and can be either connectionless or connection-oriented. In *connectionless* systems such as the Internet, each packet contains full addressing information, which is evaluated by each switch along the way to determine where to send the packet next. In *connection-oriented* systems such as Frame Relay, each path is predetermined, and packets carry only information required to identify the path through the network. In Frame Relay, this identifier is called the *Data-Link Connection Identifier (DLCI)*. The switch determines the path by looking up the identifier in tables that it holds in memory. Figure 2-8 shows an example of a packet-switched network.

Figure 2-8   Packet-Switched Network

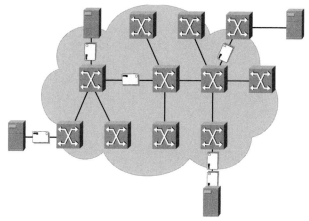

In packet-switched networks, the circuits exist only while the packet travels through them; they are called *virtual circuits (VCs)*. Two types of VCs exist:

- *Switched Virtual Circuit (SVC)*—In an SVC, a connection request is sent through the network to establish the path. This SVC can exist for various lengths of time but eventually is dissolved.

- *Permanent Virtual Circuit (PVC)*—The service provider configures a PVC by loading entries in the switch at boot time. Because the path is predetermined, it is always available for data transfer. PVCs are usually used by Frame Relay circuits, although some service providers allow the use of SVCs.

In packet-switched technology, the subscriber connects through the local loop to the nearest point where it can connect to the service provider's network. This connection point is called the service's *point of presence (POP)*. The local loop is usually a leased line and often carries several VCs simultaneously.

WAN Technologies

Many different technologies are encountered in the WAN. Each one has specific characteristics that make it suitable for specific types of data but that limit its usefulness for other traffic types. A general understanding of the available technologies is necessary for proper WAN design, as discussed later in this chapter.

Analog Dialup

For many organizations, intermittent, low-volume data transmissions occur irregularly, so simple *analog dialup* connectivity is sufficient. For example, a salesperson might have to connect to the main office to check e-mail and download technical specifications for and prices of his or her products while on the road. Often a phone line and access to the PSTN are the only network connection available for a highly mobile workforce. In addition, analog dialup connections might be used to provide temporary bandwidth above that available from the main WAN connection or as a backup connection in case the main WAN connectivity fails. Although the use of analog dialup connections was once common, technologies such as ISDN, DSL, and cable are taking over this role in most networks. One place that analog dialup connections are still deployed is to provide access to network devices. An analog modem can be connected to the AUX port of most Cisco routers to allow a network administrator to dial into the device even if the main network is nonfunctional. Figure 2-9 shows some common uses of analog dialup.

Figure 2-9   Analog Dialup Connections

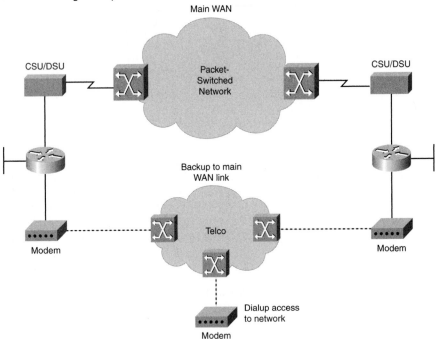

The benefits of analog dialup include low cost, high availability, and simplicity of implementation and use. The local loop connecting the subscriber site to the PSTN was not designed to carry digital data directly. Therefore, digital information must be modulated before being placed on the copper wire and then demodulated at the receiving end to extract the data from the carrier signal. Physical limitations of the local loop limit the data rate to approximately 33 kbps unless the data is coming directly through a digital connection, in which case the rate can be increased to approximately 56 kbps.

The extremely low bit rate available with analog dialup connections translates into long connect times for the transfer of large amounts of data. Scheduling the transfer of files during off-peak hours can decrease the cost, but this type of connection is unsuitable for time-sensitive data such as voice and video.

ISDN

As the technology of the PSTN advanced, frequency-division multiplexing of analog signals gave way to time-division multiplexing of digital signals on the trunks. *Integrated Services Digital Network (ISDN)* extends this time-division multiplexing to the local loop. ISDN, like analog dialup, provides a dedicated circuit-switched network between locations and eliminates the problems associated with latency and jitter.

ISDN uses *bearer* or *B channels* to carry data and *delta* or *D channels* for control information. Most small businesses that deploy ISDN technology use a *Basic Rate Interface (BRI)*, which consists of two 64-kbps B channels and one 16-kbps D channel. If more bandwidth is required, a *Primary Rate Interface (PRI)* can be deployed. In North America, the PRI is composed of 23 B channels and one D channel, each 64 kbps in size. In Europe, Australia, and other parts of the world, the ISDN PRI is composed of 30 B channels and one D channel. When synchronizing overhead is added, this equates to the bandwidth available in a T1 line (1.544 Mbps) in North America and an E1 line (2.048 Mbps) in other parts of the world, as shown in Figure 2-10.

Figure 2-10   ISDN Interfaces

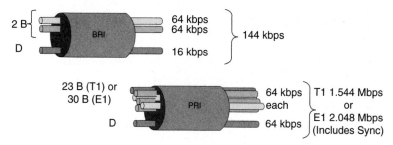

ISDN technology allows B channels to be used either individually or in combination. With the BRI interface, this means that if only one B channel is deployed, the available bandwidth is 64 kbps, which is more than the fastest available analog dialup connection. If the second B channel is activated in combination with the first, the available bandwidth jumps to 128 kbps. In addition to greatly increased bandwidth, the use of *out-of-band signaling* by ISDN allows call setup times of less than a second. Although it is normally used only for control information, some service providers allow data to be carried on the D channel of the ISDN BRI. This is possible because with only two B channels to control, the D channel is underused. With an ISDN PRI, multiple B channels can be joined between sites to provide bandwidth sufficient for all types of data, including voice and video.

ISDN technology is available in most locations around the world, including rural and underdeveloped regions where DSL and cable might not be an option. ISDN is commonly deployed to provide bandwidth-on-demand to supplement the WAN bandwidth provided by other technologies such as Frame Relay. It is also used to provide backup services in case the main WAN connection fails. Chapter 4, "ISDN and DDR," discusses ISDN in more detail.

Leased Line

If traffic flow characteristics dictate that a permanent dedicated circuit is required between locations, it is possible to purchase a leased-line connection from a service provider. The leased line provides a dedicated point-to-point connection through the service provider's network and is available in connection speeds up to 2.5 Gbps. Table 2-1, shown earlier in the chapter, lists some of the commonly available line types and connection speeds.

The cost of a leased-line connection depends on the bandwidth required and the distance between endpoints. Additionally, leased-line charges vary depending if the line is running within a local access and transport area (LATA) or must cross between different LATAs. The use of leased lines can quickly become cost-prohibitive when multiple sites must be connected or the distance between sites is great. The benefits of a leased line include a constantly available circuit of dedicated capacity that has no jitter or latency.

A serial port is required on the router at both ends of each connection to take advantage of a leased line. In addition, a CSU/DSU is required to connect to the circuit provided by the service provider. WAN traffic is not uniform, and the bandwidth available on the leased line seldom matches what is required. This means that line capacity must be purchased based on the maximum required bandwidth and that most of this bandwidth goes unused.

Today, leased lines are usually deployed to connect a remote site into a service provider's packet-switched network. Several connections can be multiplexed over a single leased line, minimizing the number of interfaces, and subsequently the cost of the border router.

X.25

Service providers introduced packet-switched technology in response to the high cost of leased-line technology. This technology allows the lines to be shared, thus reducing the cost associated with any one connection. The first packet-switched technology to be deployed was the *X.25* group of protocols. X.25 is a low bit rate network layer technology that can use either SVCs or PVCs, as shown in Figure 2-11. Access to the X.25 network is usually through either a leased-line or dialup connection.

Figure 2-11   WAN Deployment Using X.25

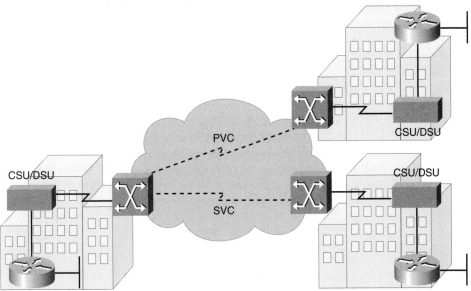

In X.25, virtual circuits are constructed using call request packets that are sent to the destination address. As soon as the SVCs are built, they are assigned a channel number. Subsequent packets labeled with the *channel number* are moved through the network to the destination address. PVCs can be used when the channels between end users are predefined. Multiple channels are possible on a single leased-line or dialup connection.

Because data is being moved on a shared network, the cost of X.25 technology is significantly lower than that of either leased-line or circuit-switched technology. Costs are usually based on the amount of data transferred rather than distance or connect time. These networks typically function at a maximum bit rate of 48 kbps, which is less than that currently available with most other technologies, including analog dialup. Data is subject to delays because the bandwidth must be shared between multiple users.

Although X.25 has been widely replaced by Frame Relay and ATM technology in North America, many countries around the world have significant investments in X.25 technology and continue to rely on it to move data. In North America, X.25 is still used for dialup point-of-sale (POS) terminals and Electronic Data Interchange (EDI) applications, where the low bandwidth and high latency are not a problem.

Frame Relay

As communication media improved, data transmission became more reliable, and the extensive error checking found in X.25 was no longer required. *Frame Relay* is much simpler than X.25 and functions at the data link layer. Frame Relay provides the benefits of a packet-switched network and has a much higher transmission speed than is available from X.25. Although most Frame Relay networks run at speeds less than that of a T1 line (1.544 Mbps), some vendors currently offer Frame Relay services at DS-3 (45 Mbps) port speeds.

Frame Relay reduces the latency associated with packet switching technology by eliminating error checking and flow control. Additionally, it uses techniques to reduce network congestion, which could introduce jitter. This makes Frame Relay ideal for voice, video, and data transmission.

Frame Relay networks are normally accessed through either leased lines or dialup connections from the end user. PVCs are usually created between the network's endpoints, but some service providers allow SVCs to be used. If ISDN is used to connect to the Frame Relay cloud, the D channel is used to build one or more SVCs on the B channel. A Data Link Connection Identifier (DLCI) is used to identify PVCs between the end user and the local Frame Relay switch. These DLCIs are usually mapped to IP addresses on the destination network, as shown in Figure 2-12.

Figure 2-12   Typical Frame Relay Network

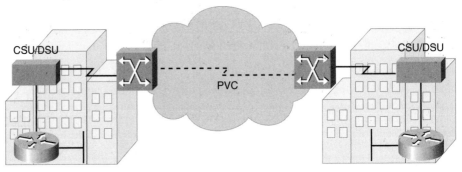

A single physical interface on a router can be configured to handle multiple VCs. This allows organizations to purchase a single access circuit into the Frame Relay cloud, thus minimizing the costs associated with connecting to multiple remote sites. Service providers usually sell the subscriber a PVC connection through their network to the destination site.

Many factors contribute to the cost of a Frame Relay circuit. The major factor is the amount of data that the service provider guarantees to transfer on the circuit. This value is known as the *Committed Information Rate (CIR)*. If bandwidth is available on the network, most service providers allow subscribers to exceed this CIR for short periods of time. The amount of data that the service provider allows the subscriber to burst also contributes to the circuit's cost. Understand that any data moved on the Frame Relay network in excess of the purchased CIR runs the risk of being discarded if congestion occurs on the network. Chapter 5, "Frame Relay," covers this topic in greater detail.

ATM

Asynchronous Transfer Mode (ATM) was developed to overcome the problems encountered in moving voice and video over shared-bandwidth networks. Typical ATM circuits exhibit speeds in excess of 155 Mbps and introduce very little latency or jitter into the circuit. This is accomplished by using small, fixed-length cells to move traffic instead of the large frames encountered in earlier technologies.

An ATM *cell* is 53 bytes in size and consists of a 5-byte header followed by 48 bytes of payload. Because the ATM cells are small, voice and video traffic do not have to wait behind a large data frame to be transmitted. Although this is a definite advantage for traffic that is sensitive to delay, it is not a benefit for segmented Layer 3 payloads. If the ATM network is carrying this type of traffic, each 48-byte payload must have a 5-byte ATM header that the ATM switch uses to reassemble the data at the destination. When this increased overhead is taken into account, an ATM circuit requires approximately 20 percent more bandwidth to move the same amount of data as a Frame Relay circuit.

ATM is usually deployed over PVCs, but it also can use an SVC. Multiple VCs can be carried over a leased-line connection to the edge of the ATM network. An ATM deployment would be very similar to the Frame Relay deployment illustrated in Figure 2-12.

DSL

Digital Subscriber Line (DSL) is family of technologies that use the unused bandwidth available in the copper wires that run into most business and residential locations. Telephone services typically use only the frequency range from 330 Hz to 3.3 kHz. DSL technologies carry broadband signals by moving them at frequencies above 4 kHz.

Collectively, these technologies are often referred to as *xDSL*. All forms of DSL are classified as either symmetric or asymmetric based on the relationship between the upload and download speeds. Asymmetric DSL provides a higher download speed than upload, whereas Symmetric DSL has the same speed in both directions. Many different forms of DSL exist, including the following:

- *Asymmetric DSL (ADSL)*
- *Symmetric DSL (SDSL)*
- *High Bit Rate DSL (HDSL)*
- *ISDN (like) DSL (IDSL)*
- *Consumer DSL (CDSL)*

ADSL is the most commonly encountered form of DSL in North America. This form of DSL offers download speeds greater than the provided upload speed. Although this might be ideal for most home users, who generally download far more than they upload, it is unacceptable for hosting servers. Consumer DSL is also known as G.Lite or DSL-lite. DSL data rates are available at speeds up to 8.192 Mbps through the use of complex modulation and encoding schemes. Table 2-5 lists the characteristics of some of the currently available forms of DSL.

Table 2-5   DSL Characteristics

DSL Service	Download Speed	Upload Speed
ADSL	64 kbps–8.192 Mbps	16 kbps–640 kbps
SDSL	1.544 Mbps–2.048 Mbps	1.544 Mbps–2.048 Mbps
HDSL	1.544 Mbps–2.048 Mbps	1.544 Mbps–2.048 Mbps
IDSL	144 kbps	144 kbps
CDSL	1 Mbps	16 kbps–160 kbps

Each end user has a dedicated connection back to the service provider's network. Multiple DSL subscriber lines are multiplexed together at the service provider, into a single high-capacity line. This is accomplished by the use of a *DSL Access Multiplexer (DSLAM)*. The DSLAM uses TDM to put multiple signals together on the line, as shown in Figure 2-13.

Figure 2-13   DSL Deployment

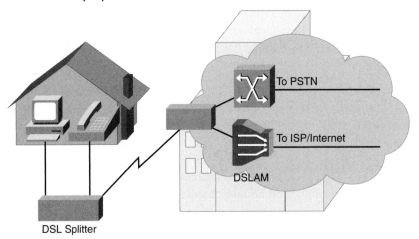

Because xDSL uses frequencies above the 4-kHz window used by standard telephone services, having both telephone services and broadband DSL active at the same time on a local loop is usually possible. This is true for all forms of DSL except SDSL, which does not allow simultaneous telephone and DSL services. The xDSL family of technologies provides an always-on connection and dedicated bandwidth to the service provider's network.

Unfortunately, DSL is not widely available in all parts of the world. To function properly, a DSL subscriber must be no farther han 5.5 km (3.5 miles) from the central office (CO). Local loops in excess of this do not allow DSL to function properly. This makes DSL unavailable in most rural or underdeveloped areas. Additionally, the condition of the cabling between the DSLAM and the subscriber plays an important role in a DSL link's speed and reliability.

DSL is used to connect to the service provider's network. It is not commonly deployed as a technology to connect directly to a remote network. After connection to the service provider's network occurs, alternative technologies are deployed to allow Layer 3 access to the remote network. Most service providers currently deploy either ATM or leased-line technology on their core WAN. If security is a consideration, a VPN can be deployed across the DSL connection.

Cable

The installation of cable television in most urban environments has brought with it the ability to use the coaxial cable that carries the television signal to also carry digital data. Like DSL, cable provides an always-on connection between the service provider's network and the end user, which is subject to attack from the outside world. Figure 2-14 illustrates a typical cable installation.

Figure 2-14   Typical Cable Installation

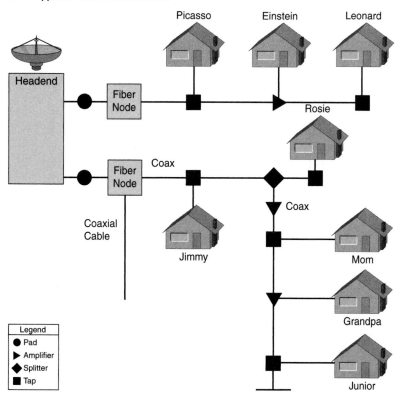

Cable technology has the potential to provide enormous amounts of bandwidth in a symmetrical manner by assigning a 6-MHz-wide channel to carry data between the service provider and the end user. This single channel can carry data at speeds up to 40 Mbps, which is many times faster than a standard T1 or E1 leased line. This makes cable technology ideal for applications that require the transfer of large amounts of data, such as multimedia applications.

Unfortunately, cable connections are shared-bandwidth connections, meaning that this bandwidth must be shared between multiple users. The actual data rate that an end user can expect depends on the use of the medium by others on the same medium. As more users join the network, the bandwidth available to individual users declines. Many service providers limit bandwidth allocated to individual users to ensure a certain level of service to all subscribers. In addition, this technology lets individuals connected to the same medium share files and access each others' computers unless the end user takes precautions to prevent this. Most cable service providers now take measures to prevent the security problems associated with shared media access. For secure transmission of data, VPN technology should be deployed between the user and the remote network.

Figure 2-15 Cable Networks

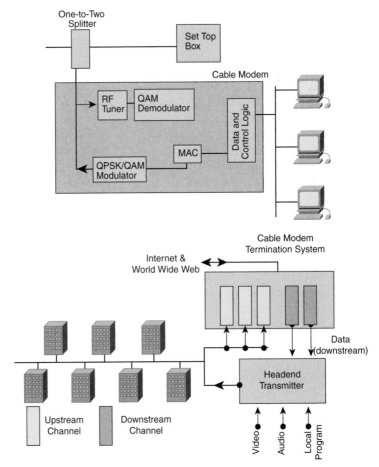

At the headend, the service provider combines video and data services and places them on the shared medium. At the end-user site, these signals are separated by a splitter and are sent to the appropriate device, as shown in Figure 2-15. Cable subscribers can enjoy high-bandwidth data connections and television signals simultaneously. In addition, most cable service providers now offer voice over IP (VoIP) services over the same connection.

WAN Design

It's not easy to design an efficient WAN. You need a thorough understanding of the organization's current and future requirements, as well as the characteristics and limitations of the available technologies, to determine which technology or combination of technologies most closely matches the organization. Additionally, WAN design is a dynamic process of trying to strike the optimum balance between technical requirements and the available financial and technical resources.

WAN Communication

WANs generally are considered a collection of data links that interconnect LANs, which in turn house servers and other end devices. Routers interconnect LANs to form a WAN, as shown in Figure 2-16. WANs function at the lower three layers of the OSI model, as shown in Figure 2-17.

Figure 2-16   Typical WAN

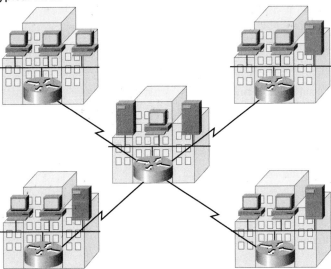

Figure 2-17   WAN OSI Layers

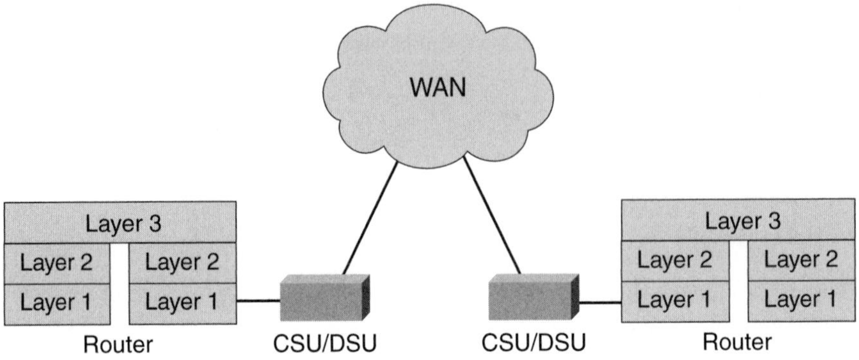

Due to legal issues and the high cost of WAN technology, these data links are usually owned and maintained by a communications service provider and are made available to subscribers for a fee. These links are then used to interconnect LANs or to provide access to remote networks. Charges for link provision are a major cost element of a WAN. WANs usually function at data rates much less than that normally encountered on LANs.

Data links terminate at routers, which continually exchange address information about directly connected LANs. These routers then use this information, along with the network layer information contained in the data stream, to determine the correct data link to facilitate data delivery. Routers might also implement *quality of service (QoS)*, which can prioritize the different data streams. WANs do not provide services to end users.

WAN design is not an easy task. Users continually demand increases in speed and availability. At the same time, financial constraints work to restrict the network designer's ability to accomplish this. To complicate things even further, WANs typically carry a variety of traffic types, including voice, video, and data. A proper WAN must be designed to handle all traffic types that might be encountered in an enterprise and provide adequate bandwidth at an acceptable cost. WAN design and implementation have two primary goals:

- Application availability

- Reduced total cost of ownership

In addition, WAN design must take into account three general factors:

- **Environmental variables** include such things as the location of hosts, servers, and terminals; the environment's projected traffic; and the projected costs of delivering different levels of service.

- **Performance constraints** consist of such things as network reliability, traffic throughput, and host/client computer speeds. For example, the speed of the NICs and the hard drive access speeds are considered performance constraints.

- **Networking variables** include networking topology, line capacities, and packet traffic. A thorough characterization of traffic is critical to the successful planning of a WAN.

Steps in WAN Design

Enterprises install WANs to move information between their branches in a timely manner. As changes occur in the enterprise, the WAN design must be revisited to determine if the existing WAN is still meeting these requirements. WAN design is a very challenging process. Most WANs have evolved over time and will continue to do so as technology, business practices, and business structure continue to change. A systematic approach to WAN design or redesign helps minimize expenses and maximize the network's availability and responsiveness. Figure 2-18 illustrates this systematic approach.

Figure 2-18   WAN Design Process

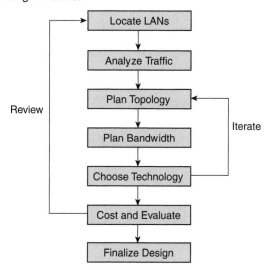

When designing a WAN, it is important to know what types of traffic will be carried on the network, as well as their source and destination. Different types of traffic have different requirements or tolerances for bandwidth, latency, and jitter, as shown in Table 2-6.

Table 2-6   WAN Traffic Types

Traffic	Latency	Jitter	Bandwidth
Voice	Low	Low	Medium
Videoconferencing	Low	Low	High
Transaction data (for example, SNA)	Medium	Medium	Medium
Messaging (for example, e-mail)	High	High	High
File transfer	High	High	High
Batch data	High	High	High
Network management	High	High	Low

You must determine traffic characteristics for each pair of endpoints. If this is an upgrade or a modification of an existing WAN, statistics and traffic analysis can be conducted. If this is a new WAN, consultation with the end users forms the basis of this information.

When you collect information from users, you must focus on a number of key areas. It is important to separate the end users' desires from the actual network requirements. Although every end user stresses response time as being critical, some applications, such as financial applications, have a genuine requirement for short response times. Throughput-intensive applications usually involve some sort of file transfer and quite often can be scheduled to occur at off-peak times, thus minimizing their impact on response-time-sensitive applications. A third area to pay particular attention to in WAN design is the requirement for network reliability. Military organizations and organizations that conduct much of their business online have a real need for near-100 percent uptime. Thus, they require a high level of redundancy to be built into the network design.

The type of information that must be collected includes the following:

- Connectivity and volume flows
- Client/server data
- Connection or datagram orientation
- Latency tolerance, including length and variability
- Network availability tolerance
- Error rate tolerance

- Priority

- Protocol type

- Average packet length

Knowledge of the traffic flow's endpoints helps determine the *topology* to be deployed. Topology depends not only on geographic considerations but also on the requirements of the network itself. For example, if network availability is important, redundant links should be deployed. The topological design should help minimize unnecessary flow of traffic between areas of the network.

The next step in the design process is selecting appropriate link technologies. This decision is made based on the required bandwidth plus the characteristics of the traffic moving on the network. As mentioned previously, different technologies introduce different levels of latency and jitter into a network, and some traffic, such as voice, is very intolerant of these.

After the topology is determined and the technology chosen, the next step is to determine both the installation and operational costs and see how these match the organization's requirements. At this stage, you might decide to go forward with the design or revisit the design process and alter the design based on the business needs and resources.

It must be stressed that the process shown in Figure 2-18 should be used whenever a new WAN is to be designed or an existing one modified or expanded. It should also be mentioned that this process is seldom linear. Several design modifications are usually required before a final design is chosen.

Identifying and Selecting Networking Capabilities

WAN design consists of determining both the interconnection pattern and the technology to be deployed on the data links. Many WANs deploy a classic star topology, with the company's head office usually configured as the star's center. As new branch offices are added to the WAN, they are connected back to the head office. Although this strategy can decrease costs by minimizing the number of circuits required to deploy the WAN, it can be problematic due to the lack of redundant links. If a satellite office, or the link between the head and satellite office, goes down, only the satellite office is unable to connect to the network. The problem is that if the head office goes offline, the entire network is shut down, and nobody can communicate. To minimize the risk of total network failure should the central hub go down, many WANs interconnect the satellite offices to form either a full- or partial-mesh network. Figure 2-19 illustrates these topologies.

Figure 2-19 Common WAN Topologies

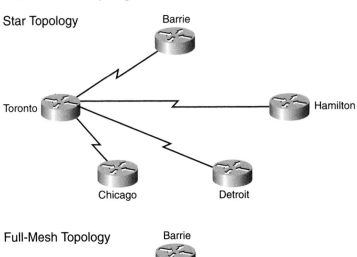

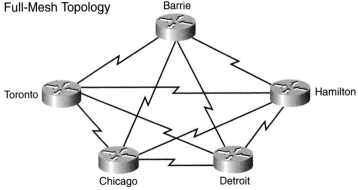

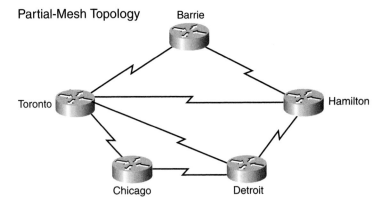

The addition of devices into a network to provide redundant data links might produce a more reliable network, but it also increases the cost of deployment. WAN technologies usually require that the entire packet be received before it can be moved onto another data link. This means that each device introduces a certain amount of latency and the more devices inserted into a data path, the more latency is introduced.

As previously discussed, many different technologies are available for deployment on WAN data links, each exhibiting characteristics that make its deployment suitable in certain scenarios. Table 2-7 lists some of these technologies.

Table 2-7   Common WAN Technologies

Technology	Charge	Maximum Bit Rate	Connection
Leased line	Distance, capacity	Unlimited	Permanent, fixed capacity
Basic telephone	Distance, time	33 to 56 kbps	Dialed, slow connection
ISDN	Distance, capacity	64 or 128 kbps (BRI), < 2 Mbps (PRI)	Dialed, fast connection
X.25	Volume	< 48 kbps	Switched, fixed capacity
Frame Relay	Capacity	< 4 Mbps	Permanent, variable capacity
ATM	Capacity	> 155 Mbps	Permanent, variable capacity

Technologies that require network connections to be established on demand, such as POTS and ISDN, are unsuitable for networks that require rapid response time or low latency. After it is established, ISDN provides a low-latency network and is often deployed to connect the small office/home office (SOHO) or a small branch office to the enterprise network. ISDN is also used to provide *bandwidth-on-demand (BOD)* or as backup to the main WAN link. Even though other choices such as cable and DSL exist, these are not globally available, so ISDN is still the technology of choice.

Leased lines can provide a high-bandwidth network with low latency and jitter, but they are not commonly used to interconnect end users. Leased lines are charged for based on both the link's distance and capacity, among other factors, and a WAN constructed of only leased lines would be prohibitively expensive. Leased lines are normally deployed as a short access circuit into a shared-bandwidth technology network, such as Frame Relay or ATM. The leased line connects the end user to the POP of a shared network.

Shared-access networks such as Frame Relay and ATM carry data from several subscribers over the same data links. Individual subscribers have no control over the path the data takes through the cloud or how long data must wait at each node in the network. This uncertainty in latency and jitter can make shared-bandwidth networks unsuitable for many types of traffic. The benefit of a shared network is that the cost to the individual subscriber is usually substantially less than the cost of the same bandwidth on a dedicated network. Many techniques have been developed to help reduce latency and jitter in this type of network to make it more suitable for all types of traffic. These include traffic shaping and QoS.

ATM is a shared-network technology that reduces latency and jitter by using high-speed data links and fixed-size cells. Because each cell contains 48 bytes of data and a 5-byte ATM header, delay-sensitive data such as voice traffic is not held up behind large data frames.

Modern WANs make use of several technologies:

- Leased lines, Frame Relay, ISDN, and DSL are often deployed to connect individual sites into an area.

- Frame Relay, ATM, or leased lines are then used to connect these areas to the backbone.

- ATM or leased-line technology form the backbone.

Three-Layer Design Model

As WANs continue to grow, it becomes impractical to continue with a star or mesh topology. For example, consider a network to be deployed for an organization that is operational in ten countries around the world and that has offices in five different cities in each of these countries. Linking these sites in a full-mesh topology would require 1225 WAN links. Clearly, this would be cost-prohibitive. If a standard star topology were deployed, the hub router would require either 50 dedicated interfaces or interfaces that could handle 50 virtual circuits, depending on the WAN technology deployed. Consider the problems that would be encountered in scaling this network as more sites came on board. For example, one additional country with five connected cities would require the addition of 260 circuits for a full-mesh connection or the addition of another five interfaces or VCs if a star topology were deployed.

An excellent example of a *hierarchical network design* is the PSTN. This network is available around the world and supplies reliable and predictable service. A hierarchical network design offers many advantages over other network designs:

- **Scalability**—A network's ability to grow with an organization without sacrificing control or manageability.

- **Ease of implementation**—Assigning clear functionality to each layer of the network makes implementation easier.

- **Ease of troubleshooting**—Assigning clear functionality to each layer makes it much easier to locate and isolate a network problem. This design also allows a network to be temporarily segmented to reduce the problem's scope.

- **Predictability**—Network behavior is predictable in a hierarchical design, thus allowing modeling of network performance for capacity planning.

- **Protocol support**—The logical arrangement of the networking infrastructure allows for the support of multiple protocols and applications.

- **Manageability**—All the preceding benefits contribute to a highly manageable network.

Figure 2-20 illustrates a *three-layer hierarchical design* similar to that deployed by the PSTN. The design clearly defines the functionality of each of the layers, making implementation, management, and troubleshooting much easier than they would be if a nonhierarchical design were deployed. In this design, individual LANs are interconnected in a star topology through access links to form *areas*. These areas are then joined through distribution links to form *regions*, which in turn can be linked through core links.

Figure 2-20   Three-Layer Hierarchical Network Design

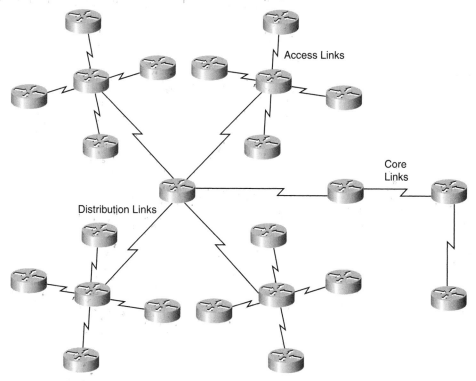

Proper WAN design contains the majority of traffic locally. Each LAN is responsible for its own local services. The central LAN not only provides services to its local users but is also responsible for providing area-wide service.

Each layer in the hierarchical design model has specific functionality:

- The *core layer* is used only to move traffic between regions. It can carry a variety of traffic types, some of which may be sensitive to delay and jitter. Redundant high-speed links are common at this layer to allow the core layer to continue to function even if individual circuits fail. There should be no manipulation of the packets at this layer. *Core links* usually deploy either ATM or leased-line technology.

■ The *distribution layer* is the demarcation point between the access layer and the core layer. This layer provides boundary definition of the network and is the layer where packet manipulation can occur. This layer of a WAN design can perform the following functions:

— Address or area aggregation

— Departmental or workgroup access to the core layer

— Broadcast/multicast domain definition

— Virtual LAN (VLAN) routing

— Media transitions

— Security

The distribution layer would include the campus backbone and all of its connecting routers. Routers in this layer are usually programmed to control which traffic is permitted on the campus backbone. Therefore, this layer is said to provide policy-based connectivity. This is also the layer where any remote access to the corporate network is permitted. *Distribution links* are usually either Frame Relay or ATM.

■ The *access layer* is the layer where end users are allowed to connect. This layer may use access control lists to optimize the needs of a set of users. The access layer connects LANs into the WAN and isolates broadcast traffic to the individual workgroup. *Access links* can be dialup, leased line, or Frame Relay connections, depending on the traffic volume and type.

Other Layered Design Models

Although the three-layer design shown in Figure 2-21 offers many benefits, the complexity it introduces is often more than many networks require. In cases such as this, either a one-layer or a two-layer design may suffice.

Figure 2-21   Three-Layer Design Model

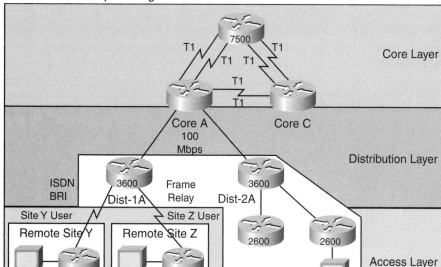

A *one-layer design* might be sufficient in enterprises that have few branches and the traffic flow between the branches is minimal. Originally, the cost of leased lines made this type of design impractical because of the high cost of long-haul leased lines. The implementation of Frame Relay technology provides a means to connect branches in a one-layer design without incurring the costs associated with long leased lines. Figure 2-22 shows a one-layer design. In a one-layer design, the area hub also serves as the regional and core hubs.

Figure 2-22   One-Layer Design

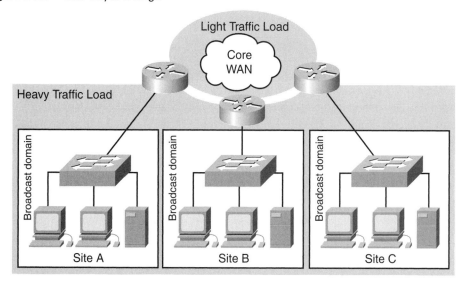

A *two-layer design* allows for some geographic concentration of the network traffic flow. Essentially, this design model produces a "star of stars," as shown in Figure 2-23. In this design, the central router serves the purpose of a core router even though it is not connected to any other core routers. This model allows the basic structure to be easily replicated, allowing for network growth.

Figure 2-23   Two-Layer Design

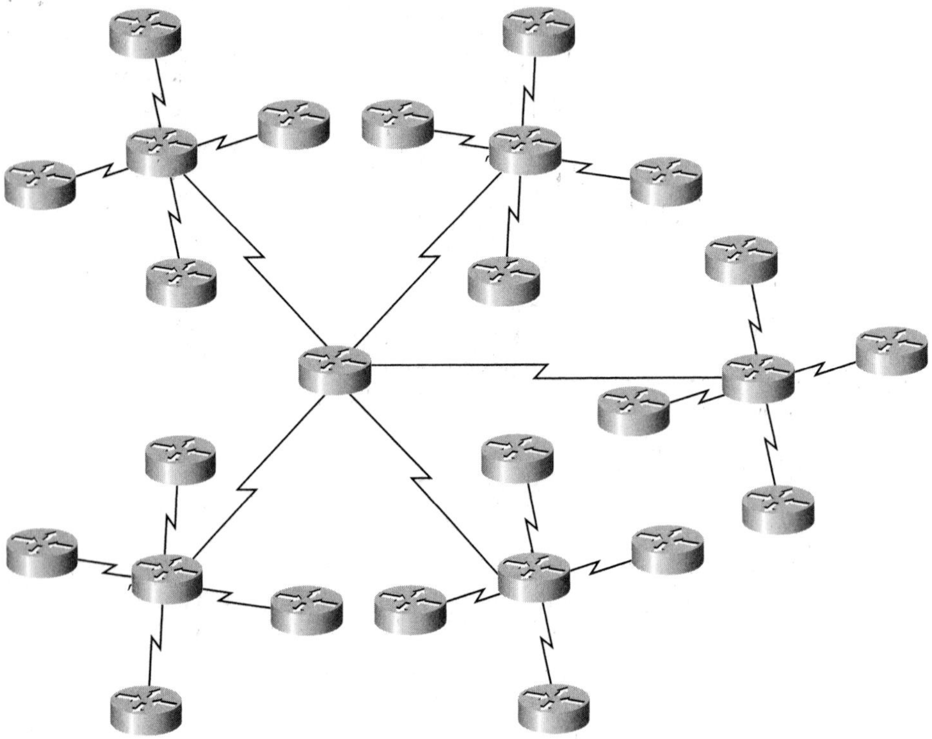

Other WAN Design Considerations

With the wide availability of the Internet, traffic flow into or out of the Internet must be considered during any WAN design. Because the Internet is probably available wherever the enterprise has a branch, each branch can connect independently to the Internet through an ISP. Alternatively, a core router can be connected to the Internet, with all traffic to or from the Internet going through this core router.

The advantage of the first design is that some traffic can be moved through the Internet instead of the enterprise WAN, thus reducing the WAN's complexity and also reducing costs. A disadvantage is that the enterprise network is vulnerable to attack at multiple locations, making management and security extremely complex. The alternative scenario is to move all traffic destined for or coming from the Internet through a core router. This simplifies management and security issues but increases the cost and complexity of the enterprise WAN.

If interbranch traffic is low and each branch has a separate connection to the Internet, it is possible to move all traffic across the Internet, eliminating the need for a separate WAN. The increased costs of securing the individual LAN connections to the Internet can be compensated for by the savings incurred by not having to install and manage a separate WAN.

The location of servers and services in an enterprise WAN is an extremely complex task requiring a good understanding of traffic flow dynamics. Generally, servers should be placed in the enterprise WAN closest to the site where they will be accessed, and replication of servers across links should be scheduled to occur during off-peak times. This minimizes unnecessary traffic flow in the WAN and also minimizes security risks.

Summary

This chapter examined the various standards, equipment, and technologies that comprise a modern WAN. Each available technology exhibits specific characteristics that govern the appropriate scenario for its implementation. These technologies, their characteristics, and common usage can be summarized as follows:

- Leased line:
  - Offers dedicated bandwidth.
  - The link cost is proportional to the bandwidth and the length of line required.
  - Offers high bandwidth with low latency and jitter.
  - Usually used to connect the subscriber into service providers shared access the network.
  - Used as core links in some WAN designs.
- Circuit-switched:
  - Common examples include the PSTN (analog) and ISDN (digital).
  - Forms a complete path from source to destination before sending any information.
  - Delay is encountered during call setup.
  - Cost is proportional to the connection's duration.
  - Usually deployed as a backup to the main WAN connectivity.
- Packet-switched:
  - Common examples include X.25 and Frame Relay.
  - Media is shared between multiple subscribers, thus lowering the total cost to any individual subscriber.
  - Small voice packets may become trapped behind larger data packets.

— Data may experience delay and jitter due to network congestion and path determination.

— Cost is based on bandwidth requirements and the number of connections required.

■ Cell-switched:

— ATM is an example of a cell-switched network.

— It is similar to packet switching, except that fixed-size cells are used. For example, each ATM cell consists of a 5-byte ATM header and a 48-byte payload.

— Offers high bandwidth and low latency on a shared-access network.

— Prevents small voice packets from being trapped behind large data trains.

— Commonly used for WAN core links.

WAN design, or redesign, must start with a complete analysis of traffic flow, including type, source, and destination. The source and destination are used in conjunction with network reliability requirements to determine the topology to be deployed. Common examples of WAN topology include star and full or partial mesh. The type of traffic moving on a WAN helps you determine the proper link technology to deploy. The goal of any WAN is to provide for the timely delivery of many different types of traffic without introducing latency or jitter that would disrupt this traffic. Each traffic type exhibits a different level of tolerance to these factors, so the link technology you select must be appropriate to the type of traffic being carried.

Regardless of the type of traffic being moved on the WAN, a systematic approach must be taken to its design or redesign. Care must be taken to confine traffic to the area of the WAN where it is needed and to minimize the unnecessary flow of traffic between areas. A three-layer hierarchical design model should be considered whenever possible, but for smaller organizations, either a one- or two-layer model may be sufficient.

Check Your Understanding

Complete all the review questions listed here to test your understanding of the topics and concepts in this chapter. Answers are listed in Appendix A, "Answers to Check Your Understanding and Challenge Questions."

1. What is another name for the equipment located at the subscriber's site?

A. CSU

B. CPE

C. DSU

D. DCE

E. DTE

2. What device prepares data and also places it on the local loop for transmission to the service provider?

A. CSU

B. CPE

C. DCE

D. DTE

3. What device is required to prepare digital data for transmission on an analog network?

A. CSU/DSU

B. DTE

C. Local loop

D. Modem

4. What device is responsible for formatting data to be transmitted on a purely digital network?

A. CSU/DSU

B. DTE

C. Local loop

D. Modem

5. WAN technologies function primarily at which two layers of the OSI model?

A. Physical

B. Data link

C. Network

D. Transport

E. Session

F. Presentation

G. Application

6. What ISO standard frame type forms the basis of most serial line encapsulations?

A. ARPA

B. HDLC

C. PPP

D. SLIP

7. Which two of the following are examples of a circuit-switched network?

A. ATM

B. ISDN

C. Frame Relay

D. PSTN

8. What WAN technology uses equal-sized cells to transmit data?

A. ATM

B. ISDN

C. Frame Relay

D. PSTN

E. X.25

9. What can be used to allow a single leased-line or circuit-switched connection to carry multiple conversations?

A. ATM

B. CSU

C. DTE

D. TDM

10. What type of packet-switched virtual circuit is created by loading entries into the switch at boot time?

A. Boot virtual circuit

B. Predefined virtual circuit

C. Permanent virtual circuit

D. Switched virtual circuit

11. What is a POP?

   A. The point where the customer's network connects to the local loop

   B. The nearest point where the service provider's network can be accessed

   C. The point where local network control is turned over to the service provider

   D. The connection between the local network and the service provider's network

12. What type of signal multiplexing is available on analog networks?

   A. Analog-division multiplexing (ADM)

   B. Frequency-division multiplexing (FDM)

   C. Time-division multiplexing (TDM)

   D. Wavelength-division multiplexing (WDM)

13. What describes the composition of an ISDN BRI interface in Europe and Australia?

   A. B+2D

   B. B+23D

   C. B+30D

   D. 2B+D

   E. 23B+D

   F. 30B+D

14. What is the total bandwidth available from an ISDN PRI in North America?

   A. 128 kbps

   B. 144 kbps

   C. 192 kbps

   D. 1.544 Mbps

   E. 2.048 Mbps

15. What two devices are required to connect a branch office to a service provider using leased-line technology?

   A. CPE

   B. CSU/DSU

   C. FastEthernet interface

   D. ISDN BRI

   E. Modem

   F. Serial interface

16. What does X.25 use to move data packets through the network?

    A. Channel number

    B. DLCI

    C. SPID

    D. Telephone number

17. What measures does Frame Relay use to reduce latency compared to X.25 technology?

    A. Frame Relay deploys extensive error checking to minimize the retransmission of lost data.

    B. Frame Relay eliminates error checking and flow control.

    C. Frame Relay uses Layer 3 addressing, and X.25 uses Layer 2 addressing.

    D. Frame Relay uses small, 53-byte cells to move data, and X.25 uses larger frames.

18. What does Frame Relay use to identify the PVC between the end user and the local Frame Relay switch?

    A. Channel number

    B. DLCI

    C. SPID

    D. Telephone number

19. If a subscriber purchased 20 Frame Relay PVCs from a service provider, what is the minimum number of serial interfaces required on the subscriber's router?

    A. None, because Frame Relay does not use a serial interface.

    B. One, because multiple VCs can be configured on each serial interface.

    C. Two, because each physical interface can carry a maximum of 16 VCs.

    D. 20, because each VC requires a dedicated interface.

20. What technology was developed to overcome the problems of moving voice and video over shared-bandwidth networks?

    A. ATM

    B. Frame Relay

    C. ISDN

    D. Leased line

    E. X.25

21. Why is Frame Relay preferred over ATM for moving segmented Layer 3 data?

    A. ATM does not have a mechanism to track the segment number.

    B. ATM functions at Layer 2, and segmentation occurs at Layer 4.

    C. The overhead associated with ATM makes it less efficient than Frame Relay for moving segmented data.

    D. The addressing scheme used in ATM is incompatible with segmented data.

22. What is the most common form of DSL in North America?

    A. Asymmetric DSL (ADSL)

    B. Symmetric DSL (SDSL)

    C. High Bit Rate DSL (HDSL)

    D. ISDN (like) DSL (IDSL)

    E. Consumer DSL (CDSL)

23. What does the term *asymmetric* refer to in ADSL?

    A. The upstream speed is greater than the downstream speed.

    B. The downstream speed is greater than the upstream speed.

    C. Frames destined for the service provider are larger than those originating from the service provider.

    D. Frames destined for the subscriber are larger than those originating from the subscriber.

24. What has prevented DSL technology from becoming universally available?

    A. DSL can function only with the PSTN technology installed in North America.

    B. DSL technology is extremely expensive to implement.

    C. DSL technology requires the installation of a DSLAM at every subscriber's site.

    D. DSL functions only over a local loop less than 5.5 km (3.5 miles) long.

25. How does cable technology provide bandwidths up to 40 Mbps?

    A. TDM is used to provide multiple time slices to data.

    B. The frequencies normally assigned to any unwatched channels are reassigned to carry data.

    C. A 6-MHz-wide channel is allocated to carry data.

    D. Data is carried on the cable by encoding it on frequencies above the 4-kHz window used to carry regular channels.

26. Which of the following two statements accurately compare ADSL and cable technology?

    A. ADSL offers different speeds in the upstream and downstream directions, and cable offers the same speed in both directions.

    B. ADSL offers maximum speeds greater than those available through cable.

    C. Cable is a shared-bandwidth technology, and ADSL offers dedicated bandwidth to the service provider.

    D. Cable speeds are unaffected by the number of users connected, whereas xDSL speeds decrease as more users join the network.

27. What two pieces of information should be considered in a WAN design or redesign?

    A. ACLs deployed on the LAN

    B. Physical location of end users

    C. Addressing scheme deployed on the LAN

    D. Types of traffic that will move on the WAN

    E. Traffic source and destination LAN

28. What is a major source of information used to design a new WAN?

    A. Traffic flow statistics

    B. Network performance statistics

    C. Interviews with end users

    D. WAN design documents

29. What two factors should you consider when designing the topology of a new WAN?

    A. Bandwidth requirements

    B. Installation costs

    C. Network availability requirements

    D. Source and destination addresses

    E. Traffic type

30. What two factors should you consider when deciding on the link technology to be deployed in a new WAN installation?

    A. Bandwidth requirements

    B. Installation costs

    C. Network availability requirements

    D. Source and destination addresses

    E. Traffic type

31. What WAN design model would be appropriate for an organization with three branch offices located in close proximity to each other, and requiring only limited amounts of data to be exchanged between the sites?

    A. One-layer design model

    B. Two-layer design model

    C. Three-layer design model

    D. Four-layer design model

32. What WAN design model would be appropriate for an organization with ten branch offices each in six different countries located around the world?

    A. One-layer design model

    B. Two-layer design model

    C. Three-layer design model

    D. Four-layer design model

33. In the three-layer WAN design model, what two types of technology are commonly deployed on the core links?

    A. ATM

    B. Frame Relay

    C. ISDN

    D. Leased line

    E. X.25

34. In the three-layer WAN design model, what is the purpose of the core links?

    A. To provide services to regional sites

    B. To provide services to both regional and local sites

    C. To move data between regional hubs

    D. To move data between core hubs

Challenge Questions and Activities

Complete the following questions as well. These questions are purposefully designed to be similar to the more complex styles of questions you might expect to see on the CCNA exam. This section may also list activities that will help you prepare for the exams.

1. You have been hired to help design a new WAN that will be deployed across seven countries in the EU. Each country will require the connection of between five and 12 cities into the new WAN for the purpose of exchanging financial and security information between the participants. Because of the sensitive nature of the data being moved, the network requires near-100-percent uptime. Which type of WAN design model would be appropriate? Which type of technology should be deployed?

2. A small interior design company has opened a second office in a city approximately 80 km (50 miles) from the main office. The company occasionally will need to move e-mail and design specifications between the two offices. Which type of WAN deployment would you suggest, and why?

3. XYZ Inc. wants to replace its high-cost leased-line network with a lower-cost alternative. The company currently connects ten offices using a full-mesh topology for its voice over IP (VoIP) network. All offices are located in urban areas. What solution would you recommend as a replacement for the current network?

Objectives

Upon completion of this chapter, you should be able to answer the following questions:

- How does TDM enable multiple conversations to be carried over a single link?

- What are the functions of DTE and DCE devices, and how can they be interconnected?

- What are the differences between the ISO standard HDLC and Cisco's implementation?

- What advantages does PPP have over HDLC?

- How does the PPP frame format compare to the standard HDLC frame format?

- What are the key components of the PPP layered architecture, and what is the purpose of each?

- What steps are involved in establishing and terminating a fully functioning PPP link carrying multiple Layer 3 protocols?

- How do PAP and CHAP function?

- Which commands can be used to configure and troubleshoot a serial link, and when is it appropriate to use each?

Key Terms

This chapter uses the following key terms. You can find the definitions in the glossary at the end of the book.

continues

To move data between remote networks, WANs often deploy serial point-to-point links. The technology deployed on these links must be both efficient and secure to allow multiple simultaneous conversations to be carried. This chapter examines some of these technologies, paying particular attention to High-level Data Link Control (HDLC) and Point-to-Point Protocol (PPP). The similarities and differences between these are discussed, along with configuration and troubleshooting methodology.

Serial Point-to-Point Links

WAN technologies are based on serial transmissions at the physical layer. The bits that make up the Layer 2 frame are signaled one at a time by physical layer processes onto the physical medium. Common signaling methods include *Nonreturn to Zero Level (NRZ-L)*, *High-Density Binary 3 (HDB3)*, and *Alternate Mark Inversion (AMI)*. These signaling methods help differentiate between serial communication methods. Some of the more common serial communication standards are

- EIA/TIA-232

- V.35

- High-Speed Serial Interface (HSSI)

Time-Division Multiplexing

For a serial link to carry multiple simultaneous conversations, a process known as *time-division multiplexing (TDM)* is deployed. This technique divides the media into multiple time slices and then interleaves either bits or bytes of data from multiple conversations, assigning each conversation one or more timeslots, as shown in Figure 3-1. Because this technique *multiplexes* signals from many different input channels, the output channel must have a minimum capacity equal to the sum of the inputs.

Figure 3-1   Time-Division Multiplexing

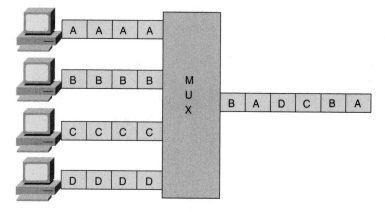

TDM functions solely at the physical layer and has no regard for the type of information it carries. In addition, if a timeslot is assigned to a conversation that has no information to transfer, the timeslot goes unused. No other traffic is assigned to the timeslot; thus, valuable bandwidth goes unused. A modification of TDM known as Statistical Time-Division Multiplexing (STDM) analyzes the bandwidth require ments of each conversation and dynamically reassigns unused timeslots to conversations that require additional bandwidth.

Integrated Services Digital Network (ISDN), which is discussed more fully in Chapter 4, "ISDN and DDR," is an example of where TDM is deployed. An ISDN BRI consists of two 64-kbps B channels for carrying data and one 16-kbps D channel for out-of-band signaling. In addition, 48 kbps is allocated to framing and synchronization information. These channels are provided by assigning TDM timeslots on the physical medium.

Demarcation Points

The demarcation point or "demarc" is the point at which the service provider's responsibility ends. In the U.S., the service provider provides the local loop, which terminates at the *channel service unit/data service unit (CSU/DSU)*. It is usually housed in the subscriber's telecommunications closet and is the responsibility of the end user. In many other countries, the service provider provides and manages the *network terminating unit (NTU)*, as shown in Figure 3-2. Managing the NTU allows the service provider to troubleshoot the local loop without relying on the customer to have the CSU/DSU properly configured. In these cases the demarcation point occurs after the NTU. The subscriber connects customer premises equipment (CPE), such as a router or Frame Relay access device (FRAD), into the NTU using either a V.35 or RS-232 serial interface.

Figure 3-2   Demarcation Points

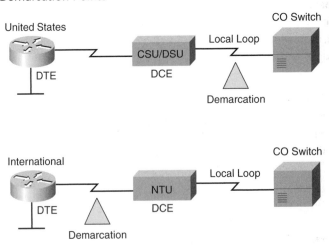

DTE and DCE

Serial connections have a data terminal equipment (DTE) device at one end and a data communications equipment (DCE) device at the other end. The service provider is responsible for connecting DCE devices together through its network. The DTE device is usually the CPE and is often the company's border router that connects to the service provider's network through a leased line. Other types of DTE equipment include computers, terminals, fax machines, and printers. DCE devices convert the data from the DTE into a form that is acceptable to the service provider's network. The DCE device is commonly a modem or CSU/DSU. The remote DCE receives the signal and decodes it back into a sequence of bits that is sent to the remote DTE. Figure 3-3 illustrates a network topology with the connection of DTE and DCE devices.

Figure 3-3   Connecting DTE and DCE Devices

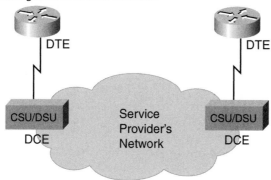

Both the *Electronic Industries Alliance (EIA)* and the *International Telecommunications Union Telecommunications Standard Sector (ITU-T)* have been active in developing standards to allow DTEs to communicate with DCEs. The ITU-T calls DCE data circuit-terminating equipment, and the EIA calls it data communications equipment. Regardless of the name, the functionality is identical.

Standardization of the DTE/DCE interface includes the following:

- **Mechanical/physical**—The connector type and number and arrangement of pins

- **Electrical**—Defines the voltage levels for both 0 and 1

- **Functional**—Specifies the functions that are performed by assigning meanings to each of the signaling lines

- **Procedural**—Specifies the sequence of events for transmitting data

It is possible to connect two DTE devices together directly by using a *null-modem cable* or adapter, as shown in Figure 3-4. If synchronous communication is required, either of the two DTE devices must generate the clocking signal, or an external clocking source must be provided.

Tip

There's a quick way to remember the difference between DTE and DCE. The T in DTE refers to the terminal and connects to the provider. The C in DCE refers to the communications provider. The DCE end also provides the clocking signal in synchronous communications.

Figure 3-4   Connecting DTE Devices with a Null-Modem Cable

The purpose of this clock signal is to align the transmitting and receiving ends of a communications link so that they agree on how data will be transmitted and received. The DCE end normally uses an internal clock, and the DTE end uses an external clock that is usually provided by the DCE device. Data received outside the expected intervals is assumed to be in error and is ignored. Synchronous communication lines require a constant signal to align the transmitting and receiving clocks but perform about 30 percent faster than asynchronous links, which require the inclusion of start and stop bits to control data flow.

Table 3-1 describes the construction of a null-modem cable or adapter. This cable/connector allows two DTE devices to communicate by establishing flow control between them. Normal serial line communication between a DTE and DCE device requires the DTE device to signal that it wants to send data using a request to send (RTS), to which the DCE device responds with a clear to send (CTS) signal. Additionally, the DTE device uses the DTR line to signal that it is ready to accept information; the DCE device uses the DSR line for the same purpose. By crossing these control lines, in addition to the transmit and receive lines, flow control can be implemented between two DTE devices.

Table 3-1   Null-Modem Cable Construction

Connect:	To:
Frame Ground (FG)	Frame Ground (FG)
Transmit Data (TD)	Receive Data (RD)
Receive Data (RD)	Transmit Data (TD)
Request to Send (RTS)	Clear to Send (CTS)
Clear to Send (CTS)	Request to Send (RTS)
Signal Ground (SG)	Signal Ground (SG)
Data Set Ready (DSR)	Data Terminal Ready (DTR)
Data Terminal Ready (DTR)	Data Set Ready (DSR)

On a router, the *synchronous* serial port can be configured as either a DTE or DCE device. Different cables are required, depending on the configuration. If the interface is configured as DTE, the clocking signal must be derived from the CSU/DSU or another DCE device. The default setting for a synchronous serial port is as a DTE device.

The DTE-to-DCE cable is a shielded serial transition cable that has connectors designed to match the interfaces on the devices to which it must connect. Cisco routers use either a DB-60 or 26-pin connector on the DTE end to connect to the router's serial port. The 26-pin connector is found on the newer *Smart Serial cables* and is much more compact than the older DB-60 connectors. The use of this connector allows more serial connections in a given amount of space or *form factor*. The connector on the DCE end of the cable is usually dictated by the WAN service provider or the specific CSU/DSU. Cisco devices support the *EIA/TIA-232*, *EIA/TIA-449*, *V.35*, *X.21*, and *EIA/TIA-530* standards.

High-Level Data Link Control (HDLC)

Serial communications can be based on *bit-oriented*, *byte-oriented*, or *character-oriented protocols*. Initially, serial communications were based on character-oriented protocols because the more efficient bit-oriented protocols were proprietary. In 1979, the ISO agreed on *High-level Data Link Control (HDLC)* as a standard bit-oriented data link layer encapsulation for data on synchronous serial links. Since that time, the ITU-T has developed a number of derivative protocols collectively known as *link access protocols*, which include the following:

- *Link Access Procedure, Balanced (LAPB) for X.25*

- *Link Access Procedure on the D channel (LAPD) for ISDN*

- *Link Access Procedure for Modems (LAPM)*

- *Link Access Procedure for Frame Relay (LAPF)*

HDLC defines a Layer 2 framing structure that allows for flow and error control using acknowledgments and windowing. Each HDLC frame has the same structure, regardless of whether it is a data or control frame. HDLC defines three different types of frames, as shown in Figure 3-5. Cisco has introduced its own proprietary version of HDLC that is incompatible with those of other vendors. This frame type is also shown in Figure 3-5 and is discussed next.

Figure 3-5   HDLC Frame Formats

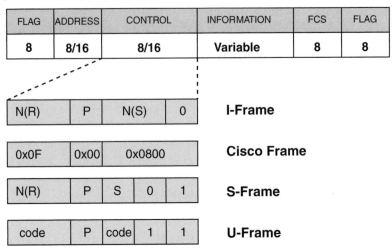

Unnumbered frames (U-frames) are used to manage links. For example, they are used to set up the logical link between the primary station and a secondary station and to tell the secondary station which mode of operation is used.

Information frames (I-frames) carry the actual data. They can piggyback acknowledgment information relating to the flow of Information frames in the reverse direction.

Supervisory frames (S-frames) are used for error and flow control.

Frame types are identified by the first 1 or 2 bits of the *Control field*. In the I-frame, the send-sequence number refers to the number of the frame to be sent next, and the receive-sequence number provides the number of the frame that will be received next. This information is maintained by both the sender and receiver.

The default encapsulation method used by Cisco devices on synchronous serial lines is HDLC. If the encapsulation has been changed to something else and must be changed back, enter serial interface configuration mode and enter the **encapsulation hdlc** command to set the encapsulation protocol on the interface.

Standard HDLC does not support multiple protocols on a single link because it has no method to identify the Layer 3 protocol being carried. The Cisco implementation of HDLC uses a proprietary Type field that acts as a Protocol field. Cisco HDLC can be used on point-to-point connections between Cisco devices. When connecting with non-Cisco devices, PPP is a more viable option because PPP is implemented in the same manner by all vendors.

Troubleshooting Serial Links

Many commands are available to help you troubleshoot problems with serial communications. The **show interfaces serial** command displays the Layer 2 encapsulation currently deployed on the interface, along with the interface's status and the line protocol, as shown in Example 3-1, in which HDLC is configured.

```
Example 3-1      show interfaces serial Command Output
Router#show interfaces serial 0/1
Serial0/1 is up, line protocol is up
  Hardware is PowerQUICC Serial
  Internet address is 10.20.15.1/30
  MTU 1500 bytes, BW 128 Kbit, DLY 20000 usec,
     reliability 255/255, txload 1/255, rxload 1/255
  Encapsulation HDLC, loopback not set
  Keepalive set (10 sec)
  Last input 00:00:07, output 00:00:03, output hang never
  Last clearing of "show interface" counters 00:01:11
  Input queue: 0/75/0/0 (size/max/drops/flushes); Total output drops: 0
  Queueing strategy: weighted fair
  Output queue: 0/1000/64/0 (size/max total/threshold/drops)
     Conversations  0/2/32 (active/max active/max total)
     Reserved Conversations 0/0 (allocated/max allocated)
     Available Bandwidth 96 kilobits/sec
  5 minute input rate 0 bits/sec, 0 packets/sec
  5 minute output rate 0 bits/sec, 0 packets/sec
     11 packets input, 1472 bytes, 0 no buffer
     Received 11 broadcasts, 0 runts, 0 giants, 0 throttles
     0 input errors, 0 CRC, 0 frame, 0 overrun, 0 ignored, 0 abort
     11 packets output, 1500 bytes, 0 underruns
     0 output errors, 0 collisions, 0 interface resets
     0 output buffer failures, 0 output buffers swapped out
     2 carrier transitions
     DCD=up  DSR=up  DTR=up  RTS=up  CTS=up
```

For data to move across a serial link, both the interface and line protocol must appear in the up state. Because the line protocol is Layer 2, the Layer 1 physical interface must be in the up state before the protocol can come up. Five possible error conditions exist for the interface's status and the line protocol:

- Serial x is down, line protocol is down
- Serial x is up, line protocol is down
- Serial x is up, line protocol is up (looped)
- Serial x is up, line protocol is down (disabled)
- Serial x is administratively down, line protocol is down

These errors can occur at either the DTE or DCE end of the connection. Table 3-2 lists these errors, along with their interpretations and possible solutions.

Table 3-2   Interpretation of Serial Interface and Line Status Messages

Status	Condition	Possible Solution
Serial x is up, line protocol is up	Proper status.	No action is required.
Serial x is up, line protocol is down (DTE mode)	The router is not sensing a CD signal. A WAN carrier service provider problem has occurred, which means that the line is down or not connected to the CSU/DSU. The cabling is faulty or incorrect. Hardware failure has occurred. (CSU/DSU)	1. Check the LEDs on the CSU/DSU to see whether the CD is active, or insert a breakout box on the line to check for the CD signal. 2. Verify that the proper cable and interface are being used by checking the documentation. 3. Insert a breakout box and check all control leads. 4. Contact the service provider to see if there is a problem. 5. Swap faulty parts. 6. If faulty router hardware is suspected, change the serial line to another port. If the connection comes up, the previously connected interface is faulty.

Table 3-2   Interpretation of Serial Interface and Line Status Messages   *continued*

Status	Condition	Possible Solution
Serial x is up, line protocol is down (DTE mode)	A local or remote router is misconfigured. Keepalives are not being sent by the remote router. A leased-line or other carrier service problem has occurred, which means a noisy line or misconfigured or failed switch. A timing problem has occurred on the cable, which means that serial clock transmit external (SCTE) is not set on CSU/DSU. SCTE is designed to compensate for clock phase shift on long cables. When the DCE device uses SCTE instead of the internal clock to sample data from the DTE, it is better able to sample the data without error even if a phase shift occurs in the cable. A local or remote CSU/DSU has failed. Router hardware, which could be either local or remote, has failed.	1. Put the modem, CSU, or DSU in local loopback mode and use the **show interfaces serial** command to determine whether the line protocol comes up. If the protocol comes up, a WAN carrier service problem or failed remote router is the likely problem. 2. If the problem appears on the remote end, repeat step 1 on the remote modem, CSU, or DSU. 3. Verify all cabling. Make certain that the cable is attached to the correct interface, the correct CSU/DSU, and the correct WAN carrier service provider network termination point. Use the **show controllers** EXEC command to determine which cable is attached to which interface. 4. Enable the **debug serial interface** command. 5. If the line protocol does not come up in local loopback mode, and if the output of the **debug serial interface** EXEC command shows that the keepalive counter is not incrementing, a router hardware problem is likely. Swap the router interface hardware. 6. If the line protocol comes up and the keepalive counter increments, the problem is not the local router. 7. If faulty router hardware is suspected, change the serial line to an unused port. If the connection comes up, the previously connected interface is the problem.

Table 3-2   Interpretation of Serial Interface and Line Status Messages   *continued*

Status	Condition	Possible Solution
Serial x is up, line protocol is down (DCE mode)	The **clockrate interface** configuration command is missing.	1. Add the **clockrate interface** configuration command on the serial interface.
	The DTE device does not support or is not set up for SCTE mode (terminal timing).	2. Set the DTE device to SCTE modem if possible. If the CSU/DSU does not support SCTE, you might need to disable SCTE on the Cisco router interface.
	The remote CSU or DSU has failed.	3. Verify that the correct cable is being used.
		4. If the line protocol is still down, there is a possible hardware failure or cabling problem. Insert a break out box and observe leads.
		5. Replace faulty parts as necessary.
Serial x is up, line protocol is up (looped)	A loop exists in the circuit. The sequence number in the keepalive packet changes to a random number when a loop is initially detected. If the same random number is returned over the link, a loop exists.	1. Use the **show running-config** privileged EXEC command to look for any loopback interface configuration command entries.
		2. If a **loopback interface** configuration command entry exists, use the **no loopback interface** configuration command to remove the loop.
		3. If no **loopback interface** configuration command exists, examine the CSU/DSU to determine whether they are configured in manual loop back mode. If they are, disable manual loopback.

Table 3-2   Interpretation of Serial Interface and Line Status Messages   *continued*

Status	Condition	Possible Solution
		4. Reset the CSU or DSU and inspect the line status. If the line protocol comes up, no other action is needed.
		5. If the CSU or DSU is not configured in manual loopback mode, contact the leased-line or other carrier service for line troubleshooting assistance.
Serial x is up, line protocol is down (disabled)	A high error rate has occurred due to a WAN service provider problem. A CSU or DSU hardware problem has occurred. Router hardware (interface) is bad.	1. Troubleshoot the line with a serial analyzer and breakout box. Look for toggling CTS and DSR signals. 2. Loop CSU/DSU (DTE loop). If the problem continues, a hardware problem is likely. If the problem does not continue, a WAN service provider problem is likely. 3. Swap out bad hardware as required (CSU, DSU, switch, local or remote router).
Serial x is administratively down, line protocol is down	The router configuration includes the **shutdown interface** configuration command. A duplicate IP address exists.	1. Check the router configuration for the **shutdown** command. 2. Use the **no shutdown** interface configuration command to remove the **shutdown** command. 3. Verify that there are no identical IP addresses using the **show running-config** privileged EXEC command or the **show interfaces** EXEC command. 4. If there are duplicate addresses, resolve the conflict by changing one of the IP addresses.

The **show controllers** command is also a valuable troubleshooting tool. This command displays the state of the interface channels and whether a cable is attached to the interface. This command is an excellent way to verify the attached cable type remotely. Example 3-2 shows partial output from the **show controllers** command where a V.35 DCE cable is attached to the interface and the clock rate is set. The syntax of this command varies between router platforms.

Example 3-2   Partial Output from the **show controllers** Command

```
Router#show controllers serial 0/1
Interface Serial0/1
Hardware is PowerQUICC MPC860
DCE V.35, clock rate 56000
idb at 0x828A2A54, driver data structure at 0x828A5858
SCC Registers:
General [GSMR]=0x2:0x00000030, Protocol-specific [PSMR]=0x8
Events [SCCE]=0x0000, Mask [SCCM]=0x001F, Status [SCCS]=0x06
Transmit on Demand [TODR]=0x0, Data Sync [DSR]=0x7E7E
<output omitted>
```

If the electrical interface is displayed as UNKNOWN instead of V.35, EIA-TIA-449, or some other electrical interface type, an improperly connected cable is the likely problem. It also is possible that a problem has occurred with the internal wiring of the interface card itself.

Table 3-3 outlines a number of useful **debug** commands available to aid in the troubleshooting process.

Table 3-3   Troubleshooting the Serial Interface Using **debug**

Command	Description
debug serial interface	Determines if the HDLC keepalive packets are incrementing. If not, a problem with either the interface or network is indicated.
debug arp	Indicates whether the router is sending information about or learning about routers (with ARP packets) on the other side of the WAN cloud. Use this command when some nodes on a TCP/IP network are responding but others are not.
debug frame-relay lmi	Obtains Local Management Interface (LMI) information, which is useful for determining if a switch and router are sending and receiving LMI packets.
debug frame-relay events	Determines if exchanges are occurring between a router and a Frame Relay switch.
debug ppp negotiation	Displays PPP packets being transmitted at startup when options are being negotiated.

Table 3-3   Troubleshooting the Serial Interface Using **debug**   *continued*

Command	Description
debug ppp packets	Displays PPP packets being sent and received. This command displays low-level packet dumps.
debug ppp errors	Displays PPP errors associated with PPP operation, such as illegal or malformed frames.
debug ppp authentication	Displays PPP Challenge Handshake Authentication Protocol (CHAP) and Password Authentication Protocol (PAP) packet exchanges.

Lab 3-1   Troubleshooting a Serial Interface (3.1.7)

In this lab, you configure a serial interface on the London and Paris routers.

PPP Authentication

Serial line communication protocols have been developed to meet the evolving needs of the communications industry. These protocols can carry data from multiple Layer 3 protocols, ensuring the authenticity of remote devices and optimizing the use of available bandwidth. Many protocols have evolved in a vendor-neutral environment and allow interoperability between equipment produced by various manufacturers.

Serial Line Internet Protocol (SLIP)

Serial Line Internet Protocol (SLIP), as described in IETF RFC 1055, is used to carry TCP/IP packets over a point-to-point connection. It was originally designed to work over low-speed dedicated serial lines and was often deployed over dialup links. SLIP is a packet-framing mechanism; it does not provide packet type identification, addressing, or error detection. In addition, standard SLIP does not provide a method of compression, even though a version of SLIP known as *Compressed SLIP* or *CSLIP* uses Van Jacobson header compression on outgoing IP packets. Because of SLIP's many limitations, it has been widely replaced by the more feature-rich and flexible PPP.

Point-to-Point Protocol (PPP)

Point-to-Point Protocol (PPP), as originally defined by IETF RFC 1661, provides a standard method for transporting multiprotocol datagrams over point-to-point links. PPP is a data link layer protocol and was designed as a replacement for the nonstandard SLIP, which also functions at Layer 2 of the OSI model. PPP can carry many different Layer 3 protocols simultaneously, including AppleTalk, DECnet, IP, and IPX. SLIP works only with IP traffic. Additionally, PPP supports the negotiation of many features, including *compression*, *authentication*, and *multilink* capabilities. PPP can support the following essential features that SLIP does not support:

- Dynamic address allocation

- PAP authentication

- CHAP authentication

- Multilink

PPP can be configured on the following types of physical interfaces:

- Asynchronous serial

- HSSI

- ISDN

- Synchronous serial

PPP uses a layered architecture, as shown in Figure 3-6. It is composed of the following main components:

- A method for encapsulating multiprotocol datagrams

- A *Link Control Protocol (LCP)* for establishing, configuring, and testing the data-link connection

- A family of *Network Control Protocols (NCPs)* for establishing and configuring different network layer protocols

Figure 3-6   PPP Layered Architecture

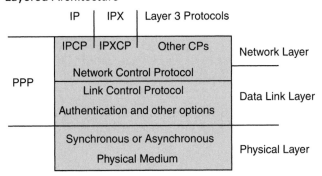

The structure of the PPP frame is shown in Figure 3-7 and is described in Table 3-4.

Figure 3-7   PPP Frame

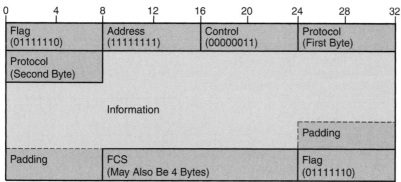

Table 3-4   PPP Frame Fields

Field Name	Size (in Bytes)	Description
Flag	1	Indicates the start of the PPP frame. Always has the value 01111110 binary.
Address	1	In HDLC this is the frame's destination address. Because PPP is a direct link between two stations, this field has no meaning and is set to 11111111 binary.
Control	1	This field is used in HDLC for various control functions. In PPP this field is set to 00000011 binary.
Protocol	2	Identifies the protocol of the datagram encapsulated in the Information field.
Information	Variable	For regular PPP frames, the network layer data gram is encapsulated here. For control frames, the control information is placed here instead.
Padding	Variable	This field may be used to increase the size of the PPP frame.
FCS	2 (or 4)	The Frame Check Sequence is a CRC code used to determine the frame's integrity. THE FCS is calculated over the Address, Control, Protocol, Information, and Padding fields.
Closing Flag	1	Indicates the end of the PPP frame. This field always has the value 01111110 binary.

The *Protocol field* identifies the purpose of the PPP frame. It identifies the network layer protocol to which the datagram belongs if the PPP frame is carrying data or identifies it as a control protocol. Table 3-5 shows the ranges used for the various functions; Table 3-6 presents specific examples.

Table 3-5   PPP Protocol Field Ranges

Protocol Field Range (Hex)	Description
02xx–1Exx xx01–xx1F	Not used (compression inefficient)
0xxx–3xxx	Datagram belonging to a specific network layer protocol
8xxx–Bxxx	Datagram belonging to associated Network Control Protocol
4xxx–7xxx	Datagram belonging to low-volume protocols with no NCP
Cxxx–Exxx	Datagram is a control protocol

Table 3-6   PPP Protocol Field Values

Protocol Value (Hex)	Protocol Name
8021	Internet Protocol Control Protocol
8023	OSI Network Layer Control Protocol
8029	AppleTalk Control Protocol
802B	Novell IPX Control Protocol
C021	Link Control Protocol
C023	Password Authentication Protocol
C223	Challenge Handshake Authentication Protocol

PPP uses Link Control Protocol (LCP) to negotiate and set up control options on the WAN data link. LCP is used to negotiate the encapsulation format options, including the following:

- **Authentication**—Authentication requires that the calling side of the link enter credentials to verify to the called side that it has permission to make the call. PPP can use either PAP or CHAP. Cisco devices also support Microsoft's version of CHAP (MS-CHAP), allowing Microsoft OS-based machines to authenticate with a Cisco router or access server acting as a Network Access Server (NAS).

- **Compression**—Compression reduces the amount of data in a frame and therefore increases its efficiency. Cisco routers can use either Stacker or Predictor.

- **Error detection**—Error detection allows PPP to identify a fault condition. The Quality and Magic Number options help ensure a reliable, loop-free data network.

- **Multilink**—Cisco IOS 11.1 and later allows PPP to load-balance over multiple interfaces.

- **PPP callback**—Cisco IOS 11.1 and later allow a router to act as either a *callback server* or a *callback client*. The client makes the initial call and requests that it be called back. The initial call is then terminated, and the callback server calls back the client based on its configuration. This provides for enhanced security.

In addition, LCP does the following:

- Handles varying limits on packet size

- Detects common misconfiguration errors

- Terminates the link

- Determines when a link is operating properly and when it is failing

NCPs are used to establish and configure options for multiple network layer protocols.

PPP session establishment progresses through three phases:

1. Link establishment

2. Authentication phase (optional)

3. Network layer protocol

Session establishment is carried out by LCP frames. Three types of LCP frames are used to establish a PPP session:

- *Link-establishment frames* are used to establish and configure a link.

- *Link-maintenance frames* are used to manage and debug a link.

- *Link-termination frames* are used to terminate a link.

During the link-establishment phase, each device sends LCP frames to configure and test the data link. These LCP frames contain a configuration option field that allows them to negotiate the use of such options as compressing certain fields and the link-authentication protocol. If a configuration option is not included in the LCP, the default value for that configuration option is assumed. The LCP must open the connection and successfully negotiate the configuration options before any network layer packets can be exchanged. This phase is complete when a configuration acknowledgment frame has been sent and received.

PPP authentication methods are described in RFC 1334. The LCP negotiates the optional authentication phase during the initial link establishment. If used, authentication must take place before the network layer protocol phase is entered. Two types of authentication are available for use over a PPP link:

- PAP

- CHAP

An optional link-quality determination test can also be conducted before the network layer protocol phase is entered.

Password Authentication Protocol (PAP)

Password Authentication Protocol (PAP) provides a simple method for a peer to establish its identity by using a *two-way handshake*. This is done only upon initial link establishment, as shown in Figure 3-8. The *peer* repeatedly sends an ID/password pair to the *authenticator* until either authentication is acknowledged or the connection is terminated. The authenticator maintains a database of username/password pairs that it compares to the information received from the peer that wants to be authenticated.

Figure 3-8   PAP Authentication

PAP is not a strong authentication method because the password is sent across the wire in clear text, allowing it to be easily "sniffed." In addition, there is no protection from *playback* or repeated *trial-and-error attacks*. The peer is in control of the frequency and timing of authentication attempts. After authentication, no repeat authentication is requested, leaving the connection open for *hijack*.

Challenge Handshake Authentication Protocol (CHAP)

Challenge Handshake Authentication Protocol (CHAP) is defined by IETF RFC 1994 and overcomes many of the limitations inherent in PAP. CHAP uses a *three-way handshake* and never sends the password across the link. In addition, CHAP uses repeated challenges—the frequency of which is controlled by the authenticator, as shown in Figure 3-9.

Figure 3-9   CHAP Authentication

CHAP uses four types of PPP frames, all of which have the Protocol field set to 0xC223. In these control frames, the Information field contains a CHAP header that is composed of the following:

- A 1-byte Code field that describes the frame's function

- A 1-byte Identifier used to match challenges, responses, and replies

- A 2-byte Length field that specifies the size of the CHAP package, including the Code, Identifier, Length, and Data fields

Data follows the CHAP header and can consist of zero or more bytes, as specified by the Length field. Part A of Figure 3-10 shows the PPP Challenge and Response frame format, and Part B of Figure 3-10 shows the PPP CHAP Success and Failure frame format. Table 3-7 lists the four control frames.

Figure 3-10   PPP CHAP Control Frames

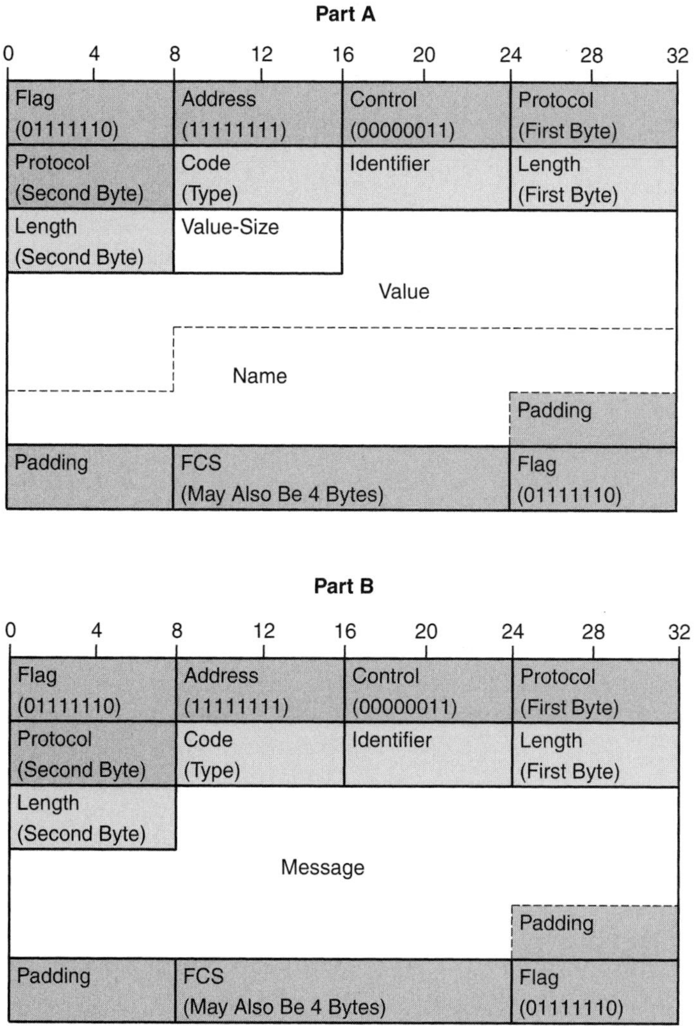

Table 3-7   CHAP Control Frame Codes

Code	Description
1	Challenge
2	Response
3	Success
4	Failure

To avoid sending the password between peers, each device is configured with a database containing the username of the other peer and a common shared secret. The authenticator sends a code 1 *Challenge* frame to the remote peer containing an incrementally changing identifier and a random and unpredictable challenge value. This challenge is received by the peer, which uses its own database to determine the shared secret associated with the authenticator. The peer then places the challenge value, the identifier, and the shared secret in a *one-way hash* algorithm such as *Message Digest 5 (MD5)*. A one-way hash is one that cannot be reversed.

This hash is then sent back to the authenticator, as a code 2 *Response* frame, as shown in Figure 3-11. The authenticator uses its database to determine the shared secret associated with the peer. It places this secret, the challenge string, and the identifier through the same hashing algorithm. It then compares the hash generated locally to the one received from the peer to determine if authentication was successful.

Figure 3-11   CHAP Challenge-Response

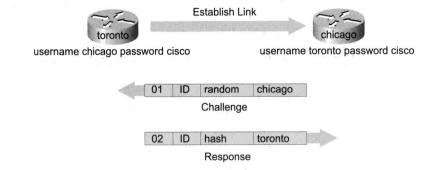

If the hashes match, a code 3 *Success* frame is sent back to the peer, but if the hashes do not match, a code 4 *Failure* frame is returned. At no time is the shared secret sent over the medium, except as part of the hash. After authentication, the authenticator sends challenges to the peer at random intervals, asking it to reauthenticate. The frequency of authentication can be controlled by a third-party software package or a product such as Cisco Secure ACS. The Microsoft version of CHAP (MS-CHAP) is supported; it allows Windows-based machines to authenticate with a Cisco-based Network Access Server.

Although it isn't perfect, CHAP is much more secure than PAP. Because the password is never sent over the link, it is not possible to "sniff" it from the wire or use replay attacks against the network. The authentication process is initiated by the authenticator, which hinders the use of trial-and-error attacks. Random variable challenges to the peer by the authenticator also make hijack-type attacks extremely difficult by limiting the time of exposure for any single attack. CHAP has widely replaced PAP for authentication on PPP links, although PAP may still be encountered in situations where either the peer or the authenticator cannot support CHAP.

The final phase in establishing a PPP session is the network layer protocol phase. In this phase, the PPP devices send NCP frames to choose and configure one or more network layer protocols. Each network layer protocol that will move across the PPP link must have a corresponding NCP to control and configure that link. For example, if both IP and IPX traffic will move across the link, both IPCP and IPXCP are brought up at this time. After they are configured, packets from each protocol may flow across the link.

The network layer remains active until an activity timer expires, a user intervenes, or the link is closed by the LCP or NCP frames. If the LCP frames close the link, they notify network layer protocols so that they may take appropriate action.

Figure 3-12 illustrates the entire PPP session establishment and termination process.

Figure 3-12   PPP Session Establishment/Termination

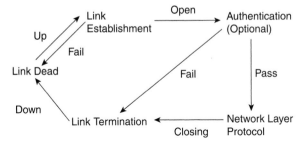

Configuring PPP

You configure PPP encapsulation by entering the **encapsulation ppp** command in the appropriate serial interface configuration mode. After PPP is configured, you may specify a number of options, including compression, error detection, multilink, and authentication.

Lab 3-2   Configuring PPP Encapsulation (3.3.2)

In this lab, you configure a serial interface on the Washington and Dublin routers with the PPP protocol.

Configuring Compression on PPP Links

Point-to-point compression can be configured on PPP links. Compression reduces the size of the PPP frame via lossless data compression. Most Cisco devices support only software compression, which can seriously degrade system performance. You must carefully analyze the overall effect of compression on any system before deciding to implement it. PPP encapsulations support both Predictor and Stacker compression algorithms. *Predictor* uses a RAND compression algorithm, and *Stacker* uses an LZS algorithm. For compression to function, both ends of a PPP link must be properly configured. To enable PPP compression, use the following command:

```
Router(config-if)#compress [predictor | stac]
```

If the bottleneck is caused by the load on the router, you should select the Predictor algorithm. If the bottleneck is a result of the line bandwidth, you should select the Stacker algorithm. You should also disable compression if the router CPU load exceeds 40 percent or if the majority of the data is already compressed. To determine the CPU load, use the **show processes cpu** EXEC command.

Configuring Error Detection on PPP Links

Data communications links are rarely perfect. Packets can be dropped or corrupted for a number of reasons, including line noise, buffer overruns, and equipment failures. Sometimes it is desirable to determine when and how often the link is dropping data to allow a router to use another route or link. PPP fully supports *Link Quality Report (LQR)* packets, which keep track of data loss in both the inbound and outbound directions. When *Link Quality Monitoring (LQM)* is enabled, LQRs are sent in place of keepalives, every keepalive period. To monitor the data dropped on a link, use the following command:

```
Router(config-if)#ppp quality percentage
```

The *percentage* argument specifies the link quality threshold. If this percentage is not maintained, the link is deemed to be of poor quality and is taken down.

Configuring Multilink Support on PPP Links

The multilink feature provides *load balancing* functionality over multiple WAN links while providing multivendor interoperability, packet fragmentation and proper sequencing, and load calculation on both inbound and outbound traffic. *Multi-Link Protocol (MLP)* allows packets to be fragmented and the fragments to be sent simultaneously over multiple point-to-point links to the same remote address. The multiple links come up in response to a defined load threshold on the line, which must be configured separately. To configure multilink on an interface, issue the following command:

```
Router(config-if)#ppp multilink
```

Configuring Authentication on PPP Links

Authentication is designed to verify that a remote device has permission to make a connection. Usually authentication is configured on both ends of a PPP link to allow mutual authentication. To configure authentication, a username and password must be created on each router for the router that will connect to it. You do this in global configuration mode by issuing the following command:

```
Router(config)#username name password secret
```

where *name* is the (case-sensitive) hostname of the remote router and *secret* must be the same on both routers.

After creating the user accounts, enter the appropriate interface configuration, and configure the interface for PPP encapsulation as follows:

```
Router(config-if)#encapsulation ppp
```

Next, you must specify the PPP authentication method. The options available are CHAP and PAP, and they can be specified either alone or in combination. If both are specified, the first one listed is tried. If authentication cannot be negotiated using the first method specified, the second method is tried. Note that if authentication fails on the first method listed, the second method is not tried. To specify the authentication method, use the following interface configuration command:

```
Router(config-if)#ppp authentication {chap | chap pap | pap chap | pap | ms-chap}
```

In Cisco IOS Software Release 11.1 and later, PAP is disabled by default and must be enabled on the interface. This is accomplished with the following command:

```
Router(config-if)#ppp pap sent-username username password password
```

If authenticating Microsoft-based hosts, the ms-chap option should be specified. It is also possible to specify an interface-specific CHAP username or password using the following commands:

```
Router(config-if)#ppp chap hostname hostname
```

```
Router(config-if)#ppp chap password password
```

Quite often these commands are necessary if the username and password allocated by the service provider are not the same as the remote router's hostname. In this case, an alternative name can be specified for authentication purposes.

Figure 3-13 shows two routers, Toronto and Chicago, that must communicate using PPP. Examples 3-3 and 3-4 show the appropriate configurations for PAP and CHAP, respectively.

Figure 3-13   Sample Network for PPP Session Establishment

Toronto   Chicago

Example 3-3   Router Configurations: PAP

```
Toronto Router
!
hostname toronto
!
username chicago password 0 cisco
!
!interface Serial0/1
 ip address 10.20.15.1 255.255.255.252
 encapsulation ppp
 clockrate 56000
 ppp authentication pap
 ppp pap sent-username toronto password 0 cisco
!
```

```
Chicago Router
!
hostname chicago
!
username toronto password 0 cisco
!
interface Serial0/0
 ip address 10.20.15.2 255.255.255.252
 encapsulation ppp
 no fair-queue
 ppp authentication pap
 ppp pap sent-username chicago password 0 cisco
!
```

Example 3-4   Router Configurations: CHAP

```
Toronto Router
!
hostname toronto
!
username chicago password 0 cisco
!
interface Serial0/1
 ip address 10.20.15.1 255.255.255.252
 encapsulation ppp
 clockrate 56000
 ppp authentication chap
!
```

```
Chicago Router
!
hostname chicago
!
username toronto password 0 cisco
!
interface Serial0/0
 ip address 10.20.15.2 255.255.255.252
 encapsulation ppp
 no fair-queue
 ppp authentication chap
!
```

 Lab 3-3   Configuring PPP Authentication (3.3.3)

In this lab, you configure a serial interface on the Madrid and Tokyo routers.

For any serial link to become fully functional, the encapsulation on each end of the link must be the same. To verify the Layer 2 encapsulation, use the **show interfaces serial** command. Example 3-5 shows the output when PPP is configured. When PPP is configured, this command displays the status of both the LCP and NCP.

Example 3-5   show interfaces serial Command Output

```
Router#show interface serial 0/1
Serial0/1 is up, line protocol is up
  Hardware is PowerQUICC Serial
  Internet address is 10.20.15.1/30
  MTU 1500 bytes, BW 128 Kbit, DLY 20000 usec,
      reliability 255/255, txload 1/255, rxload 1/255
  Encapsulation PPP, loopback not set
  LCP Open
  Open: IPCP, CDPCP
  Last input 00:00:09, output 00:00:09, output hang never
  Last clearing of "show interface" counters 01:38:26
  Input queue: 0/75/0/0 (size/max/drops/flushes); Total output drops: 0
  Queueing strategy: weighted fair
  Output queue: 0/1000/64/0 (size/max total/threshold/drops)
      Conversations  0/2/32 (active/max active/max total)
      Reserved Conversations 0/0 (allocated/max allocated)
      Available Bandwidth 96 kilobits/sec
  5 minute input rate 0 bits/sec, 0 packets/sec
  5 minute output rate 0 bits/sec, 0 packets/sec
      1257 packets input, 54696 bytes, 0 no buffer
      Received 0 broadcasts, 0 runts, 0 giants, 0 throttles
      3 input errors, 0 CRC, 2 frame, 0 overrun, 0 ignored, 0 abort
      1258 packets output, 55417 bytes, 0 underruns
      0 output errors, 0 collisions, 7 interface resets
      0 output buffer failures, 0 output buffers swapped out
      28 carrier transitions
      DCD=up  DSR=up  DTR=up  RTS=up  CTS=up
```

You can use the **debug ppp** command to examine the PPP process in real time. Many options can be specified, as shown in Table 3-8.

Table 3-8   Debugging PPP

Command	Description
debug ppp packet	Displays PPP packets being sent and received
debug ppp negotiation	Displays PPP packets transmitted during PPP startup
debug ppp error	Displays protocol errors and error statistics associated with PPP negotiation and operation
debug ppp chap	Displays CHAP packet exchanges

Lab 3-4   Verifying PPP Configuration (3.3.4)

In this lab, you configure a serial interface on the Brasilia and Warsaw routers with the PPP protocol.

Lab 3-5   Troubleshooting PPP Configuration (3.3.5)

In this lab, you configure a serial interface on the London and Paris routers and troubleshoot the connection.

To observe the authentication process, use the **debug ppp authentication** command. Example 3-6 shows partial output from the **debug ppp authentication** command on the Toronto router in our example when PAP is configured. With two-way authentication configured, each router authenticates the other before the NCPs are allowed to come up.

Example 3-6   Partial Output of debug ppp authentication

```
01:54:04: Se0/1 PPP: Phase is AUTHENTICATING, by both
01:54:04: Se0/1 PAP: Using hostname from interface PAP
01:54:04: Se0/1 PAP: Using password from interface PAP
01:54:04: Se0/1 PAP: O AUTH-REQ id 2 len 18 from "toronto"
01:54:04: Se0/1 PAP: I AUTH-REQ id 2 len 18 from "chicago"
01:54:04: Se0/1 PAP: Authenticating peer chicago
01:54:04: Se0/1 PPP: Phase is FORWARDING, Attempting Forward
01:54:04: Se0/1 PPP: Phase is AUTHENTICATING, Unauthenticated User
01:54:04: Se0/1 PPP: Phase is FORWARDING, Attempting Forward
01:54:04: Se0/1 PPP: Phase is AUTHENTICATING, Authenticated User
01:54:04: Se0/1 PAP: O AUTH-ACK id 2 len 5
01:54:04: Se0/1 PAP: I AUTH-ACK id 2 len 5
01:54:04: Se0/1 PPP: Phase is UP
```

Table 3-9 provides further explanation of the highlighted lines in Example 3-6.

Table 3-9   Two-Way Authentication Using PAP

Output	Description
01:54:04: Se0/1 PPP: Phase is AUTHENTICATING, by both	Two-way authentication
01:54:04: Se0/1 PAP: O AUTH-REQ id 2 len 18 from "toronto"	Outgoing authentication request

Table 3-9   Two-Way Authentication Using PAP

Output	Description
01:54:04: Se0/1 PAP: I AUTH-REQ id 2 len 18 from "chicago"	Incoming authentication request
01:54:04: Se0/1 PAP: Authenticating peer chicago	Authenticating incoming
01:54:04: Se0/1 PAP: O AUTH-ACK id 2 len 5	Outgoing acknowledgment
01:54:04: Se0/1 PAP: I AUTH-ACK id 2 len 5	Incoming acknowledgment

Example 3-7 shows output from the **debug ppp authentication** command when CHAP is properly configured. After the challenge response is evaluated and determined to be correct, the NCPs are brought up on the line. Example 3-8 shows the same output when the passwords are misconfigured.

Example 3-7   Successful Authentication Using CHAP

```
02:01:34: %LINK-3-UPDOWN: Interface Serial0/1, changed state to up
02:01:34: Se0/1 PPP: Treating connection as a dedicated line
02:01:34: Se0/1 PPP: Authorization NOT required
02:01:34: Se0/1 CHAP: O CHALLENGE id 7 len 28 from "toronto"
02:01:34: Se0/1 CHAP: I CHALLENGE id 7 len 28 from "chicago"
02:01:34: Se0/1 CHAP: Using hostname from configured hostname
02:01:34: Se0/1 CHAP: Using password from AAA
02:01:34: Se0/1 CHAP: O RESPONSE id 7 len 28 from "toronto"
02:01:34: Se0/1 CHAP: I RESPONSE id 7 len 28 from "chicago"
02:01:34: Se0/1 PPP: Sent CHAP LOGIN Request to AAA
02:01:34: Se0/1 PPP: Received LOGIN Response from AAA = PASS
02:01:34: Se0/1 CHAP: O SUCCESS id 7 len 4
02:01:34: Se0/1 CHAP: I SUCCESS id 7 len 4
02:01:35: %LINEPROTO-5-UPDOWN: Line protocol on Interface Serial0/1, changed state to
  up
```

Example 3-8   Unsuccessful Authentication Using CHAP: Misconfigured Passwords

```
00:11:14: %LINK-3-UPDOWN: Interface Serial0/1, changed state to up
00:11:14: Se0/1 PPP: Treating connection as a dedicated line
00:11:14: Se0/1 PPP: Authorization NOT required
00:11:14: Se0/1 CHAP: O CHALLENGE id 41 len 28 from "toronto"
00:11:14: Se0/1 CHAP: I CHALLENGE id 42 len 28 from "chicago"
00:11:14: Se0/1 CHAP: Using hostname from configured hostname
00:11:14: Se0/1 CHAP: Using password from AAA
00:11:14: Se0/1 CHAP: O RESPONSE id 42 len 28 from "toronto"
00:11:14: Se0/1 CHAP: I RESPONSE id 41 len 28 from "chicago"
00:11:14: Se0/1 PPP: Sent CHAP LOGIN Request to AAA
00:11:14: Se0/1 PPP: Received LOGIN Response from AAA = FAIL
00:11:14: Se0/1 CHAP: O FAILURE id 41 len 26 msg is "Authentication failure"
```

The **debug ppp authentication** command can also detect misconfigured authentication types, as shown in Example 3-9.

Example 3-9   Misconfigured Authentication Types

```
00:35:40: Se0/1 PPP: I pkt type 0xC021, datagramsize 18
00:35:40: Se0/1 LCP: I CONFREQ [ACKrcvd] id 105 len 14
00:35:40: Se0/1 LCP:    AuthProto PAP (0x0304C023)
00:35:40: Se0/1 LCP:    MagicNumber 0x0DDF2A13 (0x05060DDF2A13)
00:35:40: Se0/1 LCP: O CONFNAK [ACKrcvd] id 105 len 9
00:35:40: Se0/1 LCP:    AuthProto CHAP (0x0305C22305)
```

Viewing PPP Link Establishment and Authentication

The entire PPP negotiation and authentication process is clearly seen in Example 3-10, which is output generated by the **debug ppp negotiation** command. This shows the LCPs bringing up the line, authentication, multiple NCPs coming up, and finally bringing up the appropriate Layer 3 line protocols.

Example 3-10   Successful PPP Negotiation

```
01:37:44: %LINK-3-UPDOWN: Interface Serial0/1, changed state to up
01:37:44: Se0/1 PPP: Treating connection as a dedicated line
01:37:44: Se0/1 PPP: Phase is ESTABLISHING, Active Open
01:37:44: Se0/1 LCP: O CONFREQ [Closed] id 4 len 15
01:37:44: Se0/1 LCP:    AuthProto CHAP (0x0305C22305)
01:37:44: Se0/1 LCP:    MagicNumber 0x0D81F0BE (0x05060D81F0BE)
01:37:44: Se0/1 LCP: I CONFREQ [REQsent] id 138 len 15
01:37:44: Se0/1 LCP:    AuthProto CHAP (0x0305C22305)
01:37:44: Se0/1 LCP:    MagicNumber 0x0E31CFAB (0x05060E31CFAB)
01:37:44: Se0/1 LCP: O CONFACK [REQsent] id 138 len 15
01:37:44: Se0/1 LCP:    AuthProto CHAP (0x0305C22305)
01:37:44: Se0/1 LCP:    MagicNumber 0x0E31CFAB (0x05060E31CFAB)
01:37:44: Se0/1 LCP: I CONFACK [ACKsent] id 4 len 15
01:37:44: Se0/1 LCP:    AuthProto CHAP (0x0305C22305)
01:37:44: Se0/1 LCP:    MagicNumber 0x0D81F0BE (0x05060D81F0BE)
01:37:44: Se0/1 LCP: State is Open
01:37:44: Se0/1 PPP: Phase is AUTHENTICATING, by both
01:37:44: Se0/1 CHAP: O CHALLENGE id 4 len 28 from "toronto"
01:37:44: Se0/1 CHAP: I CHALLENGE id 4 len 28 from "chicago"
01:37:44: Se0/1 CHAP: Using hostname from configured hostname
01:37:44: Se0/1 CHAP: Using password from AAA
01:37:44: Se0/1 CHAP: O RESPONSE id 4 len 28 from "toronto"
01:37:44: Se0/1 CHAP: I RESPONSE id 4 len 28 from "chicago"
01:37:44: Se0/1 PPP: Phase is FORWARDING, Attempting Forward
01:37:44: Se0/1 PPP: Phase is AUTHENTICATING, Unauthenticated User
01:37:44: Se0/1 PPP: Phase is FORWARDING, Attempting Forward
01:37:44: Se0/1 PPP: Phase is AUTHENTICATING, Authenticated User
01:37:44: Se0/1 CHAP: O SUCCESS id 4 len 4
01:37:44: Se0/1 CHAP: I SUCCESS id 4 len 4
01:37:44: Se0/1 PPP: Phase is UP
01:37:44: Se0/1 IPCP: O CONFREQ [Closed] id 4 len 10
01:37:44: Se0/1 IPCP:    Address 10.20.15.1 (0x03060A140F01)
01:37:44: Se0/1 CDPCP: O CONFREQ [Closed] id 4 len 4
01:37:44: Se0/1 IPCP: I CONFREQ [REQsent] id 4 len 10
01:37:44: Se0/1 IPCP:    Address 10.20.15.2 (0x03060A140F02)
01:37:44: %Se0/1 IPCP: O CONFACK [REQsent] id 4 len 10
01:37:44: Se0/1 IPCP:    Address 10.20.15.2 (0x03060A140F02)
01:37:44: Se0/1 CDPCP: I CONFREQ [REQsent] id 4 len 4
01:37:44: Se0/1 CDPCP: O CONFACK [REQsent] id 4 len 4
01:37:44: Se0/1 IPCP: I CONFACK [ACKsent] id 4 len 10
01:37:44: Se0/1 IPCP:    Address 10.20.15.1 (0x03060A140F01)
```

Example 3-10   Successful PPP Negotiation   *continued*

```
01:37:44: Se0/1 IPCP: State is Open
01:37:44: Se0/1 IPCP: Install route to 10.20.15.2
01:37:44: Se0/1 IPCP: Add link info for cef entry 10.20.15.2
01:37:44: Se0/1 CDPCP: I CONFACK [ACKsent] id 4 len 4
01:37:44: Se0/1 CDPCP: State is Open
01:37:45: %LINEPROTO-5-UPDOWN: Line protocol on Interface Serial0/1, changed state to
  up
```

Summary

This chapter examined the functionality of DTE and DCE devices and how they transform data in a manner that allows it to be moved across WAN serial links. The role of TDM in allowing the media to carry multiple simultaneous conversations was considered.

This chapter also examined the structure of both the HDLC and PPP frames, with emphasis on the functionality of the various fields. The role of the Link Control Protocol (LCP) and Network Control Protocols (NCPs) in establishing, configuring, maintaining, and terminating a PPP link was covered, as were PAP and CHAP authentication. Configuration and troubleshooting commands were presented.

The next chapter shows you how to implement PPP to allow multiple, secure, simultaneous conversations over a digital network.

Check Your Understanding

Complete all the review questions listed here to test your understanding of the topics and concepts in this chapter. Answers are listed in Appendix A, "Answers to Check Your Understanding and Challenge Questions."

1. What is the role of the CSU/DSU?

    A. To transform the data into a format acceptable for transmission on the service provider's network

    B. To transform the data into a format acceptable to the CPE DCE device

    C. To transform the data into a format acceptable to the local DCE device

    D. To transform the data into a format acceptable to the serial interface

2. What is used to connect two DCE devices?

    A. Local loop

    B. Null-modem cable

    C. Serial cable

    D. Service provider's network

3. What is used to directly connect two DTE devices?

    A. Local loop

    B. Null-modem cable

    C. Serial cable

    D. Service provider's network

4. What is used to connect a DTE device to a DCE device?

    A. Local loop

    B. Null-modem cable

    C. Serial cable

    D. Service provider's network

5. What is the default Layer 2 serial line encapsulation used on Cisco routers?

    A. CHAP

    B. HDLC

    C. PPP

    D. SLIP

6. When would PPP be selected over HDLC as a Layer 2 serial line encapsulation?
   (Choose three.)

   A. When working in a multivendor environment

   B. When working with high-speed serial links

   C. When working in a Cisco-only environment

   D. When CHAP must be configured

   E. When both IP and IPX traffic must be carried on the same link

   F. When working with low-speed serial links

7. A network technician must configure a remote connection into the corporate network. The
   connection must be able to carry both IP and IPX traffic over a secure link. What should
   the technician configure?

   A. SLIP using PAP

   B. SLIP using CHAP

   C. PPP using PAP

   D. PPP using CHAP

8. What is a role of the NCP?

   A. Configuring authentication

   B. Configuring Layer 3 protocols

   C. Setting the MTU

   D. Testing link quality

9. What type of authentication uses a three-way handshake?

   A. CHAP

   B. PAP

   C. PPP

   D. SLIP

10. What command sets the Layer 2 encapsulation to the Cisco default on the serial interface?

   A. Router(config)#**encapsulation hdlc**

   B. Router(config)#**encapsulation default hdlc**

   C. Router(config-if)#**encapsulation hdlc**

   D. Router(config-if)#**encapsulation default**

   E. Router(config-if)#**encapsulation ppp**

11. What command can be used to determine the Layer 2 encapsulation in use on serial 0/0?

A. Router#**show encapsulation serial 0/0**

B. Router#**show interface serial 0/0**

C. Router#**show serial 0/0 encapsulation**

D. Router#**show interface serial 0/0 encapsulation**

12. What command can be used to determine problems with CHAP?

A. Router#**show chap**

B. Router#**show authentication chap**

C. Router#**debug ppp chap**

D. Router#**debug ppp session**

E. Router#**debug ppp authentication**

13. A remote site reports that it cannot connect to the corporate WAN. The link has been configured to use PPP with CHAP. A partial output of the **debug ppp authentication** command is shown here:

```
00:11:14: Se0/1 PPP: Sent CHAP LOGIN Request to AAA
00:11:14: Se0/1 PPP: Received LOGIN Response from AAA = FAIL
00:11:14: Se0/1 CHAP: O FAILURE id 41 len 26 msg is "Authentication failure"
```

What is the most likely cause of the problem?

A. The passwords are misconfigured.

B. The encapsulations are misconfigured.

C. The authentication protocols are misconfigured.

D. The physical layer is malfunctioning.

14. What is responsible for completing the authentication process in a PPP session?

a. LCP

b. NCP

c. IP

d. CHAP

15. What PPP frame type is sent in response to a successful CHAP authentication?

    A. 1

    B. 2

    C. 3

    D. 4

16. What happens to a TDM timeslot when the conversation to which it is assigned has no data to transmit?

    A. The timeslot is reassigned to another conversation.

    B. The timeslot remains unused.

    C. The timeslot is eliminated from the data stream.

    D. The timeslot is held until there is data to transmit.

17. At what layer of the OSI model does TDM function?

    A. Physical

    B. Data link

    C. Network

    D. Transport

Challenge Questions and Activities

Complete the following questions as well. These questions are purposefully designed to be similar to the more complex styles of questions you might expect to see on the CCNA exam. This section may also list activities that will help you prepare for the exams.

1. You have been asked to troubleshoot a faulty PPP link between two sites on the corporate WAN. The link was previously running HDLC with no authentication without problems. What procedure would you follow to diagnose this problem?

2. The network administrator has decided to change the currently implemented PAP authentication on the PPP link to CHAP. Which commands will be required to complete this task?

3. A Cisco router is running IOS 12.2 and must be configured for PAP authentication. The administrator has correctly created accounts for all remote routers and has issued the **ppp authentication pap** command, but authentication is not working. What is the probable cause of this problem?

4. How does CHAP authenticate a remote site without sending the password across the link?

CHAPTER 4

ISDN and DDR

Objectives

Upon completion of this chapter, you should be able to answer the following questions:

- Which standards are used for ISDN addressing, concepts, and signaling?

- What is the available bandwidth on an ISDN BRI and PRI in North America and elsewhere?

- What are the roles of the various devices encountered in an ISDN network?

- What are the characteristics of the ISDN reference points?

- How is an ISDN end-to-end connection configured and verified?

- How is interesting traffic defined for DDR?

- What advantages do dialer profiles exhibit over legacy DDR?

- What commands are used to configure, test, and troubleshoot both legacy DDR and dialer profiles?

Key Terms

This chapter uses the following key terms. You can find the definitions in the glossary at the end of the book.

continues

continued

Integrated Services Digital Network (ISDN) is a technology that allows multiple simultaneous end-to-end digital communications to occur over the same medium as ordinary analog telephone wiring. ISDN can support a wide range of services, including voice, video, and data.

Dial-on-demand routing (DDR) is a technique that allows WAN connectivity to be built up over ordinary telephone lines when required. DDR allows a router to connect using a dialup service when data needs to be sent and then disconnect when the transfer is complete.

Combining DDR with ISDN lets you establish reliable WAN connectivity when required without the expense of an "always-on" connection. This combination is ideally suited to both small office, home office (SOHO) and small remote offices, which typically have a very low volume of data to exchange with the central office. Because ISDN costs depend on both the connect time and the volume being transferred, this combination of technologies offers savings only when short connect times can be used to transfer the low volume of data required.

Although ISDN and DDR are still used in some environments and for specialized applications, the widespread availability of broadband connectivity through cable and DSL has all but eliminated their adoption in new installations. Alternative technologies provide always-on, secure connectivity at a fraction of the cost of ISDN and will soon force ISDN to the status of a legacy application.

ISDN Concepts

The Public Switched Telephone Network (PSTN) was originally designed to carry analog traffic over the local loop between the customer site and the central office (CO), as shown in part (a) of Figure 4-1. The analog technology that existed at the time created an upper limit on the available bandwidth of approximately 3 kHz. As technology advanced, the telephone companies upgraded their switches to be capable of handling digital signals, which made ISDN possible. ISDN uses a digital signal over the existing telephone circuit wiring, allowing digital end-to-end connectivity, as shown in part (b) of Figure 4-1.

Figure 4-1   Analog and Digital Connectivity

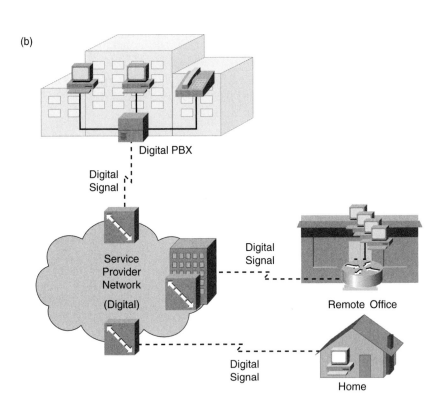

ISDN Standards and Concepts

Work on ISDN standards began in the 1960s, with a comprehensive set of ISDN recommendations published in 1984. These recommendations are continuously updated by the *International Telecommunication Union Telecommunication Standardization Sector (ITU-T)*. These standards encompass digital telephony and data communications and are organized into three general areas:

- **E series**—These recommend telephone network standards for ISDN. For example, international addressing for ISDN is covered under E.164.

- **I series**—These deal with the concepts, terminology, and general methods involved in ISDN. The I.100 series includes general ISDN concepts and the structure of other I series recommendations. I.200 deals with the service aspects of ISDN, I.300 describes network aspects, and I.400 describes how the User-Network Interface (UNI) is provided.

- **Q series**—These cover how switching and signaling should operate. Signaling is the process of establishing a call. Q.921 (Link Access Procedure on the D channel [LAPD]) and Q.931 (ISDN network layer between terminal and switch) are key examples of the Q series.,

Two main channel types are defined by ISDN standards:

- The *bearer channel (B channel)* is a 64-kbps data path that can be used to carry a full-duplex digital conversation.

- The *delta channel (D channel)* is used to carry control information for the B channel. The D channel can have a capacity of either 16 kbps for the Basic Rate Interface (BRI) or 64 kbps for the Primary Rate Interface (PRI).

The ISDN *BRI* interface consists of two B channels and one D channel (2B+D).

The ISDN *PRI* interface consists of either 23 B channels and one D channel (23B+D) in North America and Japan, or 30 B channels and one D channel (30B+D) in most other parts of the world, as shown in Figure 4-2. The difference between the two can be attributed to the fact that the standard ISDN line in North America and Japan is a T1 with bandwidth of 1.544 Mbps. In Europe and most other places in the world, a standard ISDN line is an E1 with bandwidth of 2.048 Mbps.

Figure 4-2   ISDN BRI and PRI Interfaces

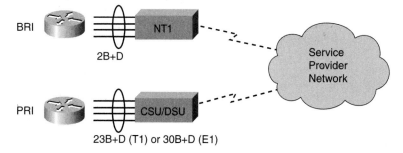

The B channel is used to carry digitized data streams, which may be voice video or data. ISDN is a circuit-switched technology and the B channels are the elemental circuit-switching unit. If voice is to be carried, specialized methods are used to encode and decode the speech at either end of the link. If data is to be carried across the connection, either *High-level Data Link*

Control (HDLC) or *Point-to-Point Protocol (PPP)* may be used at Layer 2. The advantages of PPP over HDLC include authentication and link quality management. Chapter 3, "PPP," provides a complete comparison of HDLC and PPP.

The D channel is responsible for carrying messages related to call setup and teardown. These messages, generated whenever a TCP connection is made, are usually carried over the same path that carries data and are known as *in-band signaling*. With ISDN, these messages move across the D channel while data moves across the B channel. This is known as *out-of-band signaling*. Traffic on the D channel uses *Link Access Procedure on the D channel (LAPD)*, which is based on HDLC, as discussed in Chapter 3.

Under certain circumstances the D channel also can carry user data. For example, a number of ATM/debit machines have an ISDN D channel only. These machines use this D channel both to send requests and receive responses.

ISDN spans the physical, data link, and network layers (Layers 1 through 3) of the OSI model. Various ITU-T standards define each channel, as shown in Table 4-1. The emergence of ISDN represents an effort to standardize subscriber services, user/network interfaces, and network and internetwork capabilities.

Table 4-1   ISDN Three-Layer Model

OSI Layer	B Channel	D Channel
3	IP	Q.931—ISDN network layer between terminal and switch
2	HDLC PPP	Q.921—LAPD
1	I.430—BRI I.431—PRI	

ISDN Layer 1

The ISDN BRI was designed to work over the physical path designed to carry analog phone service. Although only one physical path exists, there are three distinct information paths—two bearer channels and the delta channel. ISDN functions by *multiplexing* the signals from these three information paths to the one physical path.

The ISDN physical layer frame format differs depending on the direction in which it is traveling. If the frame is outbound, it is sent from the terminal to the network and uses the *TE frame format*. Inbound frames, sent from the network to the terminal, use the *NT frame format*. Figure 4-3 illustrates these frames.

Figure 4-3   ISDN TE and NT Frames

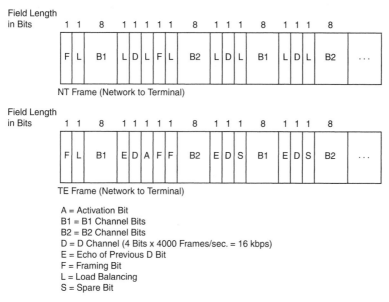

A = Activation Bit
B1 = B1 Channel Bits
B2 = B2 Channel Bits
D = D Channel (4 Bits x 4000 Frames/sec. = 16 kbps)
E = Echo of Previous D Bit
F = Framing Bit
L = Load Balancing
S = Spare Bit

These frames are 48 bits long, of which 36 bits represent data. The purpose of each bit in the frame is as follows:

- **F (framing bit)**—Provides synchronization

- **L (load-balancing bit)**—Adjusts the average bit value

- **E (echo of previous D channel bits)**—Ensures contention resolution when several terminals on a passive bus contend for a channel

- **A (activation bit)**—Activates devices

- **S (spare bit)**—Unassigned

- **B1, B2, and D**—Handle user data

Four thousand of these 48-bit-long frames are transmitted every second, specifying a bandwidth of 192 kbps (4000 frames per second * 48 bits per frame). Each B channel has a capacity of 64 kbps (4000 frames per second * 16 bits per frame), and the D channel has a capacity of 16 kbps (4000 frames per second * 4 bits per frame). This accounts for 144 kbps of the total, with the remainder assigned to the overhead required for data transmission.

Multiple ISDN user devices can be physically attached to one circuit. In this configuration, collisions can result if two terminals transmit simultaneously. Therefore, ISDN provides features to determine link contention. When an NT receives a D bit from the TE, it echoes the bit in the next E bit position. The TE expects the next E bit to be the same as its last transmitted D bit. If the TE detects a bit in the echo (E) that is different from its D bits, it must stop transmitting immediately.

Before any device can transmit to the D channel, it must determine that no other devices are transmitting by detecting a predetermined number of continuous binary 1s on the channel. The actual number of 1s that must be detected depends on the device's priority. Devices with higher priority must detect fewer continuous binary 1s than devices with lower priority. Generally, telephone connections have a higher priority than other devices, and signaling information has higher priority than nonsignaling information.

After a device transmits on the D channel, it has its priority lowered and must detect an increased number of continuous binary 1s before being able to transmit again. Devices cannot raise their priority until all other devices on the physical medium have had a chance to transmit on the D channel.

ISDN Layer 2

The Layer 2 ISDN frame uses LAPD, which is a derivative of HDLC. LAPD is used across the D channel to ensure that control and signaling information flows and is received properly. The LAPD frame format is very similar to that of HDLC, as shown in Figure 4-4. Like HDLC, LAPD uses supervisory, information, and unnumbered frames (see Chapter 3). The LAPD protocol is formally specified in ITU-T *Q.920* and ITU-T *Q.921*.

Figure 4-4   LAPD Frame Format

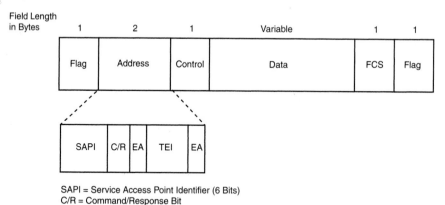

The LAPD Flag and Control fields are identical to those of HDLC. The LAPD Address field can be either 1 or 2 bytes long. The first Address field byte contains the *Service Access Point Identifier (SAPI)*, which identifies the portal at which LAPD services are provided to Layer 3. The C/R bit indicates whether the frame contains a command or a response. The *Terminal Endpoint Identifier (TEI)* field identifies either a single terminal or multiple terminals. Each piece of terminal equipment requires a unique identifier. This TEI can be either statically assigned or dynamically assigned by the switch when the device starts up. Statically assigned

TEIs range from 0 to 63, and dynamically assigned TEIs range from 64 to 127. A TEI of all 1s indicates a broadcast.

ISDN Layer 3

For one router to connect to another using ISDN, several exchanges must occur. The router communicates with the local ISDN switch using the D channel. The switches on the service provider's network use *Signaling System 7 (SS7)* to communicate.

The ISDN data-link processes (LAPD) are described by Q.921. The D channel is used for call control functions such as call setup, signaling, and termination, which are then implemented in *Q.931*. Q.931 specifies the OSI Layer 3 functions and recommends a network layer connection between the terminal endpoint and the local ISDN switch. Although the standard makes a recommendation, it does not impose an end-to-end recommendation.

Many ISDN switches were developed before Q.931 was standardized. These switches all implement this functionality in different ways. Routers must be able to communicate with all of these different implementations and accomplish this through a configuration option that allows the administrator to specify the type of switch that the router connects to.

Figure 4-5 illustrates the sequence of events that occurs during the establishment of an ISDN connection. The following list documents the specific events illustrated.

Figure 4-5   ISDN Call Setup

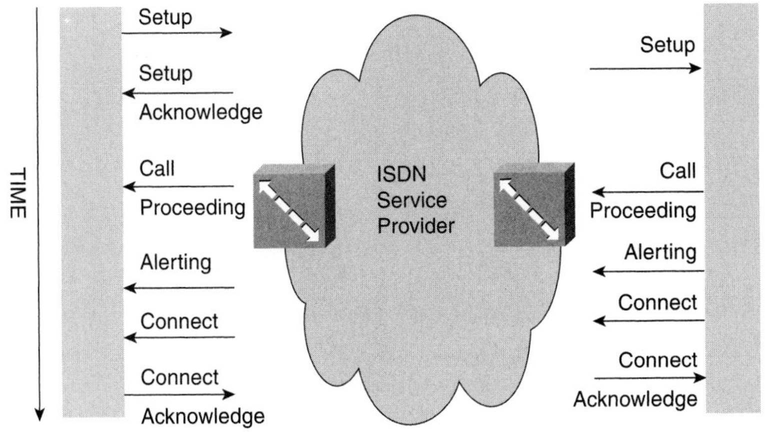

1. The called number is sent from the router to the ISDN switch over the D channel.

2. The local ISDN switch uses the SS7 signaling protocol to establish a path and pass the called number to the remote ISDN switch.

3. The remote switch signals the destination device over the D channel.

4. The destination ISDN NT1 sends the remote ISDN switch a call-connect message.

5. The remote switch sends the local switch a call-connect message using SS7.

6. The local ISDN switch connects one B channel end to end, leaving the other B channel available for a new conversation or data transfer. Both B channels may be used simultaneously.

ISDN Devices and Reference Points

ISDN devices include terminals, Terminal Adaptors (TAs), network-termination devices, line-termination equipment, and exchange-termination equipment. ISDN terminals come in two types. Specialized ISDN terminals are referred to as *Terminal Equipment type 1 (TE1)*, and non-ISDN-compatible terminal equipment is known as *Terminal Equipment type 2 (TE2)*. TE1s connect to the ISDN network through a four-wire, twisted-pair digital link. TE2s connect to the ISDN network through a *Terminal Adaptor (TA)*, which converts the signals generated by these non-ISDN terminals into BRI signals. The TE2 connects to the TA through a standard interface such as EIA/TIA 232 or V.35. TE1s and TAs then connect to a *Network Termination device type 2 (NT2)*. The NT2 is a device that typically is found in digital private branch exchanges (PBXs). It performs Layer 2 and 3 protocol functions and concentration services. It acts as a point at which all ISDN lines at the end user's site are aggregated and switched. The NT2 connects through a four-wire bus to a *Network Termination device type 1 (NT1)*, which converts the four-wire BRI signals into the two-wire signals used by the ISDN line from the service provider. Figure 4-6 illustrates the ISDN devices and reference points.

Figure 4-6   ISDN Devices and Reference Points

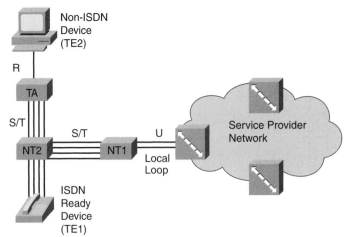

In North America, the NT1 is usually customer premises equipment (CPE). In other parts of the world, the NT1 is owned and controlled by the service provider.

To interconnect these devices, the interface between the devices must be well defined. These interfaces are known as *reference points*. The reference points at the customer side of the ISDN connection are as follows:

- *R*—This point references the connection between the non-ISDN-compatible equipment (TE2) and the Terminal Adaptor (TA). This is typically a standard serial connection such as an EIA/TIA 232.

- *S*—This point references the points that connect into the customer's switching device (NT2). It enables calls between the various types of CPE.

- *T*—This references the outbound connection from the customer's NT1 device to the NT2 device. This interface is electrically identical to the S interface.

- *U*—This references the outbound connection from the NT1 device and the service provider's ISDN network.

Because the S and T interfaces are electrically similar, they are often labeled the S/T interface.

Due to variations in ISDN implementation, regions around the world differ in the customer equipment required to connect to the ISDN circuit. In North America, a U interface can be directly connected to the connection provided by the telephone company, but if an S/T interface is used, it must first connect to an external NT1, which in turn connects to the *telco* jack. In the rest of the world, an S/T interface connects directly to the telco jack, and a U interface cannot be used. This is because in regions other than North America, the NT1 is usually built into the telephone company's network.

Caution

Never connect a U interface to an NT1, or damage to the interface will result.

If the router has an interface labeled BRI, it is a TE1 (ISDN-enabled) device. These devices can connect directly to an external NT1 using an S/T interface. If it has a U interface, the NT1 is built in. Routers without a BRI interface are TE2 devices and require a TA to connect the serial interface to the ISDN network. Modular routers without an ISDN BRI can easily be upgraded to accommodate a BRI interface, which eliminates the need for an external TA.

Routers must know which type of ISDN switch they are to communicate with. As a consequence of various implementations of Q.931, the D channel signaling protocol used on ISDN switches varies from vendor to vendor.

Services offered by ISDN service providers around the world vary considerably. Each switch type operates slightly differently and has a specific set of call setup requirements. Before a router can be connected to an ISDN network, it must be configured to communicate with the switch used at the CO. Table 4-2 lists some of the common ISDN switch types in use around the world.

Table 4-2   ISDN Switch Types

Country	Switch Type
United States and Canada	AT&T 5ESS and 4ESS Northern Telecom DMS-100
France	VN2, VN3
Japan	NTT
United Kingdom	Net3 and Net5
Europe	Net3

Some switches require the use of a *service profile identifier (SPID)* to identify the line configuration of the BRI service. SPIDs are assigned be the service provider and allow multiple ISDN devices to share the local loop. SPIDs are used only in North America and Japan and are required by the DMS-100 and National ISDN-1 ISDN switches.

SPIDs, which resemble a telephone number in appearance, are used to identify each B channel to the ISDN switch at the central office. After the channel is identified, the switch links the available services to the connection. SPIDs are processed only during the initial connection and are required for proper initialization. If SPIDs are necessary, but are improperly configured, the initialization fails, and the ISDN services are unavailable.

ISDN Configuration

Many steps are involved in configuring an ISDN BRI or PRI interface. These involve not only the physical and logical configuration of the interface itself, but also the type of traffic that causes the ISDN interface to be activated.

Configuring an ISDN BRI

The first step in configuring an ISDN BRI is to specify the type of switch that it will connect to at the service provider end. This command can be issued in either global or interface configuration mode. If a router has multiple BRI interfaces, it is easier to specify the switch type in global configuration mode and then issue it in interface configuration mode for any interfaces that differ from that specified in global mode. ISDN switch type configurations done at the interface level override those done in global mode. The syntax for this command is as follows:

```
Router(config)#isdn switch-type switch-type
```

```
Router(config-if)#isdn switch-type switch-type
```

If the connection requires a SPID, it is provided by the service provider. The SPID's exact format depends on the service provider and the switch to which the connection is being made. SPIDs are not required on all switch types but are commonly used in North America.

If required, SPIDs must be configured on each B channel separately. SPIDs are configured in interface configuration mode as follows:

```
Router(config-if)#isdn spid1 spid-number [ldn]
Router(config-if)#isdn spid2 spid-number [ldn]
```

The SPID identifies the ISDN service subscribed to, and the optional *local dial number (LDN)* must match the called-party information coming in from the ISDN switch. The service provider might configure multiple BRIs in a *hunt group* using LDNs to signal which B channel should answer the call. In such a configuration, the LDNs must be included in the SPID configuration. The BRIs should be configured with SPIDs, and each SPID must have a *unique* LDN number. If you observe that the second channel for each BRI is not accepting calls, verify that you have a correctly configured LDN.

Example 4-1 shows a sample ISDN BRI configuration.

```
Example 4-1      ISDN BRI Configuration
!
isdn switch-type basic-ni
!
 <output ommited>
!
interface BRI0/0
isdn switch-type basic-ni
 isdn spid1 51055520000001 5552000
 isdn spid2 51055520010001 5552001
!
```

Because ISDN is a circuit-switched technology and connection costs are related to the connect time, DDR is often deployed with ISDN to bring up the interface only under predefined circumstances. This is discussed later in the chapter, in the section "DDR Configuration."

Lab 4-1   Configuring ISDN BRI (U-Interface) (4.2.1)

In this lab, you configure an ISDN router to make a successful connection to an ISDN switch.

Configuring an ISDN PRI

The ISDN PRI is delivered over either a T1 or E1 leased line. Configuring an ISDN PRI involves the following steps:

Step 1.   Specify the correct ISDN switch type that the router will connect to at the CO of the ISDN service provider.

Step 2.   Specify the T1/E1 controller, framing type, and line coding for the facility of the ISDN service provider.

Step 3.   Set the PRI group timeslot for the T1/E1 facility, and indicate the speed used.

Unlike a BRI, there is no physical PRI interface. The physical interface on the router that connects to the leased line used for ISDN is called the controller. Depending on where the service is being configured, either a T1 controller or an E1 controller must be specified. As soon as this controller is properly configured to connect to the service provider's network, each channel can be configured using the **interface serial** command.

Five steps are involved in setting up an ISDN PRI after the service provider gives you the configuration information:

Step 1.   Specify the ISDN switch type.

Step 2.   Specify the controller's location.

Step 3.   Set framing, line coding, and clocking.

Step 4.   Specify the range of timeslots available.

Step 5.   Specify an interface for the PRI D channel.

The first step is to specify the ISDN switch type using the following command:

```
Router(config)#isdn switch-type switch-type
```

Table 4-3 lists the common switch types available for an ISDN PRI connection around the world.

Table 4-3   Switch Types Available for ISDN PRI Configuration

Switch Type	Description
Primary-5ess	AT&T ISDN switch deployed in the U.S.
Primary-dms100	Northern Telecom DMS-100 switch deployed in North America
Primary-ni	National ISDN switch deployed in North America
Primary-net	Net5 ISDN switch used in United Kingdom, Europe, and Australia
Primary-ntt	NTT ISDN switch used in Japan

After the ISDN switch type is specified, the PRI controller must be selected and configured. The controller to be used and the location of the PRI are specified as follows:

```
Router(config)#controller {t1 | e1} {slot/port}
```

After the controller is selected, the framing, line coding, and clocking must be specified. The options specified here depend on the type of controller and must match the configuration provided by the service provider. For a T1 line, use this command:

```
Router(config-controller)#framing {sf | esf}
```

For an E1 line, the command is

```
Router(config-controller)#framing {crc4 | no-crc4} [australia]
```

Table 4-4 explains the syntax of this command. The default framing for a T1 line is the superframe (sf), and for an E1 line it is the CRC4 frame (crc4).

Table 4-4   T1/E1 Controller Framing Syntax

Frame Type	Description
sf	Superframe is the T1 frame type.
esf	Extended superframe is the T1 frame type.
crc4	CRC4 frame is the E1 frame type.
no-crc4	CRC4 frame is not the E1 frame type.
australia	(Optional) E1 frame type used in Australia.

After the framing has been configured, the line code must be set up using the **linecode** command. For a T1 line the command is

```
Router(config-controller)#linecode {ami | b8zs}
```

For an E1 line, use

```
Router (config-controller)#linecode {ami | hdb3}
```

Table 4-5 describes the available line codes. The default value for line code on a T1 line is **ami**, but the B8ZS signaling method is most often used in North America. For an E1 line, the default line code is HDB3.

Table 4-5   T1/E1 Line Codes

Line Code	Description
ami	Alternate mark inversion (AMI) line-code type. Valid for both T1 and E1 controllers.
b8zs	B8ZS line-code type. Valid for T1 controllers only.
hdb3	High-density bipolar 3 (HDB3) line-code type. Valid for E1 controllers only.

You can specify the clock source for a T1 or E1 controller using the following controller configuration command:

```
Router (config-controller)#clock source {line ¦ internal}
```

For the first T1 or E1 controller, the clock source defaults to **line**, while subsequent controllers default to the **internal** setting. If **line** is specified, the controller obtains its clocking from the line signal and provides this clock to the internal system clock. If **internal** is specified, the controller synchronizes itself to the internal system clock. This provides a default mechanism by which each router obtains only one external clock signal. For this reason, the **clock source** command is usually omitted from the PRI configuration.

The **pri-group** controller configuration command specifies an ISDN PRI on a *channelized* T1 or E1 controller. The syntax for this command is

```
Router(config-controller)#pri-group timeslots range
```

The timeslot range is 1 to 24 if the controller is a T1 or 1 to 31 if the controller is an E1. This establishes the 24 channels (23B+D) used with a T1 connection or the 31 channels (30B+D) used with an E1 connection. Channel 24 is the D channel for a T1 connection. For an E1 connection, the D channel is specified as channel 16.

The final step is to specify an interface for the PRI D channel. This interface is seen as a serial interface to a T1/E1 on the router. Although the channels start numbering at 1 when the timeslots are established, Cisco routers start numbering their interfaces from 0. Therefore, channel 24, which is the ISDN signaling channel on a T1, is seen as 23, and channel 16, the ISDN signaling channel on an E1, is seen as 15.

To specify the interface to be used for the D channel, use the following command:

```
Router(config-controller)#interface serial {slot/port: | unit:} {23 | 15}
```

Example 4-2 shows a sample ISDN PRI configuration for both a T1 and an E1 line. Note that CDP is disabled on the interface to control costs.

Example 4-2   Sample ISDN PRI Configurations for T1 and E1 Lines

```
T1 Line
Router(config)#controller t1 1/0
Router(config-controller)#framing esf
Router(config-controller)#linecode b8zs
Router(config-controller)#pri-group timeslots 1-24
Router(config-controller)#interface serial3/0:23
Router(config-if)#isdn switch-type primary-5ess
Router(config-if)#no cdp enable


E1 Line
Router(config)#controller e1 1/0
Router(config-controller)#framing crc4
```

Example 4-2   Sample ISDN PRI Configurations for T1 and E1 Lines   (*Continued*)

```
Router(config-controller)#linecode hdb3
Router(config-controller)#pri-group timeslots 1-31
Router(config-controller)#interface serial3/0:15
Router(config-if)#isdn switch-type primary-net5
Router(config-if)#no cdp enable
```

Note

Subinterfaces on a Cisco router are designated by a dot or period, and channels are identified by a colon. For example, serial 0.23 refers to a subinterface, and serial 0:23 refers to a channel.

Verifying and Troubleshooting ISDN Configuration

Several **show** commands are available to verify that the ISDN configuration has been implemented correctly. The **show isdn status** command can be used to verify that the router is communicating with the ISDN switch. Example 4-3 demonstrates some sample output from this command.

Example 4-3   **show isdn status** Command Output

```
Toronto#show isdn status
Global ISDN Switchtype = basic-ni
ISDN BRI0/0 interface
        dsl 0, interface ISDN Switchtype = basic-ni
    Layer 1 Status:
        ACTIVE
    Layer 2 Status:
        TEI = 64, Ces = 1, SAPI = 0, State = MULTIPLE_FRAME_ESTABLISHED
        TEI = 65, Ces = 2, SAPI = 0, State = MULTIPLE_FRAME_ESTABLISHED
        TEI 64, ces = 1, state = 8(established)
            spid1 configured, spid1 sent, spid1 valid
            Endpoint ID Info: epsf = 0, usid = 70, tid = 1
        TEI 65, ces = 2, state = 8(established)
            spid2 configured, spid2 sent, spid2 valid
            Endpoint ID Info: epsf = 0, usid = 70, tid = 2
    Layer 3 Status:
        0 Active Layer 3 Call(s)
    Active dsl 0 CCBs = 0
    The Free Channel Mask:  0x80000003
    Number of L2 Discards = 1, L2 Session ID = 24
    Total Allocated ISDN CCBs = 0
```

The Layer 1 status should be ACTIVE to indicate that a proper Layer 1 connection has been made with the ISDN switch. Table 4-6 shows the other possible Layer 1 states. Most of these states are temporary and can be cleared with the **clear interface bri** *number* command or with a router reload. The Layer 2 message should state MULTIPLE_FRAME_ESTABLISHED. This command also displays the number of active Layer 3 calls.

Table 4-6   ISDN Layer 1 State Definitions

Layer 1 State	Layer 1 State Name	Layer 1 State Description
F1	Inactive	In this inactive (powered-off) state, the terminal equipment (TE) is not transmitting and cannot detect the presence of any input signals.
F2	Sensing	This state is entered after the TE has been powered on but has not determined the type of signal (if any) that the TE is receiving. When in this state, a TE may go into a low power consumption mode.
F3	Deactivated	This is the deactivated state of the physical protocol. Neither the network termination (NT) nor the TE is transmitting. When in this state, a TE may go to a low power consumption mode.
F4	Awaiting Signal	When the TE wants to initiate activation, it sends an Activation signal to the NT and awaits a response.
F5	Identifying Input	At first receipt of any signal from the NT, the TE stops sending activation signals and awaits the activation signal or synchronized frame from the NT.
F6	Synchronized	When the TE receives an activation signal from the NT, it responds with a synchronized frame and awaits a synchronized frame from the NT.
F7	Activated	This is the normal active state, with the protocol activated in both directions. Both the NT and TE transmit normal frames. State F7 is the only state in which the B channel and D channel contain operational data.
F8	Lost Framing	This is the condition when the TE has lost frame synchronization and is awaiting resynchronization.

Example 4-4 provides sample output from the **show isdn active** command. This command provides information on the current call, including the following:

- Called number

- Time until the call is disconnected

- Advice of charge (AOC)

- Charging units used during the call

- Whether the AOC information is provided during calls or at the end of calls

```
Example 4-4      show isdn active Command Output
Toronto#show isdn active
.................................................................
                          ISDN ACTIVE CALLS
.................................................................

Call    Calling     Called      Remote    Seconds Seconds Seconds  Charges
Type    Number      Number      Name      Used    Left    Idle     Units/Currency
.................................................................
Out   — -N/A— -     5551000     Hamilton    79      44      75       0
.................................................................
```

The **show dialer** command, shown in Example 4-5, displays information about the dialer interface, including information on the current call and why the interface was brought up. This command also displays the timer values.

```
Example 4-5      show dialer Command Output
Toronto#show dialer

BRI0/0 - dialer type = ISDN

Dial String     Successes   Failures    Last DNIS   Last status
5551000               23           0                00:00:53       successful
0 incoming call(s) have been screened.
0 incoming call(s) rejected for callback.

BRI0/0:1 - dialer type = ISDN
Idle timer (120 secs), Fast idle timer (20 secs)
Wait for carrier (30 secs), Re-enable (15 secs)
Dialer state is data link layer up
Dial reason: ip (s=10.10.10.1, d=209.165.201.1)
Time until disconnect 68 secs
Connected to 5551000 (Hamilton)

BRI0/0:2 - dialer type = ISDN
Idle timer (120 secs), Fast idle timer (20 secs)
Wait for carrier (30 secs), Re-enable (15 secs)
Dialer state is idle
```

You can find information about the BRI interface or a specific ISDN channel using the **show interface** command. If the channel number is appended to the end of the command, the information obtained is about a specific channel. This command provides information on the type of encapsulation being used, the status of the *LCP*, and which *NCPs* are currently running. Example 4-6 provides sample output from the **show interface bri9/0:1** command.

Example 4-6   show interface bri0/0:1 Command Output

```
Toronto#show interface bri0/0:1
BRI0/0:1 is up, line protocol is up
  Hardware is PQUICC BRI with U interface
  MTU 1500 bytes, BW 64 Kbit, DLY 20000 usec,
     reliability 255/255, txload 1/255, rxload 1/255
  Encapsulation PPP, loopback not set
  Time to interface disconnect:  idle 00:00:55
  LCP Open
  Open: IPCP, CDPCP
  Last input 00:00:01, output 00:00:01, output hang never
  Last clearing of "show interface" counters never
  Input queue: 0/75/0/0 (size/max/drops/flushes); Total output drops: 0
  Queueing strategy: weighted fair
  Output queue: 0/1000/64/0 (size/max total/threshold/drops)
     Conversations  0/1/16 (active/max active/max total)
     Reserved Conversations 0/0 (allocated/max allocated)
     Available Bandwidth 48 kilobits/sec
  5 minute input rate 0 bits/sec, 0 packets/sec
  5 minute output rate 0 bits/sec, 0 packets/sec
     30 packets input, 1196 bytes, 0 no buffer
     Received 0 broadcasts, 0 runts, 0 giants, 0 throttles
     0 input errors, 0 CRC, 0 frame, 0 overrun, 0 ignored, 0 abort
     31 packets output, 1213 bytes, 0 underruns
     0 output errors, 0 collisions, 0 interface resets
     0 output buffer failures, 0 output buffers swapped out
     1 carrier transitions
```

Caution

As always, you should take the necessary precautions when using **debug** commands in a production environment. Excessive debugging can consume large amounts of resources and quickly degrade network performance.

You can use a number of **debug** commands to view the ISDN process in real time. Because most ISDN implementations also involve PPP and authentication, the PPP troubleshooting commands introduced in Chapter 3 also form part of the ISDN troubleshooting arsenal. Table 4-7 lists some of these commands and describes the information they can provide.

Table 4-7   Common ISDN debug Troubleshooting Commands

Command	Description
debug isdn event	Displays ISDN events occurring on the user side (on the router) of the ISDN interface. The ISDN events that can be displayed are Q.931 events (call setup and teardown of ISDN network connections).
debug isdn q921	Displays data link layer (Layer 2) access procedures that are taking place at the router on the D channel (LAPD) of its ISDN interface.

Table 4-7   Common ISDN **debug** Troubleshooting Commands   *continued*

Command	Description
	The ISDN data link layer interface provided by the router conforms to the user interface specification defined by ITU-T recommendation Q.921. The **debug isdn q921** command output is limited to commands and responses exchanged during peer-to-peer communication carried over the D channel. This debug information does not include data transmitted over the B channels that are also part of the router's ISDN interface. The peers (data link layer entities and layer management entities on the routers) communicate with each other via an ISDN switch over the D channel.
debug isdn q931	Displays information about call setup and teardown of ISDN network connections (Layer 3) between the local router (user side) and the network.

The ISDN network layer interface provided by the router conforms to the user interface specification defined by ITU-T recommendation Q.931, supplemented by other specifications such as for switch type VN4. The router tracks only activities that occur on the user side, not the network side, of the network connection. The **debug isdn q931** command output is limited to commands and responses exchanged during peer-to-peer communication carried over the D channel. This debug information does not include data transmitted over the B channels, which are also part of the router's ISDN interface. The peers (network layers) communicate with each other via an ISDN switch over the D channel. |
debug ppp negotiation	Displays PPP packets transmitted during PPP startup, where PPP options are negotiated.
debug ppp authentication	Displays authentication protocol messages, including Challenge Handshake Authentication Protocol (CHAP) packet exchanges and Password Authentication Protocol (PAP) exchanges.
debug ppp error	Displays protocol errors and error statistics associated with PPP connection negotiation and operation.

DDR Configuration

Dial-on-demand routing (DDR) is commonly deployed with ISDN technology to bring up the connection only when required. Because ISDN is billed not only on the amount of data transferred but also on the actual connect time, implementing DDR with ISDN can generate substantial savings.

Legacy DDR

DDR is triggered when traffic that matches a predefined set of criteria is queued to be sent out a DDR-enabled interface. Traffic that causes the DDR call to be placed is referred to as *interesting traffic*. After the interesting traffic has moved across the link, the call is terminated. Figure 4-7 illustrates a DDR link being activated by interesting traffic.

Figure 4-7   Interesting Traffic

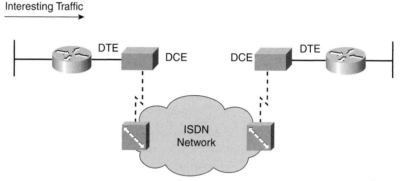

You can define interesting traffic with the **dialer-list** command. Dialer lists can define interesting traffic as all traffic from a specific protocol or may reference an access list if finer control is required. If you use an access list, you can define interesting traffic by the source or destination address or even the port number. Dialer lists do not filter traffic, but merely define which traffic is capable of activating the ISDN link.

After the link is brought up, an idle timer is activated. If the timer expires before additional interesting traffic is seen, the link is brought down. Any interesting traffic that moves across the link resets the idle timeout and keeps the link active. All traffic, both interesting and uninteresting, moves across an active link, but only interesting traffic resets the timer.

The process used to invoke a DDR session is as follows:

1. The router receives traffic and consults the routing table to determine if there is a route to the destination network. If there is a route in the routing table, the interface that the traffic must be switched to is determined.

2. The router checks the interface to see if it is configured for DDR. If DDR is configured on the interface, the router checks to see if the traffic is defined as interesting.

3. The router determines the dialing information necessary to make the call using a dialer map to access the next-hop router.

4. The router checks to see if the dialer map is in use. If the interface is connected to the desired remote destination, the traffic is sent. If the interface is not connected to the remote destination and the traffic has been defined as interesting, the router sends call setup information through the BRI using the D channel.

5. After the link is established, the router transmits both interesting and uninteresting traffic. Uninteresting traffic can include both data and routing updates.

6. The idle timer starts and runs until additional interesting traffic is detected. The call is disconnected if the idle timer reaches a preconfigured value before additional interesting traffic is detected. Interesting traffic restarts the timer.

Legacy DDR applies a single set of dialer parameters directly to an interface. This may be sufficient if the ISDN connection is always made to the same destination, but if a single interface must connect to multiple locations, dialer profiles should be used.

The steps involved in configuring legacy DDR are as follows:

Step 1.   Define static routes.

Step 2.   Specify interesting traffic.

Step 3.   Configure the dialer information.

If a dynamic routing protocol is used, hello packets and routing updates may trigger the link to come up if they are considered interesting traffic. To avoid this problem, you should define *static routes* for any connections that need to use the DDR interface. Static routes have a lower administrative distance than dynamic routes, so dynamic routes are ignored if a static route is configured. It is common practice to use a default static route or a summarized route to reduce the number of static entries in the routing table. To configure a static route, use the following command:

```
Router(config)#ip route net-prefix mask {address | interface} [distance] [permanent]
```

The *administrative distance* is an optional parameter and can be specified if the route is to be a floating static route. A *floating static route* is active only when a *dynamic route* with a more favorable administrative distance is not found in the routing table. Because ISDN connections are often used as a backup for packet or cell-switched technology, floating static routes allow the route specifying the DDR interface to be active only when learned from a dynamic protocol times out of the routing table due to failure of the primary packet-switched network.

After you configure the static routes, you need to define the interesting traffic with the **dialer-list** command. A maximum of 10 dialer lists can be defined on a router. The syntax for the **dialer-list** command is as follows:

```
Router(config)#dialer-list dialer-group protocol protocol-name {permit | deny |
  list access-list-number | access-group}
```

For example, the following command creates a dialer list that defines all IP traffic as interesting:

```
Router(config)#dialer-list 1 protocol ip permit
```

To create a dialer list to define only web and Telnet traffic as interesting, an access list must be created and referenced as follows:

```
Router(config)#dialer-list 2 protocol ip list 102
Router(config)#access-list 102 permit tcp any any eq www
Router(config)#access-list 102 permit tcp any any eq telnet
```

The dialer list is applied to the DDR interface using the **dialer-group** command as follows:

```
Router(config-if)#dialer-group dialer-group
```

The *dialer-group* value must match that specified in the **dialer-list** command.

To specify the string (telephone number) to be called for interfaces calling a single site, use the **dialer string** command in interface configuration mode. If multiple sites must be called, you must use the **dialer map** command to map the remote protocol address to the telephone number. The syntax of both commands is as follows:

```
Router(config-if)#dialer string dial-string
```

```
Router(config-if)#dialer map protocol next-hop-address [name host-name | speed 56 |
    speed 64] [broadcast] dial-string
```

To set the value of the *idle timeout*, use the **dialer idle-timeout** interface configuration command. You must specify how many seconds to wait from the last appearance of interesting traffic.

Either HDLC or PPP encapsulation may be deployed across the ISDN link. PPP is most often selected because of its advantages over HDLC, as discussed in Chapter 3. If PPP is to be deployed across the link, the encapsulation must be specified, along with the authentication method to be used. Accounts must be created on each end to allow for mutual authentication.

Figure 4-8 shows a network that requires the deployment of legacy DDR to allow traffic to move between the two LAN segments.

Figure 4-8   Sample ISDN Network

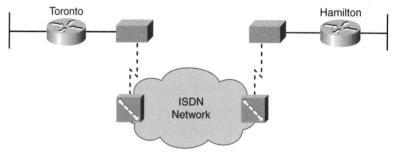

Example 4-7 shows the DDR configurations on both the Toronto and Hamilton routers required to accomplish this. PPP encapsulation has been deployed using CHAP authentication. Note that Hamilton uses a default route, sending all traffic to Toronto if it does not have another route in the routing table. But Toronto only forwards traffic destined for the Hamilton LAN across the ISDN link.

Example 4-7   Legacy DDR Configuration

```
Toronto Router
!
hostname Toronto
!
username Hamilton password 0 cisco
!
<Output Omitted>
!
isdn switch-type basic-ni
!
<output Omitted>
!
interface FastEthernet0/0
 ip address 206.165.200.225 255.255.255.224
 duplex auto
 speed auto
!
interface BRI0/0
 ip address 10.10.10.1 255.255.255.252
 encapsulation ppp
 dialer map ip 10.10.10.2 name Hamilton 5551000
 dialer-group 1
 isdn switch-type basic-ni
 isdn spid1 51055520000001 5552000
 isdn spid2 51055520010001 5552001
 ppp authentication chap
!
ip route 209.165.201.0 255.255.255.224 10.10.10.2
!
dialer-list 1 protocol ip permit
!
```

```
Hamilton Router
!
hostname Hamilton
!
<Output Omitted>
!
username Toronto password 0 cisco
!
isdn switch-type basic-ni
!
```

continues

```
Example 4-7      Legacy DDR Configuration   continued
interface BRI0
 ip address 10.10.10.2 255.255.255.252
 encapsulation ppp
 dialer map ip 10.10.10.1 name Toronto 5552000
 dialer-group 1
 isdn switch-type basic-ni
 isdn spid1 51055510000001 5551000
 isdn spid2 51055510010001 5551001
 ppp authentication chap
!
interface FastEthernet0
 ip address 209.165.201.1 255.255.255.224
 speed auto
!
ip classless
ip route 0.0.0.0 0.0.0.0 10.10.10.1
no ip http server
!
dialer-list 1 protocol ip permit
!
```

 Lab 4-2   Configuring Legacy DDR (4.3.2)

In this lab, you configure an ISDN router to make a legacy DDR call to another ISDN-capable router.

Dialer Profiles

With legacy DDR, all configuration information is applied directly to the interface, including the IP address. This prevents the DDR interface from connecting to any DDR interfaces that are not in the same subnet and forces a one-to-one relationship between the physical interfaces at both ends of the link.

Dialer profiles separate the logical configuration information from the physical interface. They allow the binding of configuration information to the physical interface on a per-call basis, allowing the physical interface to take on different characteristics for each outgoing or incoming call. Dialer profiles can be used to define encapsulation and access control lists, determine maximum or minimum calls, and turn features on and off. Dialer interfaces allow scalable circuit-switched networks to be designed and built by removing the one-to-one relationship between the interfaces.

Dialer profiles eliminate the waste of B channels by allowing ISDN BRI interfaces to belong to multiple pools, allowing them to take on logical configurations as required. The use of dialer profiles allows an interface's B channels to belong to a different subnet, use a different encapsulation, or take on different DDR characteristics.

A dialer profile has the following three elements:

- *Dialer interface*—A logical interface that uses a per-destination dialer profile.

- *Dialer pool*—A group of one or more physical interfaces associated with a dialer interface.

- *Physical interface*—Physical interfaces belong to a dialer pool. Encapsulation type, authentication, and multilink are all configured on the physical interface.

Dialer profiles behave in much the same way as legacy DDR:

1. The routing table directs a packet toward a remote DDR interface.

2. If the packet is determined to be interesting, the router looks for a dialer interface that is on the same subnet as the remote DDR interface.

3. After this dialer interface is found, it looks for an unused DDR interface that is a member of the dialer pool.

4. The configuration from the dialer profile is bound to the physical interface, and the router attempts to connect to the remote device.

5. After the call is completed, the interface is returned to the dialer pool for possible reuse.

Configuring Dialer Interfaces

You can configure multiple dialer interfaces on a single router. To configure a dialer interface, use the **interface dialer** command, specifying a number for the interface. As soon as this is done, the router is placed in interface configuration mode. From this mode, configure the IP address, encapsulation type and authentication, idle timer, and the dialer group to select interesting traffic. You must use the **dialer remote-name** and **dialer string** commands to specify the name of the remote router and the number that must be dialed to connect to it. The dialer interface must then be associated with a pool of physical interfaces using the **dialer pool** command.

You must configure the physical ISDN interfaces and assign them to a dialer pool for the dialer interface to use them. You can assign a physical interface to multiple dialer pools. To assign an interface to a dialer pool, use the **dialer pool-member** interface configuration command. A priority value may also be supplied with this command, specifying which logical interface will be given priority access to the physical interface should more than one dialer interface try to access it simultaneously. If multiple calls need to be placed and only one interface is available, the one with the highest priority is the one that dials out. Dialer pools can use any of the following interfaces:

- Synchronous serial

- Asynchronous serial

- BRI

- PRI

Example 4-8 shows a partial configuration for a router with two physical BRI interfaces but three logical dialer interfaces. Each dialer profile connects to only one of the remote sites. Dialer interface 1 can use only the first physical interface. The remaining two dialer interfaces can use either physical interface.

Example 4-8   Dialer Profiles Sample Configuration

```
!
hostname Toronto
!
!
username Hamilton password 0 cisco
username Ottawa password 0 cisco
username Detroit password 0 cisco
username Buffalo password 0 cisco
!
<Output Omitted>
!
isdn switch-type basic-ni
!
<Output Omitted>
!
interface BRI0/0
 no ip address
 encapsulation ppp
 dialer pool-member 1
 dialer pool-member 2
 isdn switch-type basic-ni
 isdn spid1 51055520000001 5552000
 isdn spid2 51055520010001 5552001
 ppp authentication chap
!
interface BRI1/0
 no ip address
 encapsulation ppp
 dialer pool-member 1
```

Example 4-8   Dialer Profiles Sample Configuration   *(Continued)*

```
 isdn switch-type basic-ni
 isdn spid1 51055530000001 5553000
 isdn spid2 51055530010001 5553001
 ppp authentication chap
!
interface Dialer1
 description Connection to Hamilton
 ip address 10.10.10.1 255.255.255.252
 encapsulation ppp
 dialer pool 1
 dialer remote-name Hamilton
 dialer string 5551000
 dialer-group 1
 ppp authentication chap
!
interface Dialer2
 description Connection to Detroit
 ip address 10.10.10.5 255.255.255.252
 encapsulation ppp
 dialer pool 2
 dialer remote-name Detroit
 dialer idle-timeout 60
 dialer string 5554000
 dialer-group 1
 ppp authentication chap
!
interface Dialer3
 description Connection to Buffalo
 ip address 10.10.10.9 255.255.255.252
 encapsulation ppp
 dialer pool 2
 dialer remote-name Buffalo
 dialer idle-timeout 100
 dialer string 5555000
 dialer-group 1
 ppp authentication chap
!
<Output Omitted>
!
dialer-list 1 protocol ip permit
!
<Output Omitted>
```

Lab 4-3   Configuring Dialer Profiles (4.3.7)

In this lab, you configure ISDN dialer profiles on the routers.

Verifying Dialer Profiles

You can verify that the dialer profiles are functioning correctly by using a number of available commands. The **show dialer** command provides statistics on the incoming and outgoing calls, as shown in Example 4-9. The message **Dialer state is data link layer up** suggests that the dialer came up properly and that the interface BRI0/0:1 is bound to the profile dialer 1.

```
Example 4-9      show dialer Partial Command Output
Toronto#show dialer

BRI0/0 - dialer type = ISDN

Dial String       Successes    Failures    Last DNIS    Last status
0 incoming call(s) have been screened.
0 incoming call(s) rejected for callback.

BRI0/0:1 - dialer type = ISDN
Idle timer (120 secs), Fast idle timer (20 secs)
Wait for carrier (30 secs), Re-enable (15 secs)
Dialer state is data link layer up
Dial reason: ip (s=10.10.10.1, d=209.165.201.1)
Interface bound to profile Di1
Time until disconnect 87 secs
Current call connected 00:00:47
Connected to 5551000 (Hamilton)

BRI0/0:2 - dialer type = ISDN
Idle timer (120 secs), Fast idle timer (20 secs)
Wait for carrier (30 secs), Re-enable (15 secs)
Dialer state is idle
```

The **show isdn active** command displays information about the currently active ISDN calls, and the **show isdn status** command displays information about the three layers involved in ISDN connectivity. The output of these commands is the same as that produced for legacy DDR connections.

Displaying ISDN Process Information

To gain information about the ISDN process in real time, a number of **debug** commands are available. To observe the data link layer exchange of information, use the **debug isdn q921** command, as demonstrated in Example 4-10. The type of message exchanged can be seen from the seventh and eighth most significant hexadecimal numbers in the output:

- 0x05 indicates a call setup message.

- 0x02 indicates a call proceeding message.

- 0x07 indicates a call connect message.

- 0x0F indicates a connect acknowledgment message (ACK).

Example 4-10   debug isdn q921 Command Output

```
Toronto#debug isdn q921
Toronto#
Toronto#ping 209.165.201.1

Type escape sequence to abort.
Sending 5, 100-byte ICMP Echos to 209.165.201.1, timeout is 2 seconds:

00:51:33: ISDN BR0/0: RX <- RRp sapi=0 tei=65 nr=1
00:51:33: ISDN BR0/0: TX -> RRf sapi=0 tei=65 nr=1
00:51:33: ISDN BR0/0: TX -> INFOc sapi=0 tei=64 ns=33 nr=25
  i=0x080109050402889018018332C0735353531303030
00:51:33: ISDN BR0/0: RX <- RRr sapi=0 tei=64 nr=34
00:51:33: ISDN BR0/0: RX <- INFOc sapi=0 tei=64 ns=25 nr=34 i=0x08018902180189
00:51:33: ISDN BR0/0: TX -> RRr sapi=0 tei=64 nr=26
00:51:33: ISDN BR0/0: RX <- INFOc sapi=0 tei=64 ns=26 nr=34 i=0x08018907180189
00:51:33: ISDN BR0/0: TX -> RRr sapi=0 tei=64 nr=27
00:51:142542387765: %LINK-3-UPDOWN: Interface BRI0/0:1, changed state to up
00:51:143919226060: %DIALER-6-BIND: Interface BR0/0:1 bound to profile Di1.!!!
00:51:33: ISDN BR0/0: TX -> INFOc sapi=0 tei=64 ns=34 nr=27 i=0x0801090F
00:51:33: ISDN BR0/0: RX <- RRr sapi=0 tei=64 nr=35!
Success rate is 80 percent (4/5), round-trip min/avg/max = 32/32/32 ms
```

You can observe call setup exchanges with the **debug isdn q931** command, as shown in Example 4-11.

Example 4-11   debug isdn q931 Command Output

```
Toronto#debug isdn q931
Toronto#
Toronto#ping 209.165.201.1

Type escape sequence to abort.
Sending 5, 100-byte ICMP Echos to 209.165.201.1, timeout is 2 seconds:

01:07:39: ISDN BR0/0: TX -> SETUP pd = 8  callref = 0x0A
01:07:39:         Bearer Capability i = 0x8890
01:07:39:         Channel ID i = 0x83
01:07:39:         Keypad Facility i = '5551000'
01:07:39: ISDN BR0/0: RX <- CALL_PROC pd = 8  callref = 0x8A
01:07:39:         Channel ID i = 0x89
01:07:39: ISDN BR0/0: RX <- CONNECT pd = 8  callref = 0x8A
01:07:39:         Channel ID i = 0x89
01:07:168312191541: %LINK-3-UPDOWN: Interface BRI0/0:1, changed state to up
01:07:169689029836: %DIALER-6-BIND: Interface BR0/0:1 bound to profile Di1
01:07:39: ISDN BR0/0: TX -> CONNECT_ACK pd = 8  callref = 0x0A..!!!
Success rate is 60 percent (3/5), round-trip min/avg/max = 32/32/32 ms
01:07:42: %LINEPROTO-5-UPDOWN: Line protocol on Interface BRI0/0:1, changed state to
  up
01:07:45: %ISDN-6-CONNECT: Interface BRI0/0:1 is now connected to 5551000 Hamilton
```

The **debug dialer events** command tells you why the call was placed. It identifies the source and destination addresses of the interesting traffic that brought up the interface. This is shown in Example 4-12, in which the traffic destined for the LAN segment on the Hamilton router causes the interface to come up. If this command has no output, the router did not identify any interesting traffic. This usually indicates an incorrectly configured dialer or access list.

Example 4-12   debug dialer events Command Output

```
Toronto#debug dialer events
Dial on demand events debugging is on
Toronto#ping 209.165.201.1

Type escape sequence to abort.
Sending 5, 100-byte ICMP Echos to 209.165.201.1, timeout is 2 seconds:

01:50:08: BR0/0 DDR: rotor dialout [priority]
01:50:08: BR0/0 DDR: Dialing cause ip (s=10.10.10.1, d=209.165.201.1)
01:50:08: BR0/0 DDR: Attempting to dial 5551000
01:50:35168270899: %LINK-3-UPDOWN: Interface BRI0/0:1, changed state to up
01:50:36531520483: BR0/0:1 interface must be fifo queue, force fifo
01:50:36545043660: %DIALER-6-BIND: Interface BR0/0:1 bound to profile Di1.!
```

Example 4-12   debug dialer events Command Output   *continued*

```
01:50:08: BR0/0:1 DDR: Remote name for Hamilton
01:50:08: BR0/0:1 DDR: dialer protocol up!!!
Success rate is 80 percent (4/5), round-trip min/avg/max = 32/32/32 ms
01:50:09: %LINEPROTO-5-UPDOWN: Line protocol on Interface BRI0/0:1, changed state to
  up
01:50:14: %ISDN-6-CONNECT: Interface BRI0/0:1 is now connected to 5551000 Hamilton
```

An improperly configured ISDN interface can continually attempt to dial out. This "flapping" can be very expensive and can make the interface unavailable for the movement of data. The **debug dialer packet** command shows which traffic is moving out of the DDR interface and is causing the interface to flap. This is often caused by improperly configured access control lists, which allow traffic such as routing updates to be seen as interesting.

Quite often, the local DDR configuration is functioning properly, and the problem rests with either the carrier network or an improperly configured remote router. To test the carrier network and the configuration of the remote router, use the following command:

```
Router#isdn call interface interface number
```

If the call goes through, both the remote router and the carrier network are functioning properly, and improperly configured DDR on the local router is probably the problem. If the call does not go through, look for a problem with either the carrier network or the configuration of the remote router.

To reset the ISDN connection between the router and the local switch, use the command **clear interface bri**. This command forces the router to renegotiate its SPIDs with the local switch. If you change SPIDs, it is sometimes necessary to use this command.

Summary

ISDN is a circuit-switched technology that functions at the lower three layers of the OSI model. ITU-T standards define the functionality of all three layers. These standards are broken into three main series:

- **E series**—These recommend telephone network standards for ISDN.

- **I series**—These deal with the concepts, terminology, and general methods involved in ISDN.

- **Q series**—These cover how switching and signaling should operate.

By using out-of-band signaling over the D channel, ISDN can achieve extremely rapid call setup and teardown times. ISDN efficiently moves digital data over a circuit that was originally designed to carry only analog traffic.

ISDN can be implemented as either a BRI or PRI, depending on the bandwidth required. BRIs consist of two 64-kbps B channels for carrying data and a single 16-kbps D channel for carrying signal information. PRIs can consist of either 23 B channels and one D channel, each having a capacity of 64 kbps in areas that use T1 lines, or 30 B channels and one D channel in areas that use E1 lines. The logical channels are multiplexed over a single physical medium.

Dial-on-demand routing (DDR) can be used in conjunction with ISDN to provide a means where the link is brought up only in response to predefined interesting traffic. To conserve B channels and maximize efficiency, the logical configuration associated with a DDR interface can be separated from the physical interface through the use of dialer profiles. This allows the logical configuration to be bound to the physical interface on a per-call basis, allowing each call to specify different configuration parameters.

Configuring, verifying, and troubleshooting ISDN DDR links often involves the use of multiple **show** and **debug** commands, each of which provides information contributing to the implementation of a properly functioning network. In addition to some ISDN-specific commands, a number of commands relating to PPP encapsulation and authentication can also provide important information.

ISDN is often used as a means to provide secondary network connectivity should a primary link fail. Primary connectivity is usually provided by a packet- or cell-switched technology because of the technology's lower costs. The next chapter examines one example of such a packet-switched technology—Frame Relay.

Check Your Understanding

Complete all the review questions listed here to test your understanding of the topics and concepts in this chapter. Answers are listed in Appendix A, "Answers to Check Your Understanding and Challenge Questions."

1. What ITU-T series covers switching and signaling?

    A. E series

    B. I series

    C. Q series

    D. S series

2. What is the capacity of the D channel on an ISDN BRI in Europe?

    A. 16 kbps

    B. 56 kbps

    C. 64 kbps

    D. 128 kbps

3. What type of signaling does ISDN use?

    A. D-band

    B. In-band

    C. Mid-band

    D. Out-of-band

4. What standard describes the ISDN PRI physical layer?

    A. I.430

    B. I.431

    C. Q.921

    D. Q.931

5. What ISDN physical layer frame format is used for outbound traffic?

    A. TA

    B. TE

    C. NT

    D. NET

6. What is the size of an ISDN frame?

   A. 36 bits

   B. 48 bits

   C. 96 bits

   D. 128 bits

7. What is the purpose of the E bit in an ISDN frame?

   A. The E bit is an error bit and indicates that a problem exists.

   B. The E bit is an echo of the B data to ensure reliable delivery.

   C. The E bit is an echo of the previous D bit and is used to help resolve contention issues.

   D. The E bit ensures compatibility with prestandard ISDN implementations.

8. What happens after a device transmits on the D channel?

   A. Its priority is lowered.

   B. It raises its priority to ensure reliable access to the channel.

   C. It lowers the priority of all other connected devices.

   D. It gains control of the channel, and other devices lose access to it.

9. What is used across the D channel to ensure that control and signaling information flows and is received properly?

   A. HDLC

   B. PPP

   C. SS7

   D. LAPD

10. What is the range used for dynamically assigned TEIs?

    A. 0 to 31

    B. 0 to 63

    C. 32 to 63

    D. 32 to 127

    E. 64 to 127

11. What is used on the ISDN service provider's network to communicate between the local and remote switch?

    A. HDLC

    B. PPP

    C. SS7

    D. LAPD

12. A router without an ISDN interface is classified as which type of device?

   A. TA

   B. TE1

   C. TE2

   D. NT1

   E. NT2

13. An ISDN-ready telephone is classified as which type of device?

   A. TA

   B. TE1

   C. TE2

   D. NT1

   E. NT2

14. What type of device converts four-wire BRI signals into the two-wire signals used by the service provider?

   A. TA

   B. TE1

   C. TE2

   D. NT1

   E. NT2

15. What type of ISDN interface would be on a router with an integrated NT1?

   A. R

   B. S

   C. T

   D. U

16. What ISDN reference point references the connection between non-ISDN-compatible equipment and the Terminal Adaptor?

   A. R

   B. S

   C. T

   D. U

17. When you configure a T1 controller as a PRI, what is the default framing?

A. sf

B. esf

C. crc4

D. Australia

18. When you configure an E1 controller for PRI operation, which channel is used for ISDN signaling?

A. 0

B. 15

C. 23

D. 31

19. What should the **show isdn status** command report for Layer 1 status in a properly configured ISDN connection?

A. Active

B. Awaiting Signal

C. Sensing

D. Synchronized

20. What **show** command displays information about the called number and the amount of time until the call disconnects?

A. **show isdn active**

B. **show interface**

C. **show isdn packets**

D. **show isdn status**

21. What **show** command provides information on the timer and why the call was initiated?

A. **show dialer**

B. **show isdn active**

C. **show interface**

D. **show isdn packets**

E. **show isdn status**

22. What **debug** command can diagnose an improperly configured password on an ISDN connection?

A. **debug isdn event**

B. **debug isdn q921**

C. **debug isdn q931**

D. **debug ppp negotiation**

E. **debug ppp authentication**

23. What **debug** command can you use to view commands and responses exchanged during peer-to-peer communications over the D channel?

    A. **debug isdn event**

    B. **debug isdn q921**

    C. **debug isdn q931**

    D. **debug ppp negotiation**

    E. **debug ppp authentication**

24. What is interesting traffic?

    A. Traffic that moves across an ISDN connection only after the link is established

    B. Traffic that triggers a DDR interface to attempt a call

    C. Traffic that is blocked by a properly configured ACL

    D. Traffic that is permitted to pass through a properly configured ACL

25. What are two reasons why static routes should be used for any traffic that must use a DDR interface?

    A. To minimize the risk of a flapping interface due to routing updates and hello packets.

    B. To provide routing information even when routing updates from dynamic protocols are unavailable.

    C. To ensure that the DDR interface is always up.

    D. To provide a path for routing updates to move across the ISDN link.

26. What command is used to attach a dialer list to a DDR interface?

    A. **access-group**

    B. **access-list**

    C. **dialer-group**

    D. **dialer-list**

27. What is the maximum number of dialer lists that can be configured on a router?

    A. One

    B. Two

    C. Three

    D. Ten

    E. Unlimited

28. What command sets how many seconds a DDR interface remains active without the appearance of interesting traffic?

   A. **connection timeout**

   B. **dialer interesting**

   C. **dialer idle-timeout**

   D. **idle timer**

29. How do dialer profiles differ from legacy DDR?

   A. Dialer profiles are applied directly to a physical interface.

   B. Dialer profiles allow each interface to connect to only one remote site.

   C. Dialer profiles allow per-call binding of the logical configuration to a physical interface.

   D. Dialer profiles function only when multiple ISDN interfaces are available.

30. What **show** command provides information about the dialer profile bound to a specific physical interface?

   A. **show dialer**

   B. **show isdn active**

   C. **show interface**

   D. **show isdn packets**

   E. **show isdn status**

31. When you view the output from a **debug isdn q921** command, which hex code indicates a connect acknowledgment message?

   A. 0x02

   B. 0x05

   C. 0x07

   D. 0x0F

32. What **debug** command provides information on why a DDR call was initiated?

   A. **debug dialer events**

   B. **debug dialer packet**

   C. **debug isdn event**

   D. **debug isdn q921**

   E. **debug ppp negotiation**

   F. **debug ppp authentication**

33. What **debug** command can help you troubleshoot a flapping interface?

   A. **debug dialer events**

   B. **debug dialer packet**

   C. **debug isdn event**

   D. **debug isdn q921**

   E. **debug ppp negotiation**

   F. **debug ppp authentication**

Challenge Questions and Activities

Complete the following questions as well. These questions are purposefully designed to be similar to the more complex styles of questions you might expect to see on the CCNA exam. This section may also list activities that will help you prepare for the exams.

1. You have just been hired as a consultant to XYZ Corporation. XYZ has several offices across Canada and the U.S. The company is experiencing problems with its ISDN BRI connection in that inbound ISDN calls are not being answered on the second B channel. Where would you start looking for the problem?

2. A small consulting company just installed ISDN BRI connections between its four offices scattered throughout Australia. Each office is on a separate network, so dialer profiles have been implemented. The company cannot connect between two of the offices and suspects that the service provider's network is at fault. How could this be verified? If the network is proven to be functioning properly, what is the most probable cause of the problem?

3. A small manufacturing company has asked you to investigate a problem with its ISDN DDR configuration. The company just received an enormous bill from its service provider that indicates that its connection has been on continuously for the past month. What is the most probable cause, and how would you verify your diagnosis?

4. A small consulting office has asked you to provide a router it can use to form a PRI connection to its service provider. The company wants to save money by configuring the device themselves. They have asked you to provide instructions on the steps involved to make certain that they do not miss any steps. What information would you provide?

CHAPTER 5

Frame Relay

Objectives

Upon completion of this chapter, you should be able to answer the following questions:

- What advantages does Frame Relay possess over circuit-switched technology?

- What is the role of LMI in a Frame Relay circuit?

- What types of LMI does a Cisco router support?

- How is flow control implemented in a Frame Relay network?

- What is Inverse ARP, and how does it function?

- What problems are inherent in Frame Relay NBMA technology, and how are they overcome?

- What commands are used to configure, test, and troubleshoot a Frame Relay circuit?

Key Terms

This chapter uses the following key terms. You can find the definitions in the glossary at the end of the book.

continues

continued

Circuit-switching technologies were the first to be widely deployed in wide-area networks (WANs). These included the analog Public Switched Telephone Network (PSTN) and the digital Integrated Services Digital Network (ISDN), which became available as network upgrades allowed digital services to be provided over the same media as the analog PSTN services.

Circuit-switched technology provides a very high *bit rate* with low *latency*, but it requires that a dedicated line on the network be allocated to each set of parties involved in data transfer. Channel capacity must be available and reserved between each pair of nodes on the path, and each node must have switching capability. Because bandwidth requirements for different types of conversations vary enormously, line utilization also varies. Although time-division multiplexing (TDM) is used to divide the line into multiple timeslots, which are then assigned to different conversations, slots assigned to low-volume conversations are frequently underutilized, making the technology very inefficient. The cost of maintaining dedicated connections is high, and end users are unable to share the connections to reduce costs. This prompted the development of packet-switching technologies, which overcome many of the limitations imposed in the circuit-switched world.

In *packet switching*, data is first broken into packets, and then each packet has both a header and trailer appended. The appended header information controls the packet's routing through the network. At each node along the path to the destination, the packet is received, stored briefly, and then passed on. Packets from multiple conversations can be multiplexed on the same physical medium, making the technology cost-effective.

Early packet-switched networks were based on *X.25* technology, which involves considerable *overhead* for *error recovery* and *redundancy*. *Frame Relay* saw its development as a result of the high data rates and low error rates available in modern high-speed communications systems. It is often referred to as a streamlined version of X.25. It was originally developed as an extension of ISDN to enable the circuit-switched technology to be transported across a packet-switched network. Since that time, Frame Relay has developed into an efficient, cost-effective, standalone technology.

Frame Relay Concepts

Frame Relay is an International Telecommunication Union Telecommunications Standardization Sector (ITU-T) and American National Standards Institute (ANSI) standard. Initial proposals for the standardization of Frame Relay were presented to the Consultative Committee on International Telephone and Telegraph (CCITT) in 1984. However, due to the lack of complete standardization and interoperability, Frame Relay was not widely deployed during the 1980s.

In 1990, Cisco, Digital Equipment Corporation (DEC), Northern Telecom, and StrataCom formed a consortium to work on the development of Frame Relay technology. The specifications developed by the consortium extended the basic Frame Relay protocol with the addition of features that provide additional capabilities for complex internetworking environments.

These extensions are collectively referred to as the *Local Management Interface (LMI)*.

Although Frame Relay can be deployed across an entire network, it is typically used to connect a LAN into the WAN cloud. The technology is most often used on the link between a LAN border device, such as a router, and the service provider's switch. If used as a WAN access technology, Frame Relay is oblivious to the type of technology used in the WAN cloud itself. The end user's border device is the data terminal equipment (DTE), and the Frame Relay switch is the data circuit-terminating equipment (DCE) device. A Frame Relay network might be privately owned, but it is more often provided as a service by a public carrier. A typical Frame Relay network consists of a number of geographically separated Frame Relay switches interconnected by *trunk lines*, as shown in Figure 5-1. End-user DTE devices usually connect to the DCE switches through leased lines.

Figure 5-1   Typical Frame Relay Network

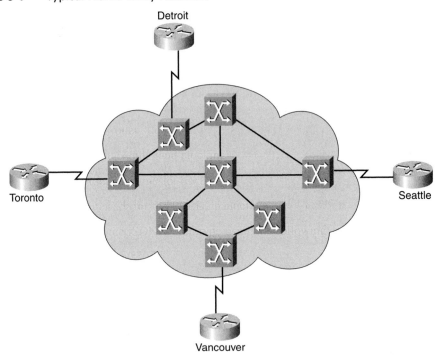

Computing equipment that is not connected to the Frame Relay network through a LAN may access the network using a *Frame Relay assembler/disassembler (FRAD)* as the DTE device. Based on its functionality, a FRAD may also be known as a *Frame Relay access device*.

Frame Relay is a high-performance WAN protocol that operates at the physical and data link layers of the OSI reference model. Frame Relay uses variable-length packets and allows end stations to dynamically share the network medium through the use of *statistical multiplexing*, which allows bandwidth to be allocated on an as-needed basis.

Virtual Circuits and DLCIs

Frame Relay provides a connection-oriented data link layer connection between pairs of communicating devices. These *virtual circuits (VCs)* are logical connections between DTE devices formed across a packet-switched network. Each VC is identified by a unique *Data-Link Connection Identifier (DLCI)* that identifies the circuit between the DTE device and the local Frame Relay switch. These DLCIs are then mapped to a remote Layer 3 address. A number of VCs can be multiplexed on a single physical circuit to help conserve equipment and optimize bandwidth utilization. If multiple VCs, each connecting to a different endpoint, are multiplexed over a single access line, that line's required bandwidth is calculated on the VCs' average bandwidth requirements, rather than the maximum requirement, as would be done in circuit-switched technology. VCs might pass through any number of intermediated DCE devices located in the Frame Relay network.

Frame Relay VCs can be either switched or permanent. A *switched virtual circuit (SVC)* is one that is built dynamically by sending signaling information through the network. As soon as the circuit is established, data can move across the network. When the connection is no longer required, the circuit is torn down, freeing the resources for use by other connections. These temporary connections are used in situations where only sporadic transfer of data is required between end devices. A communication session that uses Frame Relay SVCs has four distinct operational states:

- **Call setup**—This is the phase in which the VC between two Frame Relay DTE devices is established.

- **Data transfer**—In this phase, data is moved between the DTE devices across the Frame Relay network.

- **Idle**—In this phase, the VC still exists, but no data is flowing between the DTE devices. After a predefined idle time, the SVC connect is terminated.

- **Call termination**—The VC between the DTE devices is terminated.

After the SVC is terminated between DTE devices, a new one must be built for the same end DTE devices to communicate again. Although more efficient for sporadic traffic, the requirement to build a new VC each time a connection is required can have a negative impact on network performance. The support for SVCs is not universal and depends on the service provider.

The WAN administrator establishes a *permanent virtual circuit (PVC)* between end DTE devices across the Frame Relay network. These circuits are predefined and are loaded into the Frame Relay switches during bootup. The carrier establishes a PVC by configuring each switch along the path with input-port-to-output-port mappings. This links one switch to another until a complete path is established between communicating DTE devices, as shown in Figure 5-2.

Figure 5-2   Frame Relay Virtual Circuit

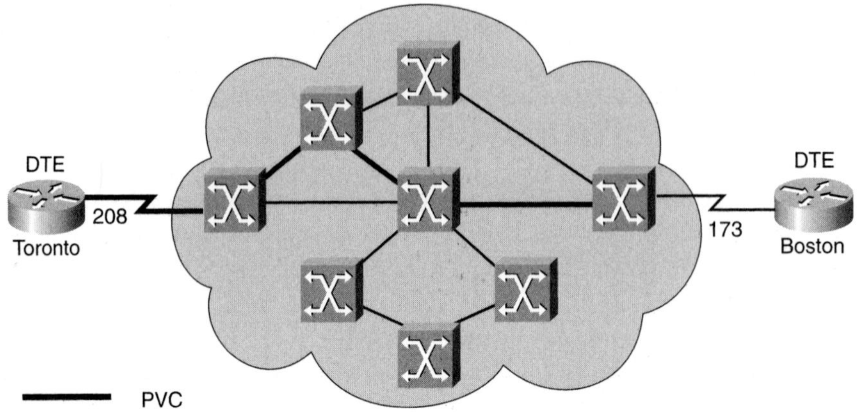

PVCs operate in one of two states:

- **Data transfer**—Data is transferred between the end DTE devices over the virtual circuit.

- **Idle**—The connection between the DTE devices is active, but no data is being transferred. Unlike a SVC, PVCs are not terminated after a predefined period of idle time.

Because PVCs are permanently established, no time is spent building the VCs between devices, and the circuit is always ready to transfer data. If the data flow characteristics are fairly regular in nature, the PVC is much more efficient for the transfer of data. Most service providers allow only PVCs to be used on their networks.

The Frame Relay Frame

Frame Relay functions by taking a packet from a network layer protocol such as IP or IPX, encapsulating this packet as the data portion of the Frame Relay frame, and then passing the frame to the physical layer for delivery. The physical layer is typically EIA/TIA-232, 449 or 530, V.35, or X.21.

Link Access Procedure for Frame Mode Services (LAPF) is an enhanced version of *LAPD* with congestion control capabilities. LAPF is used in a Frame Relay network for end-to-end signaling. Figure 5-3 illustrates the Frame Relay frame structure, the components of which Table 5-1 explains in further detail.

Figure 5-3   Frame Relay Frame Structure

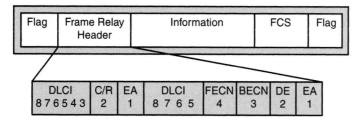

Table 5-1   Structure of a Frame Relay Frame

Field	Description
Flag (8 bits)	The Flag field is used to delimit the frame's start and end. It is always set to the hex value 7E, which is binary 01111110.
Header (16 bits)	The Frame Relay Header field is 2 bytes in size and consists of the following fields: DLCI—Data-link connection identifier C/R—Designates whether the frame is a command or response EA—Extended Address Field FECN—Forward Explicit Congestion Notification BECN—Backward Explicit Congestion Notification DE—Discard Eligibility bit The fields that comprise the Frame Relay header are discussed in detail next.
Data (Variable)	The Frame Relay standard specifies that this field must be at least 262 octets in size. To minimize fragmentation, it is suggested that this field be specified as 1600 octets.
Frame Check Sequence (FCS) (16 bits)	Even though Frame Relay is extremely reliable, there is no sense in switching frames that contain errors. This field uses the cyclic redundancy check (CRC) to verify the frames' integrity at each node. If an error in the CRC is noted, the frame is discarded. If a frame is discarded, no notification is sent to the source. Frame Relay reduces overhead by using error detection rather than error correction. Because Frame relay is usually implemented on reliable network media, it relies on the higher-layer protocols running on top of Frame Relay to handle the error correction.
Flag (8 bits)	This is identical to the start flag.

The DLCI is normally a 10-bit value used to identify the Frame Relay virtual circuit. These values are typically assigned by the service provider and usually have only local significance. They are used to identify the connection between the local DTE device and the service provider's switch, as shown in Figure 5-4. LMI allows DLCIs to take on global significance, but this then limits the number of available VCs in one network. Table 5-2 lists the DLCI assignments.

Figure 5-4   PVC Identification with DLCIs

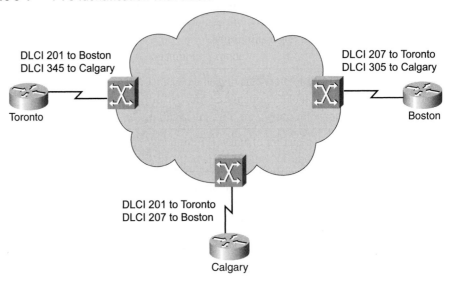

DLCI 201 to Boston
DLCI 345 to Calgary

DLCI 207 to Toronto
DLCI 305 to Calgary

Toronto

Boston

DLCI 201 to Toronto
DLCI 207 to Boston

Calgary

Table 5-2   Frame Relay DLCI Assignments

DLCI	Description
0	Reserved for LMI link management (ANSI, ITU)
1–15	Reserved
16–1007	Assignable to PVCs
1008–1018	Reserved
1019–1022	Multicasting
1023	Reserved for LMI link management (Cisco)

The Command/Response (C/R) bit is not used by the Frame Relay data link protocol and may be set to any value by the user device. This information is carried transparently by the Frame Relay network, and the use of this field is application-specific.

At the end of each DLCI byte is an extended address (EA) bit. If this bit is set to 1, the current byte is the last DLCI byte, but if it is set to 0, more address bits follow. In the standard 2-byte

address implementation, the first EA bit is set to 0, indicating that more address bits are available. The second EA bit is set to 1, indicating that the address is complete. If a 3-byte address field is used, the DLCI consists of 17 bits. If a 4-byte address field is used, the DLCI consists of 24 bits.

The Frame Relay network sets the *Forward Explicit Congestion Notification (FECN)* bit in a frame to inform the receiving DTE device that congestion was experienced in the path from the source to the destination. The Frame Relay network sets the *Backward Explicit Congestion Notification (BECN)* bit in frames traveling in the opposite direction from frames encountering a congested path (as shown in a moment in Figure 5-5). FECN bits are used for receiver-controlled flow control, and BECN bits are useful if emitter-controlled flow control is implemented. The congestion notification bit can be relayed to upper-layer protocols, which can then take the appropriate action to reduce congestion. Or the congestion notification bit might be ignored, depending on the implementation. The network administrator must decide what action should be taken when either FECNs or BECNs are received.

The *Discard Eligibility (DE)* bit is set to tell the Frame Relay network that a frame has lower importance than other frames on the network and should be discarded before any other frames. This occurs only during times of network *congestion* when available network resources become restricted. This bit might be set if the frame sent exceeds the bandwidth purchased from the service provider.

Data Movement and Flow Control

To fully understand the importance of the DE, FECN, and BECN bits, you need to understand how data actually flows on a Frame Relay network and the terminology used. The *local access rate* is the access port's clock speed. It's the maximum rate at which data can actually travel into and out of the port. The speed of this access line is typically between 64 kbps and 4 Mbps, but speeds up to 45 Mbps are available from some suppliers. The cost for a Frame Relay network is based on both the access line speeds and the *Committed Information Rate (CIR)*. CIR is the average rate of data transfer, defined over a certain interval, that the service provider guarantees to transmit through its network.

Traffic in a Frame Relay network is "bursty" by nature. The CIR is calculated as an average rate over a period of time called the *committed rate measurement interval (T_c)* and is given by this formula:

$$CIR = B_c/T_c$$

B_c is the *committed burst* and is defined as the maximum number of bits that a switch is set to transfer over any T_c. The *excess burst (B_e)* is the maximum number of uncommitted bits over and above the CIR, which the switch tries to forward. The *Excess Information Rate (EIR)* is the average rate over which bits are marked as DE. The Peak Rate is the sum of the CIR and the Excess Information Rate.

The switch maintains a bit counter on each VC. If an inbound frame pushes the counter over B_c, the frame has its DE bit set. If the frame pushes the counter over the B_e, the frame is discarded.

As frames arrive at a switch, they are buffered or queued. This buffering might introduce an unacceptable level of delay into the Frame Relay circuit. This delay might result in unnecessary retransmission of frames when the higher-level protocols do not receive an acknowledgment within the prescribed time interval. For this reason, Frame Relay switches drop frames from their queue to keep the size of the queue low and the delays to a minimum. Frames with the DE bit switched on are the first to be dropped. When the frame is dropped, no message is sent to the source device, and higher-layer protocols must detect that the frame has been dropped and request its retransmission.

When a switch is forced to drop frames, it sets the FECN bit on all traffic moving toward the destination. This informs the receiving end device that the network experienced congestion and that frames have been dropped. The destination device can then take measures to implement *flow control* and reduce the congestion on the network. In turn, this reduces the number of dropped frames and the subsequent number of FECNs that the destination receives. Flow control can also be implemented at the source if the source realizes that congestion exists in the network. To inform the source device that congestion has occurred, the Frame Relay switch sets the BECN bit on in any frames that are traveling toward the source. The source can then take appropriate actions to reduce the congestion, as shown in Figure 5-5. Note that these flow-control mechanisms are higher-layer functions and are not part of the Frame Relay technology. Only the mechanism for the notification of both sender and receiver forms part of Frame Relay.

Figure 5-5   Frame Relay Congestion Notification

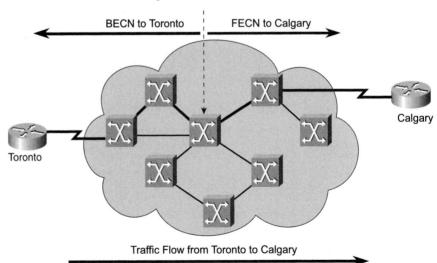

Because multiple VCs usually exist on one access circuit, each individual CIR must be less than the port speed. The sum of all the CIRs often exceeds the port speed by a significant factor. This is possible because it is very unlikely that all the VCs will use their maximum data rate simultaneously, and statistical multiplexing is used to allocate the available bandwidth based on need.

Consider an example in which a customer purchases a 9.6-kbps CIR on a 56-kbps access circuit. The customer is guaranteed the 9.6-kbps speed averaged over the committed rate measurement interval (T_c). However, what happens to any data that exceeds this value? Traffic can burst up to a maximum value of the line speed. Depending on the arrangements made with the service provider, this traffic might be either discarded or allowed to move through the network if bandwidth is available. But what happens if congestion is encountered along the way? In this case, the data that is in excess of what was contractually guaranteed should be discarded first. This is done through the use of the DE bit. The excess data would have the DE bit turned on. This signals devices along the path that this data is of lesser importance than other data on the network and should be discarded first. Some service providers allow customers to purchase a CIR of 0, which means that the DE bit is set on all data. During periods of congestion, this data is the first to be discarded. This might be a viable option if data is of very low importance and retransmission delays would not be problematic.

Note

Purchasing a CIR of 0 should not be used for applications such as VoIP, which are very intolerant of dropped packets.

Common Topologies

The most common topology deployed in Frame Relay is the *hub-and-spoke* or star topology, as shown in Figure 5-6. In this configuration, a central device, known as a hub, is connected to each remote device through a separate VC. Each remote device is located at the end of a spoke and has only one VC configured, which connects it to the hub. Although the hub has one VC configured for every spoke device, it might have only one physical access link into the Frame Relay network.

Figure 5-6   Hub-and-Spoke Topology

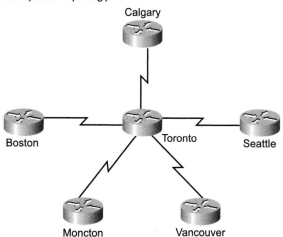

Frame Relay charges are not based on distance, so the hub device does not have to be located at the geographic center of the network. Many factors contribute to the decision of where to locate the hub device, including such things as availability of space, services, and technical support, along with the corporate structure and political climate. Often the site is selected to provide the lowest implementation and maintenance costs.

Although it's extremely cost-effective, the hub-and-spoke topology has a single point of failure and is unsuitable for networks requiring high reliability. In this situation, a full-mesh-topology, such as that shown in Figure 5-7, might be the better choice.

Figure 5-7   Full-Mesh Topology

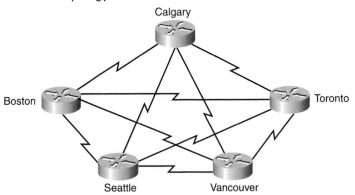

A full-mesh topology provides much greater reliability, but at a cost. Even though each site might have only one physical access link into the Frame Relay cloud, multiple VCs must be configured on each access circuit. Service providers often charge a fee for each VC. Because of address space limitations, the maximum number of VCs that can be configured in one network is less than 1000. This can prove inadequate for extremely large networks that implement a full-mesh design.

For these reasons, a full-mesh design is rarely implemented in favor of a partial mesh, as shown in Figure 5-8. In a partial-mesh design, multiple links connect each site, but each site is not connected to every other site.

Frame Relay is a *nonbroadcast multiaccess (NBMA)* technology. If multiple VCs are configured on a single access circuit, *split horizon* can cause problems for routing protocols. Split horizon is a technique that prevents the formation of *routing loops* by preventing an interface from sending routing updates on the same interface on which it received the route information. For this reason, maps must be created between the Layer 2 frame address (DLCI) and the remote Layer 3 address. These maps can be configured either manually by the network administrator or automatically through *Inverse ARP*.

Figure 5-8   Partial-Mesh Topology

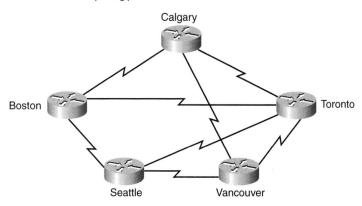

LMI

The Local Management Interface (LMI) is a set of enhancements to the basic Frame Relay specification. These enhancements were first developed in 1990 by a consortium composed of Cisco Systems, StrataCom, Northern Telecom, and Digital Equipment Corporation. LMI offers a number of extensions to the basic Frame Relay structure that are useful for managing complex internetworks. Key LMI extensions include keepalives, flow control, global addressing, virtual circuit status mechanisms, and multicasting.

The LMI global addressing extension allows Frame Relay DLCIs to take on global rather than local significance. This allows the DLCI values to identify specific DTE devices on the WAN. Individual interfaces and the DTE devices connected to them can be identified using standard address-resolution and discovery techniques. The entire Frame Relay network appears to be a typical LAN to routers on its periphery.

LMI status messages provide communication between Frame Relay DTE and DCE devices using reserved DLCIs (refer to Table 5-2). These messages periodically report on the status of the PVCs and help prevent data from being sent over PVCs that no longer exist.

The LMI multicasting extension allows *multicast* groups to be assigned. Multicasting saves bandwidth by allowing routing updates and address-resolution messages to be sent only to specific groups of routers. This extension also reports on the status of the multicast groups in the update messages.

A number of different types of LMI have been developed, all of which are incompatible with each other. The LMI type configured on the router must match that used by the service provider. If Cisco routers are connected to other Cisco routers, you can use the default LMI type; however, if you're connecting to non-Cisco equipment, you should specify the LMI type.

Newer versions of Cisco IOS support auto-sensing of the LMI type. Cisco routers support the following types of LMI:

- **Cisco**—Developed by Cisco, this is the default LMI type on Cisco devices.

- **ANSI**—Corresponds to ANSI standard T1.617 Annex D.

- **q933a**—Corresponds to ITU standard Q933 Annex A.

LMI messages are carried in modified LAPF frames. These frames have been modified by the addition of four extra fields in the header to make them compatible with the LAPD frames used in ISDN. Figure 5-9 shows a frame that conforms to the LMI specifications, and Table 5-3 discusses the fields illustrated.

Figure 5-9   Frame Relay LMI Frame

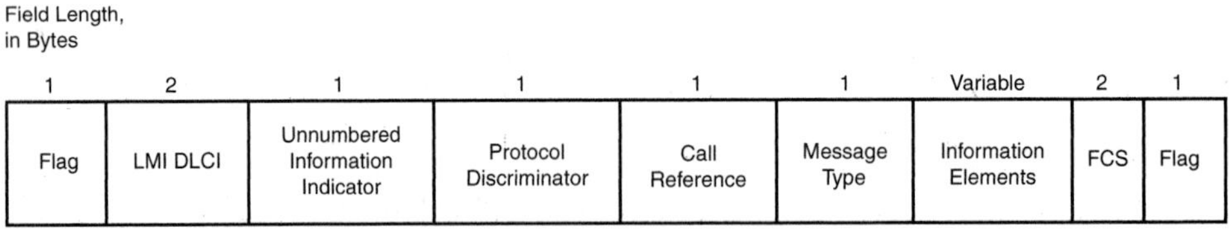

Table 5-3   Frame Relay LMI Frame

Field	Description
Flag (8 bits)	Delimits the frame's beginning and end.
LMI DLCI (16 bits)	Identifies the frame as an LMI frame instead of a basic Frame Relay frame. The LMI-specific DLCI value defined in the LMI consortium specification is DLCI =1023 for Cisco and 0 for ANSI and ITU.
Unnumbered Information Indicator (8 bits)	Sets the poll/final bit to 0.
Protocol Discriminator (8 bits)	Always contains a value indicating that the frame is an LMI frame.
Call Reference (8 bits)	Always contains 0s. This field is not currently used.
Message Type (8 bits)	Labels the frame as one of the following message types: Status-inquiry message—Allows a user device to inquire about the network's status. Status message—Responds to a status-inquiry message. Status messages include keepalives and PVC status messages.

Table 5-3   Frame Relay LMI Frame   *continued*

Field	Description
Information Elements (Variable)	Contains a variable number of individual information elements (IEs). IEs consist of the following fields: IE identifier—Uniquely identifies the IE. IE length—indicates the IE's length. Data—Consists of 1 or more bytes containing encapsulated upper-layer data.
Frame Check Sequence (FCS) (16 bits)	Ensures the integrity of the transmitted data.
Flag (8 bits)	Delimits the frame's beginning and end.

When a router is connected to a Frame Relay network, it sends an LMI *status-inquiry message* to the network. The network then responds with an LMI *status message* containing the details of every VC configured on the access link. The router periodically sends out status inquiry messages but receives only status changes. After a certain number of abbreviated messages, the network sends a full-status update.

Inverse ARP

After the router learns about the VCs that are connected, it sends an Inverse ARP request to discover the Layer 3 address information at the other end of each VC. The local DTE sends an Inverse ARP on each VC, and the remote DTE replies with the Layer 3 address. The router then builds a table mapping the Layer 3 information to the DLCIs. If multiple Layer 3 protocols are running on the network, Inverse ARP requests are issued for each. It is also possible to manually map the DLCI to the remote Layer 3 address, as discussed in the next section.

Note

If a map is created manually, Inverse ARP is disabled on the interface. It is not possible to mix static and automatic mapping of DLCIs on the same interface.

Figure 5-10 shows the Inverse ARP process.

Figure 5-10   Inverse ARP Process

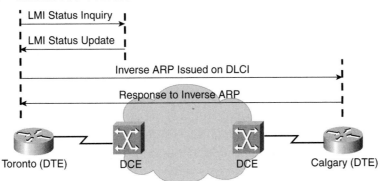

Configuring Frame Relay

Frame Relay configuration on a Cisco router is a fairly straightforward process. This is partly because the IOS can auto-sense features such as LMI type, and DLCIs can be automatically configured via Inverse ARP, which is often enough to obtain basic connectivity. The following sections outline the process of configuring Frame Relay.

Basic Configuration

Frame Relay is configured on the serial interface connecting the local DTE to the Frame Relay switch. The default encapsulation type on a Cisco router is the Cisco-proprietary version of HDLC. This should be used if you're connecting to another Cisco device or a device that supports this type of encapsulation. If you're connecting to a non-Cisco device, you should select the Internet Engineering Task Force (IETF) RFC 1490 frame type to ensure interoperability. Cisco's proprietary Frame Relay encapsulation uses a 4-byte header with 2 bytes to identify the DLCI and an additional 2 bytes to identify the packet type. To turn on Frame Relay on an interface and specify the frame type to use, issue the following command:

```
Router(config-if)#encapsulation frame-relay [cisco | ietf]
```

As soon as the encapsulation type is set, you must configure the IP address along with the bandwidth. You configure the IP address with the **ip address** command and use the **bandwidth** command to inform the routing protocols that bandwidth has been statically assigned to the interface. Routing protocols such as *Enhanced Interior Gateway Routing Protocol (EIGRP)* and *Open Shortest Path First (OSPF)* use this bandwidth to determine the metric associated with the link. The full syntax for the **ip address** and **bandwidth** commands is as follows:

```
Router(config-if)#ip address ip-address
```

```
Router(config-if)#bandwidth bandwidth-kbps
```

The **bandwidth** command is only logical and has no affect on the physical bandwidth. It is used only by some routing protocols to determine the metric associated with a route.

Configuring LMI

As previously discussed, Cisco devices support three different types of LMIs: ansi, cisco, and q933a. Cisco IOS Software Release 11.2 and later auto-sense the LMI type in use on a network, but versions of IOS before Release 11.2 require the LMI type to be manually configured. The default LMI type is **cisco**; you can change it with the following command:

```
Router(config-if)#frame-relay lmi-type [ansi | cisco | q933a]
```

Use the **show interface** command to verify the encapsulation configured, along with the LMIs' type and status, as shown in Example 5-1.

Example 5-1   Partial Output of the **show interface** Command

```
Router#show interface s0/1
Serial0/1 is up, line protocol is up
  Hardware is PowerQUICC Serial
  Internet address is 10.20.30.1/24
  MTU 1500 bytes, BW 56000 Kbit, DLY 20000 usec,
     reliability 255/255, txload 1/255, rxload 1/255
  Encapsulation FRAME-RELAY IETF, loopback not set
  Keepalive set (10 sec)
  LMI enq sent  11, LMI stat recvd 11, LMI upd recvd 0, DTE LMI up
  LMI enq recvd 0, LMI stat sent  0, LMI upd sent  0
  LMI DLCI 0  LMI type is ANSI Annex D  frame relay DTE
<output omitted>
```

Static Maps

If the remote router does not support Inverse ARP, you must create a static map to map the local DLCI to the remote router's Layer 3 address. You should also create static maps whenever broadcast and multicast traffic over the VC must be controlled. To configure a static map, use the following command:

```
Router(config-if)#frame-relay map protocol protocol-address dlci [broadcast]
```

The optional **broadcast** parameter allows broadcasts and multicasts to be sent over the VC. This permits the use of dynamic routing protocols.

Figure 5-11 shows a Frame Relay network with three sites each connecting to the Frame Relay cloud by a single access circuit. In the full-mesh design, each remote site must have a static map created to each of the other two networks. Example 5-2 shows a partial configuration of the Toronto router with maps to the Hamilton and Detroit networks.

Figure 5-11   Full-Mesh Frame Relay Network

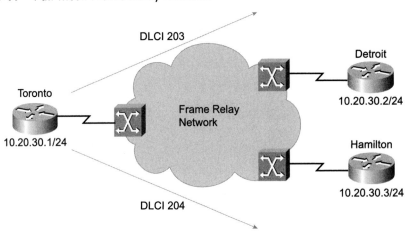

Example 5-2   Partial Configuration of the Toronto Router

```
interface Serial0/1
 bandwidth 56
 ip address 10.20.30.1 255.255.255.0
 encapsulation frame-relay IETF
 frame-relay map ip 10.20.30.2 203 broadcast
 frame-relay map ip 10.20.30.3 204 broadcast
 frame-relay lmi-type ansi
```

 Lab 5-1   Configuring Frame Relay (5.2.1)

In this lab, you configure a router to make a successful connection to a local Frame Relay switch.

 Lab 5-2   Configuring Frame Relay PVC (5.2.2)

In this lab, you configure two routers back to back as a Frame Relay PVC.

Subinterfaces

Frame Relay networks provide NBMA connectivity between remote sites. If a full-mesh topology is deployed, this is not problematic, but this type of topology is cost-prohibitive and therefore is rarely deployed. Most Frame Relay NBMA networks are built using the hub-and-spoke topology to minimize costs. In this scenario, the hub router must carry multiple PVCs, one to each remote site. If the multiple PVCs are configured on a single access circuit, two problems might result:

■ Reachability issues with routing updates

■ The need to replicate broadcasts on each PVC

The first problem stems from the fact that split horizon prevents a physical interface from sending a routing update out the same interface from which it previously received the information. This is done to prevent the formation of routing loops and means that updates received on one PVC cannot be sent out the other PVCs (see Figure 5-12).

Figure 5-12   Split Horizon Blocking Routing Updates

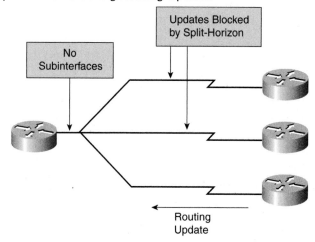

Routers that have multiple PVCs configured on a single interface must replicate broadcast packages, such as those from routing updates, on each PVC. These broadcast packets can consume large amounts of bandwidth and introduce latency into the network.

Disabling split horizon on the interface might seem like the logical solution, but this greatly increases the chance that a routing loop will form. The best solution to these problems is to implement subinterfaces on the Frame Relay network.

Subinterfaces are logical subdivisions of a physical interface. In a split-horizon environment, routing updates received on one subinterface can be forwarded through other subinterfaces. Frame Relay subinterfaces can be configured as either *point-to-point* or *multipoint* connections. When you configure subinterfaces, you specify the encapsulation type on the physical interface, and all other configuration types are assigned to the subinterface.

A subinterface configured in point-to-point mode acts in a manner similar to a leased-line connection. Each point-to-point subinterface must have its own subnet and DLCI, making it ideal for hub-and-spoke topologies. Because each subinterface is treated like a point-to-point interface, routing updates are not subject to the split-horizon rule, as shown in Figure 5-13.

Figure 5-13   Subinterfaces Allowing Routing Updates

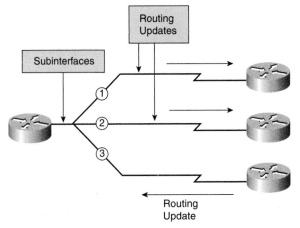

A subinterface configured in multipoint mode allows multiple PVC connections to multiple physical interfaces, or subinterfaces, on remote routers. In this mode, all interfaces must be on the same subnet. Each multipoint subinterface acts as an NBMA network, and routing updates are subject to the split-horizon rule.

The configuration of subinterfaces on a Frame Relay link requires the following steps:

Step 1.   Set the encapsulation to Frame Relay on the physical interface.

Step 2.   Remove any IP address that may be associated with the physical interface.

Step 3.   Create the logical subinterface.

Step 4.   Configure the logical subinterface.

A logical Frame Relay subinterface is created as either a multipoint connection or a point-to-point connection using the following command:

```
Router(config)#interface serial number.subinterface-number [multipoint | point-to-point]
```

The *subinterface-number* can be any value from 1 to 4294967295. If you specify the **multipoint** keyword, all router interfaces must be in the same subnet. If you specify **point-to-point**, each pair of point-to-point routers must be in the same network.

If a subinterface is configured for point-to-point connectivity, the local DLCI must be configured to distinguish it from the physical interface itself. In a multipoint configuration, the DLCI should also be configured unless a static route map has been configured. This is required because LMI does not understand subinterfaces. To configure a DLCI on a subinterface, use the **frame-relay interface-dlci** command:

```
Router(config-subif)#frame-relay interface-dlci dlci-number
```

Figure 5-14 shows a network that has been set up in the hub-and-spoke topology, with the hub router having a single access connection to the Frame Relay cloud. To prevent the formation of routing loops, point-to-point subinterfaces are configured on the hub router. Example 5-3 shows the relevant portions of the hub router configuration.

Figure 5-14   Frame Relay Hub-and-Spoke Network Using Subinterfaces

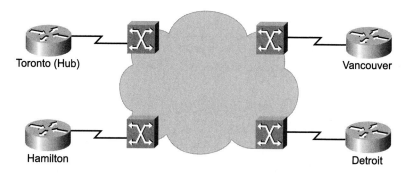

Serial 0/0.201 DLCI 201 to Hamilton
Serial 0/0.203 DLCI 203 to Detroit
Serial 0/0.204 DLCI 204 to Vancouver

Toronto (Hub)

Vancouver

Hamilton

Detroit

Example 5-3   Partial Configuration of the Hub Router Configured with Point-to-Point Subinterfaces

```
!
interface Serial0/0
 no ip address
 encapsulation frame-relay
 no fair-queue
 frame-relay lmi-type ansi
!
interface Serial0/0.201 point-to-point
 bandwidth 64
 ip address 10.20.15.5 255.255.255.252
 frame-relay interface-dlci 201
!
interface Serial0/0.203 point-to-point
 bandwidth 64
 ip address 10.20.15.9 255.255.255.252
 frame-relay interface-dlci 203
!
interface Serial0/0.204 point-to-point
 bandwidth 64
 ip address 10.20.15.13 255.255.255.252
 frame-relay interface-dlci 204
!
```

Lab 5-3   Configuring Frame Relay Subinterfaces (5.2.5)

In this lab, you configure three routers in a full-mesh Frame Relay network.

Testing and Troubleshooting

You can use a number of available commands to verify the Frame Relay operation. The **show interface** command provides information about the status of both Layers 1 and 2, as well as information about the LMI type, DLCI, and DTE/DCE equipment type (see Example 5-4).

Example 5-4   Partial Output of the show interface Command

```
Router#show interface s0/1
Serial0/1 is up, line protocol is up
  Hardware is PowerQUICC Serial
  Internet address is 10.20.30.1/24
  MTU 1500 bytes, BW 56 Kbit, DLY 20000 usec,
     reliability 255/255, txload 1/255, rxload 1/255
  Encapsulation FRAME-RELAY IETF, loopback not set
  Keepalive set (10 sec)
  LMI enq sent  8886, LMI stat recvd 8886, LMI upd recvd 0, DTE LMI up
  LMI enq recvd 0, LMI stat sent  0, LMI upd sent  0
  LMI DLCI 0   LMI type is ANSI Annex D  frame relay DTE
  Broadcast queue 0/64, broadcasts sent/dropped 19/0, interface broadcasts 0
<Output omitted>
```

To keep the LMI status exchanges between the router and the switch in synchronization, the keepalive interval configured on the router must be equal to or lower than the corresponding keepalive interval configured on the switch interface. The default keepalive interval is 10 seconds. You can change it using the interface configuration command **keepalive** *seconds*. Disabling keepalives on an interface with the **no keepalive** command disables LMI. If keepalives are enabled, the number of possible DLCI configurations on a multipoint or multicast connection is limited by the MTU size selected for the interface. To increase the number of possible DLCIs, disable keepalives.

To display information about the LMI traffic statistics, use the **show frame-relay lmi** command, as shown in Example 5-5. This command shows the type of LMI running on the interface, along with the number of LMI messages exchanged between the router and the local Frame Relay switch. If LMI information is not moving between the router and switch, check that LMI has not been disabled with the **no keepalive** command, and make sure the keepalive timers match.

Example 5-5   Output of the show frame-relay lmi Command

```
Router#show frame-relay lmi
LMI Statistics for interface Serial0/1 (Frame Relay DTE) LMI TYPE = ANSI
  Invalid Unnumbered info 0      Invalid Prot Disc 0
  Invalid dummy Call Ref 0       Invalid Msg Type 0
  Invalid Status Message 0       Invalid Lock Shift 0
  Invalid Information ID 0       Invalid Report IE Len 0
  Invalid Report Request 0       Invalid Keep IE Len 0
  Num Status Enq. Sent 8947      Num Status msgs Rcvd 8947
  Num Update Status Rcvd 0       Num Status Timeouts 0
```

To gather information about the PVCs configured on a router, use the **show frame-relay pvc** command. You can obtain detailed information about a specific PVC or the PVCs configured on a specific interface using the full version of this command:

```
Router#show frame-relay pvc [interface interface] [dlci]
```

The full **show frame-relay pvc** command is useful for viewing the number of FECN and BECN bits received on a PVC, as well as the number of packets that have had the DE bit set on. Example 5-6 shows sample output from this command when no traffic shaping is in effect.

Example 5-6   Output of the show frame-relay pvc Command

```
Router#show frame-relay pvc interface serial 0/1 203
PVC Statistics for interface Serial0/1 (Frame Relay DTE)
DLCI = 203, DLCI USAGE = LOCAL, PVC STATUS = ACTIVE, INTERFACE = Serial0/1
  input pkts 139          output pkts 29         in bytes 38130
  out bytes 1610          dropped pkts 0         in FECN pkts 0
  in BECN pkts 0          out FECN pkts 0        out BECN pkts 0
  in DE pkts 0            out DE pkts 0
  out bcast pkts 19       out bcast bytes 570
  5 minute input rate 0 bits/sec, 0 packets/sec
  5 minute output rate 0 bits/sec, 0 packets/sec
  pvc create time 1d01h, last time pvc status changed 1d00h
```

PVC status is reported by the DCE device and is received by the DTE device. The PVC status is exchanged using the LMI protocol; it can be one of the following:

- **Static**—LMI has been disabled on the interface using the **no keepalive** command.

- **Active**—The PVC is operational and can transmit packets.

- **Inactive**—The PVC is configured but down. This means that a connection exists between the DTE device and the local Frame Relay switch, but some problem is preventing information from being transferred to the remote device. This is often caused by a problem at the remote end of the network.

- **Deleted**—The PVC is not present (DTE device only), which means that no status is received from the LMI protocol. This means that the local Frame Relay switch is no longer seeing the PVC and has removed it from its table.

If information does not seem to be moving across the Frame Relay network to the correct network layer address, a problem with the map entries might be the culprit. These entries can be either dynamically configured through the use of Inverse ARP or statically configured using the **frame-relay map** command. The configuration of a static map entry on an interface automatically disables Inverse ARP. To view information on the current map entries, use the **show frame-relay map** command, as shown in Example 5-7.

Example 5-7   Output of the **show frame-relay map** Command

```
Router#show frame-relay map
Serial0/1 (up): ip 10.20.30.2 dlci 203(0xCB,0x30B0), dynamic,
              broadcast,
              IETF, status defined, active
```

In this example, 10.20.30.2 is the IP address associated with DLCI 203, and it has been dynamically learned via Inverse ARP. Frames on this PVC use the IETF frame format, and the PVC is currently active. The hex value 0xCB is the conversion of DLCI number 203, and the hex value 0x30B0 is how the DLCI would appear on the wire because of how the DLCI bits are spread out in the header.

If entries learned through Inverse ARP must be removed from the map table, use the **clear frame-relay inarp** command, as shown in Example 5-8. This works only for entries discovered dynamically. Static entries must be removed with the **no** form of the **frame-relay map** command.

Example 5-8   Clearing the Inverse ARP Table

```
Router#show frame-relay map
Serial0/1 (up): ip 10.20.30.2 dlci 203(0xCB,0x30B0), dynamic,
              broadcast,
              IETF, status defined, active
Router#clear frame-relay inarp
Router#show frame-relay map
Router#
```

You can gather much information about a Frame Relay network by observing the exchange of LMI information between the router and local Frame Relay switch in real time. You can accomplish this with the **debug frame-relay lmi** command, as shown in Example 5-9.

Example 5-9   Viewing the LMI Exchanges

```
Router#debug frame-relay lmi
Frame Relay LMI debugging is on
Displaying all Frame Relay LMI data
Router#
1d21h: Serial0/1(out): StEnq, myseq 163, yourseen 162, DTE up
1d21h: datagramstart = 0x38B7D54, datagramsize = 14
1d21h: FR encap = 0x00010308
1d21h: 00 75 95 01 01 00 03 02 A3 A2
1d21h:
1d21h: Serial0/1(in): Status, myseq 163
1d21h: RT IE 1, length 1, type 0
1d21h: KA IE 3, length 2, yourseq 163, myseq 163
1d21h: PVC IE 0x7 , length 0x3 , dlci 201, status 0x0
1d21h: PVC IE 0x7 , length 0x3 , dlci 203, status 0x2
1d21h: PVC IE 0x7 , length 0x3 , dlci 204, status 0x0
1d21h: Serial0/1(out): StEnq, myseq 164, yourseen 163, DTE up
1d21h: datagramstart = 0x38B7E94, datagramsize = 14
1d21h: FR encap = 0x00010308
1d21h: 00 75 95 01 01 01 03 02 A4 A3
1d21h:
1d21h: Serial0/1(in): Status, myseq 164
1d21h: RT IE 1, length 1, type 1
1d21h: KA IE 3, length 2, yourseq 164, myseq 164
1d21h: Serial0/1(out): StEnq, myseq 165, yourseen 164, DTE up
1d21h: datagramstart = 0x3700494, datagramsize = 14
1d21h: FR encap = 0x00010308
1d21h: 00 75 95 01 01 01 03 02 A5 A4
1d21h:
```

In this exchange, the LMIs are moving in both directions. The "out" direction is from the router to the switch, and the "in" direction is from the switch to the router. The router sends a status inquiry (StEnq) message to the switch, and the switch responds with a status update (Status) message. The inbound status message can be either type 0 or type 1. A full LMI status message is of type 0 and supplies the status of all current DLCIs. In this example, three DLCIs are known (201, 203, and 204), and the status of each is reported.

The status messages sent in a full update can be one of three possible values:

- A code of 0x2 means that the Frame Relay switch has the DLCI and everything is operational. This is the mode in which data may be transferred on the network. It displays with a status of Active with the **show frame-relay pvc** command.

- If the switch has the DLCI programmed in but is unable to use the link, the status code is 0x0, and the status is Inactive. This is most often caused by a problem at the far end of the PVC—usually a device that has lost connectivity to the network.

- A status code of 0x4 refers to a DLCI that has been deleted by the Frame Relay switch. This is usually caused by a configuration problem between the router and the local Frame Relay switch or the deliberate removal of the DLCI by the switch administrator.

Summary

Frame Relay is a very efficient technology and is extremely easy to implement. Because this technology is deployed on high-quality lines, it no longer requires the extensive error checking mechanisms that were built into its predecessor. Therefore, it is often referred to as a stream-lined version of X.25. Frame Relay relies on higher-layer protocols for error checking and the implementation of flow control. Although Frame Relay technology is still widely deployed, newer, less expensive technologies such as cable and DSL are penetrating the market. In addition, ATM offers many advantages over Frame Relay in an environment that must carry various types of traffic. These factors might soon cause Frame Relay to become a legacy technology.

Although a network that relies entirely on Frame Relay technology can be built, Frame Relay is usually deployed on the access link connecting the end user's DTE device to the service provider's Frame Relay switch. Multiple virtual circuits can be carried over a single physical access link through the use of statistical time-division multiplexing (TDM), which dynamically allocates bandwidth as required. These virtual circuits may be either switched (SVC) or perma-nent (PVC), with PVCs being the most common. PVCs eliminate the overhead encountered with SVCs, which build the circuit each time data is sent. Each virtual circuit is provided with a unique identifier called a Data-Link Connection Identifier (DLCI). The DLCI is then mapped to a network layer destination address either statically or dynamically through the use of Inverse ARP. The Local Management Interface (LMI) provides a set of extensions to the basic Frame Relay technology that provide advanced functionality such as global addresses, keepalives, link status, and multicasting.

Data is moved across a Frame Relay network by switches whose function is to receive data from one virtual circuit and then switch it to another virtual circuit, eventually moving it from source to destination. To reduce delay on the network, Frame Relay switches drop packets to keep their queues small. When packets are dropped, no notification is sent to the source, and higher-layer protocols must detect this and retransmit the packets. Frame Relay uses FECN and BECN bits to inform the destination and source, respectively, that congestion has occurred on the network so that these devices may implement appropriate flow-control options.

The next chapter introduces the concepts of network administration and management. It out-lines some of the tools and techniques available to make a network more efficient and reliable, thus providing increased user satisfaction and reduced downtime and cost.

Check Your Understanding

Complete all the review questions listed here to test your understanding of the topics and concepts in this chapter. Answers are listed in Appendix A, "Answers to Check Your Understanding and Challenge Questions."

1. Where is Frame Relay most often deployed?

   A. Between the end user's DCE device and the service provider's DTE device

   B. Between the end user's DTE device and the service provider's DCE device

   C. Between the service provider's DCE devices

   D. Between the end user's DTE devices

2. What Frame Relay device is required to connect an end device to a Frame Relay network if it is not connected through a LAN?

   A. Assembler/disassembler

   B. Modulator/demodulator

   C. Router

   D. Switch

3. At which two OSI layers does Frame Relay function?

   A. Application

   B. Presentation

   C. Session

   D. Transport

   E. Network

   F. Data link

   G. Physical

4. What is used to dynamically assign bandwidth as required for Frame Relay circuits?

   A. Channel Service Unit

   B. Data-Link Connection Identifier

   C. Time-Division Multiplexing

   D. Service Profile Identifier

   E. Statistical Time-Division Multiplexing

5. In what two operational states can a PVC function?

   A. Call setup

   B. Data transfer

   C. Idle

   D. Call termination

   E. Call maintenance

6. How many bits are assigned to the DLCI in a standard Frame Relay 2-byte address field?

   A. 6

   B. 8

   C. 10

   D. 12

   E. 16

7. How many bits are assigned to the DLCI if a 3-byte Frame Relay address field is used?

   A. 8

   B. 13

   C. 17

   D. 21

   E. 24

8. What DLCI is used for ANSI LMIs?

   A. 0

   B. 1

   C. 16

   D. 1007

   E. 1023

9. What range of DLCIs may be statically assigned to PVCs?

   A. 1–15

   B. 16–1007

   C. 1008–1018

   D. 1019–1022

10. What range of DLCIs may be dynamically assigned to SVCs?

    A. 1–15

    B. 16–1007

    C. 1008–1018

    D. 1019–1022

11. What Frame Relay header bit is used to flag a frame as having lower priority than the other frames on the network?

    A. BECN

    B. DE

    C. DLCI

    D. EA

    E. FECN

12. What Frame Relay header bit is turned off to allow 24-bit DLCIs?

    A. BECN

    B. DE

    C. DLCI

    D. EA

    E. FECN

13. What Frame Relay header bit is used to inform the sending device that congestion has occurred along the path to the destination?

    A. BECN

    B. DE

    C. DLCI

    D. EA

    E. FECN

14. What happens to a frame if it exceeds B_c on a PVC?

    A. It is immediately dropped.

    B. It has the DE bit set on.

    C. It has the BECN bit set on.

    D. Nothing. This is normal.

15. What does a Frame Relay switch do to reduce congestion on a network?

A. Increase bandwidth

B. Drop frames

C. Buffer frames

D. Queue frames

16. When does a Frame Relay switch set the FECN bit on?

A. The FECN bit is always on.

B. The FECN bit is set on when traffic drops below the CIR.

C. The FECN bit is set on when traffic flow exceeds B_e.

D. The FECN is no longer used in Frame Relay.

17. Which of the following is true about the Frame Relay hub in a hub-and-spoke design?

A. The hub is always located at the network's geographic center.

B. The hub always has exactly one DLCI per physical interface.

C. The hub usually has only one access circuit to the WAN.

D. The hub deploys only multipoint subinterfaces.

18. What topology is most often deployed in Frame Relay technology?

A. Hub-and-spoke

B. Extended star

C. Partial mesh

D. Full mesh

19. What topology is usually deployed in a Frame Relay network when high reliability is required?

A. Hub-and-spoke

B. Extended star

C. Partial mesh

D. Full mesh

20. What is the default LMI type on Cisco devices?

A. ANSI

B. Cisco

C. IETF

D. q933a

21. What two message types are carried in an LMI frame?

A. Inverse ARP

B. DLCI multicast

C. Status inquiry

D. Status

22. What does a router use to discover the DLCIs associated with connected VCs?

A. DLCI multicast

B. LMI

C. Inverse ARP

D. Reverse ARP

23. What does a router use to determine the network layer address of remote devices?

A. DLCI multicast

B. DLCI inquiry

C. LMI

D. Inverse ARP

24. What Frame Relay frame type should be used when interconnecting devices from various manufacturers?

A. ANSI

B. Annex D

C. Cisco

D. IETF

E. q933a

25. What LMI type should be configured on a Cisco router connected to another Cisco device if the router is running IOS version 11.1?

A. ANSI

B. Annex D

C. Cisco

D. IETF

E. q933a

F. The router should be allowed to auto-detect the LMI type.

26. How should reachability issues on a Frame Relay network be handled?

A. Disable split horizon

B. Implement subinterfaces

C. Enable Inverse ARP

D. Specify IETF for the frame type

27. What **show** command looks for signs of congestion on a PVC connected to a specific serial interface?

A. **show interface**

B. **show interface congestion**

C. **show frame-relay lmi**

D. **show frame-relay pvc**

E. **show frame-relay congestion**

28. What **show** command checks the Frame Relay encapsulation type?

A. **show interface**

B. **show interface congestion**

C. **show frame-relay lmi**

D. **show frame-relay pvc**

E. **show frame-relay congestion**

29. What does it mean if the **show frame-relay pvc** command reports a status of Static?

A. The PVC is not present.

B. The PVC is configured but down.

C. The PVC is operational and can transmit packets.

D. LMI has been disabled on the interface using the **no keepalive** command.

30. What command removes a map entry that has been learned through Inverse ARP?

A. **clear inverse-arp**

B. **clear frame-relay inarp**

C. **clear map inverse-arp**

D. **clear frame-relay inverse-arp**

Challenge Questions and Activities

Complete the following questions as well. These questions are purposefully designed to be similar to the more complex styles of questions you might expect to see on the CCNA exam. This section may also list activities that will help you prepare for the exams.

1. You have been asked to troubleshoot connectivity issues in the corporate Frame Relay network. Users are reporting that they no longer can connect to the Tokyo office from the Paris office network and that this problem has occurred over the past 24 hours. You immediately issue a **show frame-relay map** command from the Paris router and notice that there is no map to the Tokyo office. Consulting the journal entries for the Paris network, you notice that they recently configured a static map to the Toronto office. You immediately test this connection and determine that you can Telnet to the Toronto office without problems. All other branch offices can connect to the Tokyo office without problems. What is the most probable cause of this problem, and how would you remedy the situation?

2. XYZ Inc. has just acquired ABC Inc. and must provide the ability for three new remote offices to connect to the corporate headquarters. The router at the corporate headquarters currently has a leased line between it and a branch office located in another state; it has been working without problems for the past several years. The network administrator created a new multipoint subinterface on the same physical interface of the headquarters router to provide connectivity to the three new sites using Frame Relay. After it was connected, nobody on the network could communicate. As soon as the new subinterface was shut down, connectivity between the headquarters and the original remote office was restored. A partial output of the running configuration is shown next. What steps would you take to correct this problem?

Partial Running Configuration for the Headquarters Router

```
<output omitted>
interface s0/0
 encapsulation frame-relay
 ip address 10.20.30.1 255.255.255.252
interface s0/0.101 multipoint
 bandwidth 64
 ip address 10.20.40.1 255.255.255.248
 frame-relay interface dlci  101
<output omitted>
```

3. You have just connected the corporate network to the service provider's Frame Relay switch, but you can't move data through the link. Your DTE device is a Cisco router, but the ISP is using equipment from another vendor. A partial running configuration is shown next. The keepalive interval, LMI type, and IP address and mask have been verified. What is the probable cause of the problem, and how would you correct it?

Partial Configuration of the Corporate Router

```
interface s0/0
 encapsulation frame-relay
 frame-relay lmi-type ansi
 bandwidth 56
 keepalive 15
 ip address 10.10.15.1 255.255.255.252
```

Introduction to Network Administration

Objectives

Upon completion of this chapter, you should be able to answer the following questions:

- What are the hardware characteristics of both workstation and server computer systems?

- How does a peer-to-peer arrangement differ from a client/server arrangement?

- What is the role of both clients and servers in a client/server arrangement?

- What are the differences between an operating system and a network operating system?

- What are some common operating systems and network operating systems?

- What is the goal of network management?

Additional Topics of Interest

The Additional Topics of Interest go into more detail about topics in this chapter, or they cover related topics that are less important to this chapter's primary focus. This information provides supplemental knowledge that helps you understand the presented material but does not directly form part of the CCNA certification exam. This additional coverage can be found on the CD-ROM. The following topics are covered:

- Network Services

- Choice of NOS

- Network Management Essentials

- RMON

- Syslog

Key Terms

This chapter uses the following key terms. You can find the definitions in the glossary at the end of the book.

workstation   page 189

terminal   page 189

application   page 189

client   page 189

mainframe   page 189

CPU   page 189

random-access memory (RAM)   page 189

diskless workstation   page 189

read only memory (ROM)   page 189

virus   page 189

laptop   page 189

Personal Computer Memory Card Industry Association (PCMCIA)   page 189

wireless NIC   page 189

continues

continued

This chapter introduces the concepts of workstations, servers, and the client/server relationship. It discusses the requirements of a network operating system and provides some common examples. This chapter also introduces network management and outlines why it is important.

Workstations and Servers

A LAN environment contains many different components. Peripherals such as printers, scanners, and storage devices are interconnected with various computing devices through intranetworking devices such as switches. Often these computing devices take on very specific roles in the network environment, functioning as either a workstation or server.

Workstations

The term *workstation* has many different definitions, one of which is often used simply to identify a *terminal* or computer that is connected to a LAN and that is used to run *applications*. In this context, the workstation is merely a *client* as opposed to a server or *mainframe*. Another, more accurate definition of a workstation is a high-performance, single-user computer usually used for graphics, CAD, technical, and scientific applications. As the power and complexity of PCs continue to increase, the distinction between these definitions is diminishing.

A workstation is usually a machine with a fast *CPU* and large amounts of *random-access memory (RAM)* and disk space. It is usually geared toward the professional user rather than the consumer or home user. A variation on the typical workstation is one that does not have a disk drive installed. These *diskless workstations* must retrieve programs and data from the network. The software required to connect the workstation to the network is stored in *read-only memory (ROM)* in the workstation and is loaded when the workstation boots.

Because diskless workstations do not have any disk drives, it is not possible to upload outside data from the workstation to the network or to download and remove information from the network via the workstation. This prevents *viruses* from being uploaded and also stops users from removing data in an unauthorized manner. Diskless workstations are often deployed in networks where security is essential.

In modern networks, *laptops* are taking on the role of workstations. This is possible because the processing capabilities of modern laptops are comparable to the most sophisticated desktop system. Laptops usually connect to the LAN through the use of either an integrated network adaptor or a *Personal Computer Memory Card Industry Association (PCMCIA)* network card. Many newer laptops have integrated *wireless NICs* installed or use *USB* network devices for connectivity. Some network installations use *docking stations* and/or *port replicators* to simplify the process of connecting to and disconnecting from networked resources.

Workstations often connect to a server from which they obtain shared data and applications. To allow this to occur, the workstation *operating system (OS)* contains a *redirector*, whose job is to intercept user data and application commands and decide if they are for the local OS or the network operating system (NOS). If the information and/or commands are destined for the NOS, the redirector sends them to the network interface card (NIC) for processing and transportation across the network. The redirector also accepts commands and information from the network and sends it to the local application.

Many different operating systems are available for use on a workstation. Some provide both OS and NOS capabilities, and others are dedicated OS only. In the Microsoft family, Windows 9x and Me are designed for workstation use, and Windows NT/2000/XP products may be used on either workstations or servers. The Windows 2003 platform is currently a dedicated network operating system. UNIX and Linux are found in both workstation and server applications. When run on workstations, these operating systems are usually found on high-end workstations running scientific or engineering applications.

Servers

In a networked environment, clients access the resources on one or more servers. *Servers* are usually dedicated machines that handle multiple concurrent requests from clients for specific *services* or information. To accomplish this, servers are usually configured on advanced hardware platforms with large amounts of high-speed storage, RAM, and processing power. In addition, these machines often have multiple high-speed NICs, and many support multiple CPUs.

Although many different network operating systems are available, most use the *TCP/IP* protocol stack for communications. Network operating systems have advanced network management tools and features that allow the connection of many simultaneous clients.

One of the most common services for a network server is *authentication*. Before any client may access shared network resources, its identity must be verified. To accomplish this, a centralized database is established that contains a listing of all clients that have permission to access these resources and their associated passwords. When a client connects to the network, it supplies its *authentication credentials* to the *authentication server*. The server then checks the username and password against those stored in the *authentication database*. If the supplied credentials can be verified, the client is allowed to access the appropriate network resources. *Authentication* merely verifies the supplied credentials against a database. Determining which resources an authenticated user has access to is called *authorization*. If the supplied credentials do not match those on record in the authentication database, the client is denied access to network resources. This centralized management of user accounts and security greatly simplifies the task of network administration.

A second common function of a network server is providing file and print services. *File services* are when the client accesses and stores shared files on the server. *Print services* are when the server caches and controls access to network printers. Having one copy of user data in a centralized location greatly simplifies file backup and *version control*. Version control ensures that all users access only the most current version of a file. These functions necessitate that the server have large amounts of physical storage as well as RAM for caching applications.

Dynamic Host Configuration Protocol (DHCP) allows a network server to automatically provide network configuration information to clients. The details of DHCP are discussed in Chapter 1, "Scaling IP Addresses." Although it is possible to run DHCP on a router, it is more common to deploy a DHCP server on the LAN segment to perform this function. To conserve address space and minimize costs, most network administrators configure their DHCP servers to provide private addresses on the internal network. Because this private address space is not routable on the Internet, traffic destined for the Internet must have its source address translated into a routable address as it moves from the internal network to the Internet. Replies must have their destination address translated from the routable address back to the appropriate private address before being placed on the internal network. This translation process is called Network Address Translation (NAT) and is also discussed in Chapter 1. Because NAT shields the internal addresses from the outside world, it provides some limited *firewall* capability. NAT can be configured on either a server or a router. Because NAT occurs as data passes between the inside and outside networks, it is usually configured on the border device.

Because servers must be able to handle multiple concurrent connections and perform many simultaneous tasks, they must be equipped with a fast CPU to provide a level of performance that is acceptable to the end users. It is now common for servers to come equipped with multiple CPUs to obtain an acceptable level of execution speed. These multiprocessor systems divide the processing requests between multiple CPUs, allowing many tasks to be run in parallel, thus greatly increasing the system's overall performance.

In large networks, administrators often maintain multiple servers, each dedicated to a specific task. For example, a server may be designated as a web server or a mail server. This allows the server hardware and software to be optimized for a single task, thus greatly increasing performance. It also allows the network administrator to allocate upgrade funds to the services most crucial to the organization. To eliminate a single point of failure in any network resource, most enterprise-level establishments have multiple servers running each of the key services.

Servers function as a central point of the network, providing files and services to clients. They must be able to handle varying loads at acceptable performance levels and also must be able to withstand the failure of one or more components without experiencing a general system failure. This *robustness* is achieved through *redundancy* in the system design. *Fault-tolerant* systems have additional resources built into the design and can compensate for component failure by using these duplicate resources. This may include such things as redundant power supplies, CPUs, RAM, and storage drives. Many systems allow you to remove and replace failed components without shutting down the system. Devices that can be replaced without powering down the system are called *hot-swappable*. The added cost of implementing component redundancy is justified by the minimized server downtime it provides, especially when you consider that server functionality is essential to network operations.

In larger networks, redundancy is often taken to the server level. Many organizations maintain redundant servers so that if one server experiences a system failure that takes it offline, the backup server assumes the functionality of the one that has failed. The nonfunctional server can then be repaired and returned to operation without users experiencing any downtime or loss of data.

Some common server applications and functions include web services using *Hypertext Transfer Protocol (HTTP)*, *File Transfer Protocol (FTP)*, and *Domain Name System (DNS)*. In addition, e-mail protocols such as *Post Office Protocol (POP)*, *Simple Mail Transfer Protocol (SMTP)*, and *Internet Messaging Access Protocol (IMAP)* are commonly supported, as is file sharing through Microsoft's *Server Message Block (SMB)* and Sun Microsystems' *Network File System (NFS)*.

The centralized storage of user data and resources on servers greatly simplifies the process of data backup and security. Most networks now incorporate large amounts of redundant storage in the form of network attached storage (NAS). Some larger networks connect multiple servers to a network of high-speed storage disks called a storage area network (SAN). Centralized file servers often have high-speed robotic tape backup systems configured to automatically back up user data during off-peak hours. If data loss occurs, it can be easily recovered from these backups. In a distributed system, file backup and version control is an extremely complicated and expensive process.

Client/Server Relationship

Small networks are often constructed in a *peer-to-peer* arrangement, in which each computer can function as either a client or a server at different times (see Figure 6-1). It is also possible for a machine to act as both a client and a server at the same time. In this arrangement, all computers are equal, and whoever physically controls the computer also controls access to all connected resources. This arrangement is not acceptable in large networks where centralized control of network resources is required. A *client/server* arrangement greatly simplifies the centralized control and management of network resources.

Figure 6-1   Peer-to-Peer Network

The client/server computing model, shown in Figure 6-2, distributes processing over multiple

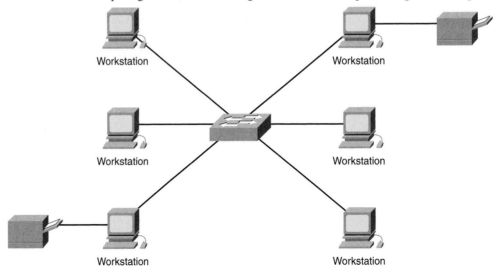

Workstation

Workstation

Workstation

Workstation

Workstation

Workstation

machines. *Distributed processing* enables access to remote systems for the purpose of sharing information and network resources. Most network operating systems are designed around the client/server model, in which the server provides services to the client. All computers on a network that are running TCP/IP are considered hosts. It should be made clear that not all hosts need to run TCP/IP. A host is any device that attempts to use a network resource. These hosts may be servers or clients, also known as workstations. A client requests information and services from a server, and a server provides services to the client. The local host is the machine from which the user is currently working, and a remote host is the machine being accessed.

Figure 6-2   Client/Server Network

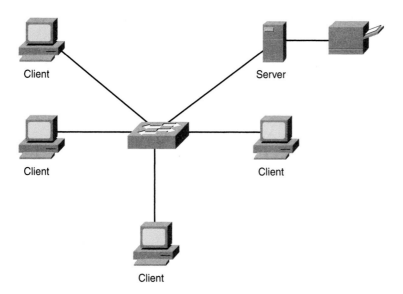

A common example of a client/server relationship is the *World Wide Web (WWW)*. In this case, the client software running on the local host is a *web browser*, such as Internet Explorer or Opera. The browser formulates a request for a resource and forwards this request to the correct destination using the *Uniform Resource Locator (URL)*, which identifies a specific resource on the remote host. The remote host (web server) formulates a response to the request and returns the information to the local host. The browser then interprets the returned information and formats the data in an appropriate manner for presentation to the user, as shown in Figure 6-3.

Figure 6-3   Requesting a Web Page from a Web Server

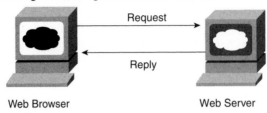

Web Browser   Web Server

Another example of a client/server relationship is that of a database server and a data entry/query client running on a local host. The end user enters the required information into the client on the local host. This client then formulates a request and sends it to the database server for processing. The server accepts the information from the client and carries out the appropriate search, returning the result to the client. The client accepts the information and presents it to the user on the local host, as shown in Figure 6-4.

Figure 6-4   Database Query

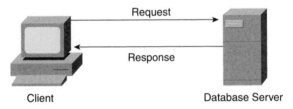

Client   Database Server

These examples have no requirement for large amounts of data to be transferred between the local and remote hosts. If the server were acting only as a file server, large volumes of data would have to be returned to the local host for processing. In the client/server model, only the results of the processed data are exchanged between the server and client. In addition, servers are usually optimized for the task at hand, making their capability to process data much greater than the local host. If data processing were offloaded to the local host, each local host would have to be constructed with sufficient resources to carry out the task. This would greatly increase the expense of the individual client machines.

Client/server technology offers many advantages, including centralized control of resources and increased security. However, it also creates a single point of failure for the network. Servers typically must contain redundant systems to ensure their continued functionality. In addition, servers must be constructed with sufficient hardware and software resources to be able to handle the processing of multiple simultaneous requests. Although this greatly increases the cost of server systems, this cost is offset by the lower level of resources required by the client-side systems. In addition, highly skilled network administrators are required to support client/server architectures.

Introduction to Network Operating Systems (NOS)

An operating system works with local hardware to provide a user interface and services to application programs that run on the local hardware. Operating systems provide these services for only a single user at a time. A *network operating system (NOS)* must provide the same functionality as an OS, but it must also allow multiple concurrent connections and access to shared network resources. Network operating systems function with the local OS to provide these services. Some common network operating systems include Novell NetWare, Microsoft Windows NT/2000/2003, UNIX, and Linux.

Workstations function as clients in a NOS environment. Specialized software added to the workstation OS allows the client to interact with the NOS, which in turn gives it access to remote resources. The local user can treat these network resources as though they are locally connected.

A server running a NOS must be able to support multiple concurrent users. The NOS allows the administrator to create accounts for each user and control the resources that each user may access. After the user provides the proper credentials to the NOS, it authenticates the user and then provides access to the appropriate shared resources.

A NOS server must be able to execute multiple tasks at the same time. To provide this capability, the NOS contains sophisticated scheduling software. This software functions by allocating processor time, memory, and other resources to different tasks in a way that allows sharing of system resources. As users authenticate, the NOS dynamically assigns them a set of system resources. When the user logs out of the system, these resources are returned to the pool for reallocation.

When selecting a NOS, you must consider several factors:

- Performance
- Management and monitoring tools
- Security
- Scalability
- Robustness/fault tolerance
- Ease of use

A NOS must provide the capability to quickly transfer files between the server and client. It also must be able to maintain a level of performance that is acceptable to the users under varying loads. Consistent *performance* under varying loads is one important characteristic of a NOS.

The management interface provides access to the tools required to manage users, files, print, and storage. This interface provides tools to install new services as well as monitor and configure existing services. A user-friendly, functional interface makes network management much easier.

A NOS must protect the shared resources under its control. This can be accomplished by authenticating all users and then restricting access only to authorized resources. Many NOSs also *encrypt* data to protect it as it traverses the network connection.

Scalability is the capability of a NOS to grow with the network. It is important that the NOS handle the addition of new users without degradation in the level of service. In addition, a scalable NOS must be able to handle the addition of new servers to a network to support existing or new users. Because much time and money go into developing a successful client/server implementation, this is a long-term investment, and anticipated future growth must be taken into account.

Robustness or fault tolerance is a network's capability to maintain a constant level of performance under varying loads even if components or processes fail. This is accomplished by adding redundant devices such as disk drives, processors, and memory. Balancing the workload across multiple servers can greatly improve network robustness.

Network Management

In the early 1980s, computer networks began to grow and become interconnected. As these networks became more complicated, the requirement for a way to manage them became obvious. Early forms of *network management* involved using remote login to monitor or configure network devices. However, as networks became increasingly complex, this was no longer sufficient, so more-sophisticated tools were developed.

Users continually demand improved levels of service. They are no longer willing to accept the inability to access network resources whenever they are required. In addition, this access must be provided at an acceptable level of performance. Network managers must be able to actively monitor the network and diagnose problems to maintain a level of network performance acceptable to all users. With the complexity of modern networks, this is a daunting task without the assistance of automated network monitoring tools.

Often, network growth occurs disproportionately with an organization's level of financial commitment. This requires the network administrator to be able to optimally distribute available resources to provide users with an acceptable level of performance, availability, and security. Through proper network monitoring techniques, network resources can be reallocated as required, thus controlling costs.

Network management includes the following duties:

- Monitoring network availability

- Improving automation

- Monitoring response time

- Providing security features

- Rerouting traffic

- Restoring capabilities

- Registering users

Network management tools allow the network administrator to accomplish the following:

- Control corporate assets

- Control network complexity

- Control costs

- Improve service

- Improve performance

- Minimize downtime

Networks continue to grow in both size and complexity. They have evolved from simple peer-to-peer arrangements in which all hosts are considered equal to complex client/server relationships. This ever-increasing complexity has necessitated the development of tools and techniques to allow the centralized management of network resources. Network management involves everything from simple remote access to the implementation of complex commercial tools such as HP OpenView and CiscoWorks. A number of open-source tools also exist for this purpose and are gaining acceptance in the corporate world. Among these is Multi-Router Traffic Grapher (MRTG), which monitors the traffic load on network links.

Client computers, from powerful workstations to laptops, use the resources and services offered by servers. After it is authenticated against a centralized database, the operating system software running on the client computer works with the network operating system to give the local machine access to networked resources. Many different types of network operating systems are available, all of which contain sophisticated scheduling software that allows many clients to connect to the server concurrently.

Summary

The network environment contains many components in addition to internetworking devices such as hubs, switches, and routers. Network administrators must be able to control a wide range of network resources to provide an acceptable level of performance to all users at all times. To accomplish this, many commercial and open-source tools have been developed to help you manage network traffic. Network operating systems have been developed to simplify the tasks of user authentication and authorization and to dynamically allocate resources to users and applications. A network administrator must be able to successfully integrate technologies and tools from many different vendors and continually "tune" the network to provide the level of service demanded by the end users. This task requires an extremely skilled individual.

Check Your Understanding

Complete all the review questions listed here to test your understanding of the topics and concepts in this chapter. Answers are listed in Appendix A, "Answers to Check Your Understanding and Challenge Questions."

1. What term accurately describes a workstation?

   A. A low-power standalone machine

   B. A multiuser networked machine

   C. A single-user computer used for scientific applications

   D. A dumb terminal connected to a mainframe computer

2. What are two reasons for using a diskless workstation?

   A. To prevent the theft of sensitive data

   B. To prevent the uploading of viruses and Trojans

   C. To reduce the workstation's cost

   D. To prevent unauthorized individuals from accessing sensitive data

3. What is the job of the network redirector?

   A. To send program output to the local monitor

   B. To intercept user commands and data and see if they are destined for the local hardware

   C. To transfer authentication requests to the local authentication database

   D. To move data from the standard input device to the standard output device

4. What Windows OS can be used on either the client or server?

   A. Windows 98

   B. Windows Me

   C. Windows 2000

   D. Windows 2003

5. What is the most common protocol stack used for network communications?

   A. SPX/IPX

   B. NetBEUI

   C. TCP/IP

   D. NetBIOS

6. What is authentication?

   A. Determining which network resources can be accessed after successfully logging into a network.

   B. Maintaining a record of services and files accessed during an interactive session.

   C. Checking supplied credentials against a database to determine if a client should be allowed to connect to a network.

   D. Updating user-supplied information after the client has successfully connected to the network server.

7. What is an advantage of networked file services?

   A. Control of printer access

   B. Simplified record-keeping of which network resources are accessed

   C. Increased file access speed

   D. Simplified backup and version control

8. What service allows a server to automatically provide network configuration information to a client?

   A. DHCP

   B. DNS

   C. NAT

   D. TFTP

9. What service protects an internal network by shielding the internal address space from the outside world?

   A. DHCP

   B. DNS

   C. NAT

   D. TFTP

10. How is robustness achieved in network design?

   A. By providing a dedicated server for each service that must be offered

   B. By spreading services across multiple servers

   C. By deploying only a single operating system across multiple servers

   D. By running all services on a single server

11. What three protocols are used for e-mail?

   A. SNMP

   B. SMTP

   C. POP

   D. IMAP

   E. DNS

   F. TFTP

12. In a peer-to-peer network arrangement, who controls access to resources?

A. Nobody

B. The network administrator

C. The department manager

D. The owner of the machine the resource is connected to

13. What type of network arrangement allows for centralized control of network resources?

A. Peer-to-peer

B. Client/server

C. Distributed

D. Centralized

14. What is the role of a server in a client/server relationship?

A. To request services from the client

B. To provide services to the client

C. To control access to the local workstation

D. To redirect network requests from the client

15. Which of the following is true of data transfer in a client/server relationship?

A. Data is processed on the client, and the results are sent to the server.

B. Data is sent to the server for processing.

C. Data processing is shared equally between the local host and the server.

D. Data processing may occur on either the server or the client, depending on which machine has free system resources.

16. What is a serious drawback of the client/server network arrangement?

A. Servers can produce a single point of failure.

B. Servers can handle requests from only one client at a time.

C. Server resources cannot be easily upgraded or planned.

D. Servers require specialized software to manage client connections.

17. How does a workstation treat network resources?

A. The workstation cannot access network resources.

B. The workstation connects to these resources by sending all data to the server.

C. The workstation must authenticate each time a network resource is accessed.

D. The workstation treats these resources as though they are connected locally.

18. What term describes how quickly a NOS can transfer files between the client and server?

   A. Performance

   B. Security

   C. Scalability

   D. Robustness

19. What term describes the capability of a NOS to maintain a constant level of performance even if one or more processes fail?

   A. Management

   B. Security

   C. Scalability

   D. Robustness

20. What term describes the capability of a NOS to handle additional users without a decrease in performance?

   A. Management

   B. Security

   C. Scalability

   D. Robustness

21. What is required to ensure that a network provides an acceptable level of performance as it grows in size and complexity?

   A. Management

   B. Security

   C. Scalability

   D. Robustness

22. Which of the following duties are part of network management? (Select all that apply.)

   A. Monitoring network availability

   B. Improving automation

   C. Monitoring response time

   D. Providing security features

   E. Rerouting traffic

   F. Restoring capabilities

   G. Registering users

Challenge Questions and Activities

Complete the following questions as well. These questions are purposefully designed to be similar to the more complex styles of questions you might expect to see on the CCNA exam. This section may also list activities that will help you prepare for the exams.

1. A new network is being constructed for XYZ Inc. The administrator has acquired funding for a total of three servers and must supply DHCP, DNS, Web, and e-mail services to a total of 100 users. How should these services be configured for reliability and optimum performance?

2. All sales employees of XYZ Inc. have been provided with laptop computers to remotely access corporate information. These employees must also connect in the office. The manager of sales has asked that all employees be provided with an appropriate workstation. What suggestion would you make?

Answers to Check Your Understanding and Challenge Questions

Chapter 1

Check Your Understanding

1. C

   Overloaded NAT lets you have multiple simultaneous conversations with a minimal number of registered IP addresses. Static NAT is usually used to provide outside access to internal machines. Dynamic NAT requires more registered IP addresses and is less efficient in large organizations.

2. C

   Machines on the same network see each other through local addresses. A machine on one network sees a machine on another network through a global address.

3. B

   PAT divides the available ports per global IP address into three ranges of 0–511, 512–1023, and 1024–65535. If a pool of addresses is supplied, PAT first tries to maintain the source port number. If it cannot, it searches from the start of the relevant pool to find an available port before moving to the next address in the pool.

4. C

   DHCP, like its predecessor, BOOTP, uses UDP for requests and replies. UDP 67 is used for requests, and UDP 68 is used for replies.

5. C

   The server broadcasts a DHCPNAK to inform all other machines that the resources previously offered to the host have not been assigned.

6. D

   The server issues the DHCPACK in response to a DHCPREQUEST by the client. The DHCPACK informs the client that it can use the network configuration requested and that the DHCP server has bound the IP address to the Layer 2 MAC address for the duration of the lease.

7. A, C, E, and F

   The DHCPDISCOVER message is sent as a broadcast so that all available DHCP servers can hear and respond to the request. The DHCPREQUEST, DHCPDECLINE, and DHCP-NAK messages are all sent as broadcasts so that all systems can be made aware of the availability of the offered network configuration.

8. C

   debug commands display information in real time. **show** commands display information about the system such as configurations or counters. Because you are looking for summary information rather than real-time interactions, the **show ip dhcp server statistics** command is appropriate.

9. D

   The command Router(config)#**ip dhcp excluded-address** *low-address* [*high-address*] removes addresses from the DHCP pool for assignment as static addresses to devices such as switches and servers.

10. C

   The DHCPDISCOVER and DHCPREQUEST messages sent from the client are sent as broadcasts. Routers block broadcasts, and a helper address must be deployed to forward these broadcasts to the DHCP server so that the server may respond with a unicast DHCPOFFER.

11. RFC 951 and RFC 1542 discuss BOOTP, RFC 1631 addresses NAT, RFC 1918 outlines the implementation of private address space, and RFC 2131 outlines DHCP.

12. DHCP supports three mechanisms for address allocation. Automatic allocation assigns a permanent address to the client. Dynamic allocation assigns an address for a fixed period of time or until the client relinquishes the IP address. Manual allocation, in which the administrator assigns an IP address to the client and DHCP, is used to convey the assigned address to the client.

13. Before the advent of the classless system of IP addressing, all subnets of a network had to be equal in size. Addresses were allocated to organizations as either Class A, B, or C addresses, regardless of their actual requirements. For example, if a company required only five routable addresses, it had no recourse but to acquire a Class C address, which allocated 256 addresses. The unused address space could not be used by any other organization and was wasted. The classless system removes the dependency on class boundaries and allows address space to be assigned more accurately. The organization just mentioned could be assigned a block of eight addresses, thus returning 248 addresses to the available pool.

14. A network administrator might decide to run a DHCP server on a router to avoid purchasing additional hardware to serve as a DHCP server. Running the DHCP service on a router also ensures that the service is available when it is required. Although this may be fine for small networks, it does make managing address space and troubleshooting more difficult. In addition, it forces the network administrator to use the IOS command set and not a graphical tool such as that provided by Windows. It also can add a burden to an already overtaxed device.

15. If an address is currently being translated and has an entry in the NAT translation table, it is unavailable for use by any other request. Normally addresses are returned to the pool when a reply is received. However, if network congestion or reachability issues prevent the reply from being received, the translation remains active until a timeout value expires it. In

dynamic NAT, the limited number of registered IP addresses can be quickly consumed, thus preventing internal hosts from being able to reach the outside network. Adjusting the timeout value to expire connections sooner can minimize the impact this can have.

16.

Service	Port
Time	37
TACACS	49
DNS	53
BOOTP/DHCP server	67
BOOTP/DHCP client	68
TFTP	69
NetBIOS name service	137
NetBIOS datagram service	138

Challenge Questions and Activities

Scenario A

The solution can be found in the file Static_NAT.pkt.

Scenario B

The solution can be found in the file Dynamic_NAT.pkt.

Scenario C

The solution can be found in the file PAT.pkt.

Final Implementation

The solution can be found in the file Final_NAT_Deployment.pkt.

Activity 2

Because the router blocks broadcasts by default, helper addresses have to be added to the interfaces that connect to segments hosting clients. Because many servers must be reached in the server farm, the interface leading to it should have directed broadcasts enabled.

```
Router(config)#
Router(config)#interface fastethernet 0/0
Router(config-if)#ip address 10.10.10.1 255.255.255.0
Router(config-if)#ip helper-address 10.10.50.255
Router(config-if)#interface fastethernet 0/1
```

```
Router(config-if)#ip address 10.10.20.1 255.255.255.0
Router(config-if)#ip helper-address 10.10.50.255
Router(config-if)#interface fastethernet 1/0
Router(config-if)#ip address 10.10.50.1 255.255.255.0
Router(config-if)#ip directed-broadcast
```

Chapter 2

Check Your Understanding

1. B

   All equipment installed at a customer's site is known as customer premises equipment (CPE).

2. C

   The subscriber's router is usually a DTE device that connects to the DCE, which prepares the data for transmission over the local loop to the service provider.

3. D

   To carry digital data on an analog network, it is necessary to modulate the signal onto an analog carrier wave. At the receiving end, the signal must be demodulated to remove the data. The device that modulates and demodulates the signal is called a modem.

4. A

   A purely digital network has no need to modulate the signal, but the data must be transformed into a form that is acceptable to the local loop. The device responsible for this is called a channel service unit/data service unit or CSU/DSU.

5. A and B

   WAN standards specify the connection's physical, electrical, and mechanical characteristics, along with the Layer 2 encapsulation format.

6. A

   Most Layer 2 encapsulations are based on the High-level Data Link Control frame format standard.

7. B and D

   Both the Public Switched Telephone Network (PSTN) and the Integrated Services Digital Network (ISDN) are examples of a circuit-switched technology. ATM uses cell switching, and Frame Relay uses packet-switching technology.

8. A

   ATM technology uses equal-sized 53-byte cells to move data. Each cell has a 5-byte ATM header followed by 48 bytes of payload.

9. D

Time-division multiplexing (TDM) allows a single connection to be shared between multiple conversations by allocating time slices to each conversation.

10. C

Permanent Virtual Circuits (PVCs) are set up by the WAN administrator and are loaded into the switch at boot time. Switched Virtual Circuits (SVCs) are built as required using the addressing information contained in the individual frames.

11. B

A Point-of-Presence (POP) is the nearest point where a subscriber can connect to the service provider's network.

12. B

Analog networks such as the PSTN use frequency-division multiplexing (FDM) to carry multiple simultaneous conversations on a single wire.

13. D

The ISDN BRI consists of two 64-kbps bearer channels to carry data and a single 16-kbps delta channel for out-of-band signaling. For this reason, it is often called 2B+D. The PRI interface differs between North America (23B+D) and Europe/Australia (30B+D). The PRI D channel is also 64 kbps in size.

14. D

In North America, the ISDN PRI consists of 23 B channels for data and a single D channel for out-of-band signaling, each of which is 64 kbps in size. When framing and synchronizing bits are added back in, this equates to the bandwidth available in a T1 interface (1.544 Mbps). In Europe/Australia, the standard PRI is 30B+D, which equates to the bandwidth available in an E1 line (2.048 Mbps).

15. B and F

Leased-line technology requires that the subscriber's router have one serial interface per line and also a CSU/DSU to put the data stream in a format that is compatible with the technology found on the local loop.

16. A

X.25 uses channels to identify data paths in the network. Frame Relay uses Data-Link Connection Identifiers (DLCIs). Service Profile IDs (SPIDs) are used to identify the connection to the local switch in ISDN technology. Telephone numbers are used on the analog PSTN to identify the endpoint.

17. B

As the quality of the media improved, it was found that the extensive error checking and flow control mechanisms built into X.25 were no longer required. Removing these from the Frame Relay technology greatly reduced the latency.

18. B

   Frame Relay uses the Data-Link Connection Identifier (DLCI) to identify the connection between the end user and the Frame Relay switch. X.25 uses channel numbers, and ISDN uses SPIDs. Telephone numbers are used on the analog PSTN.

19. B

   A single serial interface can handle multiple PVCs.

20. A

   ATM uses 53-byte cells to move data. Each cell consists of a 5-byte ATM header followed by 48 bytes of payload. Because all cells are of equal size and are very small, there is no problem with small voice packets being held up behind larger data packets.

21. C

   When moving segmented Layer 3 information, the amount of overhead required to move the data increases with ATM. This is because each ATM cell consists of a 5-byte header followed by 48 bytes of payload. It has been estimated that ATM requires 20 percent more bandwidth when moving this type of data than would Frame Relay technology.

22. A

   In North America, Asymmetric DSL (ADSL) is the most common. This form of DSL offers greater download speeds than upload.

23. B

   The word *asymmetric* in ADSL refers to the fact that ADSL offers download speeds greater than upload. This is acceptable because most end users download far more material than they upload. Unfortunately, this does not make ADSL an acceptable technology for those who want to host servers on their network.

24. D

   DSL technology works only if the local loop is kept extremely short. In rural and underdeveloped regions, this may not be possible, so DSL technology cannot be implemented.

25. C

   Cable television divides the coaxial bandwidth into channels and allocates a single 6-MHz-wide channel to the movement of data.

26. A and C

   The A in ADSL stands for asymmetric, meaning that the available download speed is different from the available upload speed. Cable is a symmetric technology, allowing equal speeds in each direction. xDSL offers a dedicated connection between the end users, whereas cable users share a common medium back to the headend.

27. D and E

   The source and destination for traffic flow help you choose the topology. The type of traffic helps you choose the type of technology that should be deployed.

28. C

For new WAN installations, it is not possible to collect information about traffic flow and type. In cases such as this, you must rely on information gathered from end users.

29. C and D

Both traffic flow dynamics and network availability requirements help you determine the topology. These can be used to help you decide if redundant links are required between sites and can help you choose the best topology to implement.

30. A and E

Traffic type and bandwidth requirements determine which technology is appropriate for a certain network. Each technology offers a certain amount of bandwidth, latency, and delay. When this is combined with knowledge of the type of traffic moving on the network and the tolerance of this type of traffic to these factors, you can select the proper technology.

31. A

For an organization with a limited number of branch offices that have to be connected and a very low volume of interbranch traffic, a one-layer design model would suffice. Although a two-layer or three-layer model should be considered, the cost and complexity of either of these designs is not required.

32. C

For larger organizations with multiple branches and a large volume of interbranch traffic, a three-layer WAN design would be appropriate. This would allow network traffic to be contained in the areas where it is required and, at the same time, provide a high-speed core layer to move traffic between branches.

33. A and D

The core links are used for the high-speed transmission of multiple types of data. The technologies deployed here must exhibit high bandwidth with low latency and jitter. The two technologies that are commonly used are ATM and leased line.

34. D

Core links are used to move various types of data between the core hubs.

Challenge Questions and Activities

1. You have been hired to help design a new WAN that will be deployed across seven countries in the EU. Each country will require the connection of between five and 12 cities into the new WAN for the purpose of exchanging financial and security information between the participants. Because of the sensitive nature of the data being moved, the network requires near-100-percent uptime. Which type of WAN design model would be appropriate? Which type of technology should be deployed?

   The key factors here are the large geographic separation, the sensitivity of the data being moved, the requirement for near-100-percent reliability, and the obvious grouping of sites both geographically and politically. It is also apparent that this is a government/military installation, so costs may be a secondary consideration. A three-layer hierarchical design should be deployed in this scenario, with the cities in each country being joined and then the collection of cities linked. Redundant links and equipment must be deployed to ensure the near-100-percent uptime. Additional data would be required to determine if a full-mesh topology were justified, but a partial mesh would be the minimal implementation consideration. Different types of technologies can be deployed on this network. It appears that the network is being designed to move segmented Layer 3 information, making Frame Relay more advantageous than ATM technology. Redundant leased lines would provide the bandwidth, security, and reliability required, but at a higher cost.

2. A small interior design company has opened a second office in a city approximately 80 km (50 miles) from the main office. The company occasionally will need to move e-mail and design specifications between the two offices. Which type of WAN deployment would you suggest, and why?

   In this scenario, the low-volume movement of non-mission-critical data between offices suggests that the Internet might be sufficient for moving the data between the offices. Each office could purchase its own connection to an ISP and use this connection to move data between offices. For low-volume applications, simple dialup might suffice, but because both offices are located in urban areas, DSL would be a viable low-cost alternative and could provide an always-on, dedicated, high-bandwidth connection.

3. XYZ Inc. wants to replace its high-cost leased-line network with a lower-cost alternative. The company currently connects ten offices using a full-mesh topology for its voice over IP (VoIP) network. All offices are located in urban areas. What solution would you recommend as a replacement for the current network?

   To reduce the cost of this network, the leased lines must be eliminated. A shared-access network would provide a viable alternative, but you must consider the type of traffic being moved. Voice traffic is very sensitive to delay and jitter, so ATM would be the technology of choice. Each office could retain a short leased line into a service provider, which could then provide ATM connections between the offices. If Frame Relay were considered, the small voice packets could be held up behind large data trains, introducing unacceptable delay into the conversations.

Chapter 3

Check Your Understanding

1. A

   The CSU/DSU transforms the data into a format acceptable to the service provider's network at the local end and then into a format acceptable to the local network on the remote end.

2. D

The role of a service provider's network is to connect DCE devices. A serial cable connects the DTE device, which is usually the CPE, to the DCE device, and a null-modem cable is used to connect two DTE devices.

3. B

A null-modem cable is used to directly connect two DTE devices. A serial cable connects a DTE device to a DCE device, and a service provider's network is used to connect DCE devices.

4. C

A serial cable is used to connect a DTE device to a DCE device. A null-modem cable connects two DTE devices, and DCE devices are connected through a service provider's network.

5. B

The default Layer 2 serial line encapsulation on a Cisco router is a proprietary form of HDLC. PPP is a standardized encapsulation that may optionally be configured. CHAP is an authentication method.

6. A, D, and E

PPP is a standards-based Layer 2 serial line encapsulation that uses individual NCPs to establish and configure multiple Layer 3 protocols on the same link. PPP also allows the use of either PAP or CHAP authentication.

7. D

SLIP allows only IP traffic to be carried. PPP can carry multiple Layer 3 protocols on the same link. Although PAP is an authentication technique, it is not as secure as CHAP, because it sends the password across the link in clear text and allows the peer to control the authentication process. With CHAP the authenticator is in control of the authentication process, and the password is not sent across the link.

8. B

NCPs establish and configure the Layer 3 protocols. Authentication, MTU, and link quality testing are all done by the LCP.

9. A

CHAP uses a three-way handshake mechanism involving a challenge, response, and success/failure. PAP uses a simple two-way handshake in which the password is sent to the authenticator and the authenticator responds.

10. C

The default Layer 2 encapsulation on Cisco routers is HDLC. This is configured at the interface level, which allows different Layer 2 encapsulations to exist on different interfaces.

11. **B**

     The **show interface** command displays the current encapsulation on a serial interface.

12. **E**

     Most problems with CHAP can be determined by watching the authentication process in real time using **debug**.

13. **A**

     Because communication is occurring, the physical layer is working fine, as are the encapsulations. The CHAP process is attempting to authenticate, which indicates that it is configured on both ends of the PPP link. The failure is caused by misconfigured passwords.

14. **A**

     Authentication is negotiated by LCP and, if configured, must be successfully completed before the NCP brings up the Layer 3 protocols.

15. **C**

     The four types of CHAP control frames are 1 (Challenge), 2 (Response), 3 (Success) and 4 (Failure).

16. **B**

     When a TDM timeslot is assigned to a conversation that has no data to transmit, it remains unused.

17. **A**

     TDM functions solely at the physical layer and does not care what data is transmitted.

Challenge Questions and Activities

1. You have been asked to troubleshoot a faulty PPP link between two sites on the corporate WAN. The link was previously running HDLC with no authentication without problems. What procedure would you follow to diagnose this problem?

    Because the link was working fine with HDLC encapsulation, the physical layer appears to be fine. Because PPP is a layered process, it is best to start by observing the LCP followed by the NCP and finally the Layer 3 protocols. Authentication is an optional phase that, if configured, must be completed before the NCPs bring up the Layer 3 protocols.

    A good place to start would be to remove the authentication and then see if the link comes up. If it does, a misconfigured authentication process is a suspect. If the link still does not come up, a **debug ppp negotiation** session should be conducted to see if the LCP phase is successful. If this phase is successful, you can suspect a problem with the NCPs or the Layer 3 configuration.

2. The network administrator has decided to change the currently implemented PAP authentication on the PPP link to CHAP. Which commands will be required to complete this task?

    To remove the currently implemented PAP authentication, issue the interface configuration command **no ppp authentication pap**. After that, you can configure CHAP authentication using the interface configuration command **ppp authentication chap**. If it isn't already configured, the **username** *name* **password** *password* global configuration command must be issued to create an account for the remote router. This configuration must be completed on both ends of the link.

3. A Cisco router is running IOS 12.2 and must be configured for PAP authentication. The administrator has correctly created accounts for all remote routers and has issued the **ppp authentication pap** command, but authentication is not working. What is the probable cause of this problem?

   On the newer versions of IOS, PAP is disabled by default. To turn it on, you must use the interface configuration command **ppp pap sent-username** *name* **password** *password.*

4. How does CHAP authenticate a remote site without sending the password across the link?

   The local device is configured with a username/password pair for the remote device. The local device sends a challenge to the remote device that contains an ID number, a random string, and the local hostname. The remote device uses the hostname to check its database to derive the shared secret associated with the specific link. The remote device then hashes this secret, the ID number, and the random string through a one-way hashing algorithm such as MD5. This hash is then sent back to the local device, along with the remote hostname. The local device computes the same hash using the random number, the ID, and the secret it obtains from looking up the remote hostname in the local database. If the hashes match, a success packet is sent. If the hashes do not match, a failure message is sent. In addition, the CHAP authentication process times out if no response is received within a predetermined amount of time.

Chapter 4

Check Your Understanding

1. C

   The E series recommends telephone network standards for ISDN. For example, international addressing for ISDN is covered under E.164. The I series deals with the concepts, terminology, and general methods involved in ISDN. The I.100 series includes general ISDN concepts and the structure of other I series recommendations. I.200 deals with the service aspects of ISDN, I.300 describes network aspects, and I.400 describes how the UNI is provided. The Q series covers how switching and signaling should operate. Signaling is the process of establishing a call. Q.921 (Link Access Procedure on the D channel [LAPD]) and Q.931 (ISDN network layer between terminal and switch) are key examples of the Q series.

2. A

   The capacity of the D channel on all BRI interfaces is 16 kbps.

3. D

   In-band signaling is when the control information is carried on the same channel as the data. ISDN reserves the D channel for the exchange of control information, thus using out-of-band signaling.

4. B

   The I.430 standard describes the physical layer of the BRI interface, whereas I.431 describes the PRI. Q.921 looks at Layer 2, and Q.931 is concerned with Layer 3.

5. B

   Frames are named depending on the direction they travel on the network. Outbound frames originate at the TE and therefore are called TE frames. Inbound frames are called NT frames.

6. B

   The ISDN frame is 48 bits long and carries 36 bits of data.

7. C

   The E bit echoes the previous D bit. If this is not detected, a collision has occurred, and transmission is immediately halted.

8. A

   After a device transmits on the D channel, it lowers its priority to allow all other devices to be able to use the connection. The device's priority can be raised only after everyone else has had a chance to access the channel.

9. D

   Both HDLC and PPP are used on the B channel. SS7 is used by switches on the service providers to set up calls. Link Access Procedure for the D channel (LAPD) is used on the D channel.

10. E

    The range from 0 to 63 is used for statically assigned TEIs, 64 to 127 is used for dynamically assigned TEIs, and all 1s signifies a broadcast address.

11. C

    Both HDLC and PPP are used on the B channel. SS7 is used by switches on the service providers to set up calls. Link Access Procedure for the D channel (LAPD) is used on the D channel.

12. C

    A device that is not ISDN-ready is called a Terminal Equipment type 2 (TE2) device. It requires a Terminal Adaptor (TA) to connect to the ISDN network.

13. B

    A device that is ISDN-ready does not require a Terminal Adaptor (TA) to connect to the ISDN network. It is called a Terminal Equipment type 1 (TE1) device.

14. D

A Network Termination device type 1 (NT1) converts the four-wire internal ISDN technology into the two-wire technology deployed on the service provider's network.

15. D

The NT1 converts the four-wire S/T interface into a two-wire U interface.

16. A

Non-ISDN-compatible equipment connects to a Terminal Adaptor (TA) through an R interface. This is usually a serial connection. The TA then converts the serial signal into a four-wire S/T ISDN signal.

17. A

The default framing for a T1 controller is super frame (sf), whereas crc4 is the default for an E1 controller.

18. B

Although 31 channels are available (30B+D) for an E1 PRI, channel 15 is used for the D channel to carry ISDN signaling information.

19. A

Although many states are possible for the Layer 1 status, most are transitional in nature. To build on the connection, the Layer 1 status should be seen as Active.

20. A

The **show isdn active** command displays information about the currently active call, including the called number and the status of the idle timer.

21. A

The **show dialer** command displays what traffic initiated the connection, as well as the status of configured timers.

22. E

The authentication process is actually part of PPP and is completed before the NCPs come up and bring up the Layer 3 protocols. To get information on the authentication process, use the command **debug ppp authentication**.

23. B

The peer-to-peer commands and responses occur at Layer 2. Therefore, the **debug isdn q921** command is the appropriate one to use to view this information.

24. B

Interesting traffic, as defined by a dialer list, includes any traffic that brings up a DDR interface or resets the idle timeout on an interface that is already active. Uninteresting traffic does not bring up a DDR interface, nor does it reset the idle timeout, but it still moves across an active link.

25. A and B

    Dynamic routing protocols generate a large amount of traffic, such as routing updates and hello packets. These go out at regular intervals and, unless the system is properly configured, can be seen as interesting traffic and cause the DDR interface to be brought up. When the DDR interface is up, routing updates can move across the link. But when the link is down, these updates cannot transverse the link, and the routing tables quickly become out of date. Static routes prevent these routing updates from triggering the DDR interface and also maintain a route in the routing table for traffic.

26. C

    An access list and a dialer list are not the same thing. An access list filters traffic, and a dialer list merely defines traffic that brings up the DDR interface. Access lists are applied with the **access-group** command, and dialer lists are applied with the **dialer-group** command.

27. D

    The maximum number of dialer lists that can be defined is ten.

28. C

    The **dialer idle-timeout** command is used to set the dialer idle value. As soon as this value is reached, the interface is brought down.

29. C

    Dialer profiles separate the logical information from the physical interface and allow a binding of this information on a per-call basis. This allows one physical interface to use many different logical configurations at different times.

30. A

    The **show dialer** command shows the binding of the dialer profile to the physical interface.

31. D

    0x02 indicates a call proceeding message, 0x05 indicates a call setup message, 0x07 indicates a call connect message, and 0x0F indicates a connect acknowledgment message (ACK).

32. A

    The **debug dialer events** command shows which traffic initiated the call.

33. B

    The **debug dialer packet** command lets you observe individual packets and determine which ones are causing the interface to come up.

Challenge Questions and Activities

1. You have just been hired as a consultant to XYZ Corporation. XYZ has several offices across Canada and the U.S. The company is experiencing problems with its ISDN BRI connection in that inbound ISDN calls are not being answered on the second B channel. Where would you start looking for the problem?

   Because the ISDN connection is functioning properly except for the second B channel answering inbound calls, the problem appears to be confined to the B channel configuration. Often if the second B channel does not answer, this can be traced back to an improperly configured LDN.

2. A small consulting company just installed ISDN BRI connections between its four offices scattered throughout Australia. Each office is on a separate network, so dialer profiles have been implemented. The company cannot connect between two of the offices and suspects that the service provider's network is at fault. How could this be verified? If the network is proven to be functioning properly, what is the most probable cause of the problem?

   To check the service provider's network and the configuration of the remote router, a call can be forced using the command **isdn call interface** *interface number*. If the call goes through, both the network and remote router are functioning properly, so other problems should be investigated. The most common problem is a misconfiguration of the DDR parameters, usually interesting traffic.

3. A small manufacturing company has asked you to investigate a problem with its ISDN DDR configuration. The company just received an enormous bill from its service provider that indicates that its connection has been on continuously for the past month. What is the most probable cause, and how would you verify your diagnosis?

   The most probable cause of this problem is that interesting traffic has not been properly configured. The DDR connection terminates only if the idle timeout value is reached before additional interesting traffic is detected. The first step would be to use the **debug dialer packet** to see what types of traffic are moving out the DDR interface. If routing updates or hello packets are seen, the dynamic routing protocols should be shut down and static routes configured.

4. A small consulting office has asked you to provide a router it can use to form a PRI connection to its service provider. The company wants to save money by configuring the device themselves. They have asked you to provide instructions on the steps involved to make certain that they do not miss any steps. What information would you provide?

   The ISDN PRI is delivered over either a T1 or E1 leased line. The configuration of an ISDN PRI involves the following steps:

   1. Specify the correct ISDN switch type that the router will connect to at the CO of the ISDN service provider.

   2. Specify the T1/E1 controller, framing type, and line coding for the facility of the ISDN service provider.

   3. Set the PRI group timeslot for the T1/E1 facility, and indicate the speed used.

Chapter 5

Check Your Understanding

1. B

   Frame Relay is usually deployed on the access link into a service provider's network. In this scenario, Frame Relay is oblivious to the technology used in the actual WAN.

2. A

   Devices that do not connect to a Frame Relay network through a LAN can be connected using a Frame Relay assembler/disassembler.

3. F and G

   Frame Relay functions at the bottom two layers of the OSI model.

4. E

   Statistical Time-Division Multiplexing allows Frame Relay to dynamically assign bandwidth on an as-needed basis.

5. B and C

   A PVC is configured by the network administrator and is loaded into the switch when the switch boots. There is no need to build this type of virtual circuit when data is being transferred. A PVC functions in two modes—data transfer and idle.

6. C

   A standard Frame Relay address field is 2 bytes long and contains 10 bits for the DLCIs.

7. C

   If a 3-byte header is used, 17 bits are assigned to the DLCI.

8. A

   LMI uses DLCI 0 (ANSI, ITU) and 1023 (Cisco).

9. B

   The range of DLCIs that can be statically or dynamically assigned to PVCs is from 16 to 1007.

10. B

    The range of DLCIs that can be statically or dynamically assigned to PVCs is from 16 to 1007.

11. B

    The DE (discard-eligible) bit flags a frame as being of lesser importance than other frames on the network. If frames need to be dropped, frames with the DE bit set are dropped first.

12. D

    If an EA bit is set to 1, it marks the end of the DLCI bits. Setting the EA bit to off signifies that more DLCI bits are to follow.

13. A

    The Frame Relay switch sends BECNs back to the source of the information to inform the sender that congestion has occurred. FECNs are sent toward the destination to inform the receiver that congestion has occurred and that frames may have been dropped.

14. B

    A frame that pushes the counter over B_c has its DE bit set. A frame that pushes the counter over B_e is immediately discarded.

15. B

    Frame Relay switches drop frames to reduce the size of their queue and reduce congestion. When frames are dropped, the sender is not notified that the information has been discarded. It is up to the higher-layer protocols to detect that frames have been dropped and to take the appropriate action.

16. C

    When Frame Relay switches are dropped because of congestion, FECNs are sent to the destination. Packets are dropped when the B_e value is exceeded.

17. C

    Many factors go into the decision of where a Frame Relay hub should be located. The hub need not be placed at the network's geographic center, because costs are not based on how far the data travels. Hubs carry multiple VCs, but usually on a single access circuit to minimize costs.

18. A

    The most common Frame Relay topology deployed is hub-and-spoke. It minimizes the expense of maintaining large numbers of VCs.

19. C

    When high reliability is required, a full-mesh design is the most desirable. However, the expense associated with the large number of VCs required usually forces a partial-mesh design.

20. B

    The default LMI on a Cisco device is Cisco.

21. C and D

    LMI messages are status inquiry and status. The status inquiry asks the DCE device for the status of connected PVCs. Then the DCE device replies with a status update.

22. B

    After a DTE device is informed about the configured DLCIs via LMI, it sends an Inverse ARP out each DLCI to detect and map the remote Layer 3 address.

23. D

    After a DTE device is informed about the configured DLCIs via LMI, it sends an Inverse ARP out each DLCI to detect and map the remote Layer 3 address.

24. D

    The two Frame Relay frame types are Cisco and IETF. Cisco should be used when interconnecting Cisco devices. When other devices are deployed, IETF should be used.

25. C

    The Cisco LMI should be used in a Cisco network. IOS version 11.2 and above auto-detect the LMI type, but older versions must be manually configured.

26. B

    Reachability issues usually occur when split horizon prevents routing updates from being sent back on the same interface from which they learned about the route. Subinterfaces eliminate the problems associated with split horizon.

27. D

    The **show frame-relay pvc** command lists the number of FECN, BECN, and DE bits that have moved across the network.

28. A

    The **show interface** command displays the encapsulation currently configured on the serial interface.

29. D

    PVCs can be in one of four status conditions. Active is when the interface is configured and working properly. Deleted is when the Frame Relay switch has removed the DLCI from its configuration. Inactive is when the DLCI is still configured in the switch but the remote Layer 3 device is unreachable. Static is when the LMI has been shut down with the **no keepalive** command.

30. B

    Dynamically learned maps may be deleted with the **clear frame-relay inarp** command.

Challenge Questions and Activities

1. You have been asked to troubleshoot connectivity issues in the corporate Frame Relay network. Users are reporting that they no longer can connect to the Tokyo office from the Paris office network and that this problem has occurred over the past 24 hours. You immediately issue a **show frame-relay map** command from the Paris router and notice that there is no map to the Tokyo office. Consulting the journal entries for the Paris network,

you notice that they recently configured a static map to the Toronto office. You immediately test this connection and determine that you can Telnet to the Toronto office without problems. All other branch offices can connect to the Tokyo office without problems. What is the most probable cause of this problem, and how would you remedy the situation?

The problem is that as soon as a static map is created on an interface, Inverse ARP is disabled. The map to the Tokyo office was created dynamically using Inverse ARP and worked fine until the static map was created. As soon as the static map was in place, the dynamic entry timed out, and connectivity was lost. The solution is to create a static map to the Tokyo office.

2. XYZ Inc. has just acquired ABC Inc. and must provide the ability for three new remote offices to connect to the corporate headquarters. The router at the corporate headquarters currently has a leased line between it and a branch office located in another state; it has been working without problems for the past several years. The network administrator created a new multipoint subinterface on the same physical interface of the headquarters router to provide connectivity to the three new sites using Frame Relay. After it was connected, nobody on the network could communicate. As soon as the new subinterface was shut down, connectivity between the headquarters and the original remote office was restored. A partial output of the running configuration is shown next. What steps would you take to correct this problem?

Partial Running Configuration for the Headquarters Router

```
<output omitted>
interface s0/0
 encapsulation frame-relay
 ip address 10.20.30.1 255.255.255.252
interface s0/0.101 multipoint
 bandwidth 64
 ip address 10.20.40.1 255.255.255.248
 frame-relay interface dlci  101
<output omitted>
```

The problem stems from the fact that the original connection used the physical interface and not a subinterface. After the new subinterface was created, an IP address was now located on both the physical interface and the subinterface. To correct the problem, the original connection should be moved to a point-to-point subinterface, and the IP address must be removed from the physical interface.

3. You have just connected the corporate network to the service provider's Frame Relay switch, but you can't move data through the link. Your DTE device is a Cisco router, but the ISP is using equipment from another vendor. A partial running configuration is shown next. The keepalive interval, LMI type, and IP address and mask have been verified. What is the probable cause of the problem, and how would you correct it?

Partial Configuration of the Corporate Router

```
interface s0/0
 encapsulation frame-relay
```

```
frame-relay lmi-type ansi
bandwidth 56
keepalive 15
ip address 10.10.15.1 255.255.255.252
```

This problem stems from the fact that the default Frame Relay encapsulation would be Cisco, and the non-Cisco equipment would be using IETF encapsulation. The solution is to switch from the Cisco encapsulation to the IETF encapsulation by issuing the command **encapsulation frame-relay ietf**.

Chapter 6

Check Your Understanding

1. C

   A workstation is a powerful standalone, single-user computer usually used for scientific or engineering applications.

2. A and B

   Diskless workstations do not have a physical drive installed, so the end user cannot easily remove data from or upload files to the network.

3. B

   The network redirector intercepts commands and data and determines if they are being directed to the local machine or destined for a networked resource. If the files or data are destined for networked resources, it is the redirector's job to send the information to the correct destination.

4. C

   Windows 98 and Me are client-side operating systems. Windows 2003 exists only in server varieties. Windows 2000 exists in both Professional (client) and Server versions.

5. C

   NetBIOS and NetBEUI protocols are found in Microsoft networks. SPX/IPX is the protocol used in older versions of Novell NetWare. All these protocols have been replaced by TCP/IP, which has become universal in its acceptance.

6. C

   Authentication is the process of verifying user credentials to determine if the user should be given access to network resources. Authorization is the process of deciding which resources an authenticated individual has access to. Accounting is recording what an authenticated user does after being connected.

7. D

With a networked file system, only one copy of an important file exists, and it is kept in a centralized location. This makes data backup and restoration much easier and also ensures that everyone is working with the same version of the file.

8. A

Dynamic Host Configuration Protocol is the process by which a client requests network configuration information from a DHCP server. DNS is the mapping of domain names to IP addresses. NAT is the translation of an internal address to an external one. TFTP is Trivial File Transfer Protocol.

9. C

NAT is the process by which an internal network address is translated to a different address as it moves from the inside to outside networks. This prevents internal addresses from being seen by machines on the outside network. Dynamic Host Configuration Protocol is the process by which a client requests network configuration information from a DHCP server. DNS is the mapping of domain names to IP addresses. TFTP is Trivial File Transfer Protocol.

10. B

Robustness is a network's capability to survive the failure of one or more services. Robustness can be enhanced by spreading services across multiple servers. In this arrangement, the failure of a single server does not eliminate the service from the network, and the network continues to function.

11. B, C, and D

SMTP, POP, and IMAP are protocols that are used to move e-mail between servers and between servers and clients. SNMP is one of the protocols used in network management. DNS maps domain names to IP addresses. TFTP is Trivial File Transfer Protocol.

12. D

In a peer-to-peer arrangement, resources connected to local computers are under the control of whoever controls the local machine.

13. B

In the client/server arrangement, allocation of network resources and user management is under the control of the network administrator. The administrator uses tools such as Novell's NDS or Microsoft's Active Directory to assist in this endeavor.

14. B

Clients request services from servers. The role of the server is to provide these services to the clients.

15. B

In the client/server arrangement, the client sends data to the server, which processes the data and then returns the results to the client. An example of this is when a web client requests a page from a web server.

16. A

One server can handle requests from many clients, but if the server fails, the entire network collapses.

17. D

Networked resources are treated as though they are directly connected to the local machine.

18. A

Performance indicates how quickly a NOS can transfer files between clients and servers. A server must be able to handle varying numbers of connections and load without any appreciable decrease in system performance.

19. D

A NOS must be able to handle the failure of one or more processes and continue providing services for connected clients. This capability indicates the operating system's robustness.

20. C

Network performance is the capability of a NOS to quickly transfer files between the server and client. As the number of users increases, the performance level must remain at an acceptable level. The capability of a NOS to provide adequate performance under varying loads is called scalability.

21. A

Network management is the capability to control network resources to ensure an adequate level of system performance under varying conditions.

22. All of the duties

Network management is an extremely complicated task. It involves monitoring and managing system resources and performance to ensure that all users have optimum access to required resources. All the noted duties are part of network management.

Challenge Questions and Activities

1. A new network is being constructed for XYZ Inc. The administrator has acquired funding for a total of three servers and must supply DHCP, DNS, Web, and e-mail services to a total of 100 users. How should these services be configured for reliability and optimum performance?

Because multiple services must be provided to 100 users, it is imperative to eliminate a single point of failure for any service. Running each service on at least two of the three machines would achieve redundancy while distributing the load over the servers, allowing for better performance.

2. All sales employees of XYZ Inc. have been provided with laptop computers to remotely access corporate information. These employees must also connect in the office. The manager of sales has asked that all employees be provided with an appropriate workstation. What suggestion would you make?

A workstation is usually a dedicated, high-power, single-user machine used for scientific and engineering applications. In this scenario the sales force does not require a high-power machine for their applications. The most economical solution would be to allow the sales force to use their laptops in the office. This can be done by providing network cards—either wired or wireless, depending on the corporate environment—or docking stations at the office, depending on their requirements.

Glossary

This glossary defines many of the terms and abbreviations related to networking. It includes all the key terms used throughout the book. As with any growing technical field, some terms evolve and take on several meanings. Where necessary, multiple definitions and abbreviation expansions are presented.

A

access control list (ACL)   A list kept by routers to control access to or from the router for a number of services. For example, an access list can be used to prevent packets with a certain IP address from leaving a particular interface on the router.

access layer   Connects workgroups to backbones and provides a logical segmentation. It isolates broadcast traffic from the workgroup.

access link   The connection from the local network to the WAN cloud.

active translation   In NAT, a mapping of one IP address to another address that is currently in use.

Address field   The portion of the frame that contains the addressing information. This field's exact format depends on the technology being used.

administrative distance   A rating of a routing information source's trustworthiness. In Cisco routers, administrative distance is expressed as a numeric value between 0 and 255. The higher the value, the lower the trustworthiness rating.

Alternate Mark Inversion (AMI)   A line-code type used on T1 and E1 circuits. In AMI, 0s are represented by 01 during each bit cell, and 1s are represented by 11 or 00, alternately, during each bit cell. AMI requires that the sending device maintain 1s density. 1s density is not maintained independent of the data stream. Sometimes called binary coded alternate mark inversion.

American National Standards Institute (ANSI) A voluntary organization composed of corporate, government, and other members that coordinates standards-related activities, approves U.S. national standards, and develops positions for the U.S. in international standards organizations. ANSI helps develop international and U.S. standards relating to, among other things, communications and networking. ANSI is a member of the International Electrotechnical Commission (IEC) and the International Organization for Standardization (ISO).

analog dialup   Using wires normally used to carry analog telephone calls to carry an analog signal transmission from a device. A modem is usually used to modulate the digital signal for analog transmission.

application   The purpose for or use of network technology. A program or group of programs designed for the end user. An application program usually requires the use of system software and utilities to carry out its function.

area   A logical set of network segments (either CLNS-, DECnet-, or OSPF-based) and their attached devices. Areas are usually connected to other areas through routers, making up a single autonomous system.

ARPANET   Advanced Research Projects Agency Network. A landmark packet-switching network that was established in 1969. ARPANET was further developed in the 1970s by BBN Technologies and was funded by the Advanced Research Projects Agency (ARPA), and later by DARPA. It eventually evolved into the Internet. The term ARPANET was officially retired in 1990.

Asymmetric DSL (ADSL)   Asymmetric Digital Subscriber Line. A modem technology that allows the unused bandwidth in ordinary telephone wires to be used to carry data. Asymmetric refers to the fact that the downstream speed is significantly faster than the upstream speed. ADSL is the most widely deployed form of DSL.

Asynchronous Transfer Mode (ATM)   The international standard for cell relay, in which multiple service types, such as voice, video, and data, are conveyed in fixed-length (53-byte) cells. Fixed-length cells allow cell processing to occur in hardware, thereby reducing transit delays. ATM is designed to take advantage of high-speed transmission media such as E3, SONET, and T3.

authentication   The process of controlling access to network resources by comparing supplied credentials against those stored in a database on the authentication server.

authentication credentials   Usually a username and password, supplied by the user, that are compared to those stored in the authentication database. These credentials may be either sent in clear text or encrypted, depending on the technology deployed.

authentication database   The record of username and password pairs that the user-supplied credentials are verified against. The authentication database resides on the authentication server.

authentication server   The actual machine on which the authentication database resides.

authenticator   The device in an authentication system that physically allows or blocks access to the network.

B

Backward Explicit Congestion Notification (BECN)   A bit set by a Frame Relay network in frames traveling in the opposite direction of frames encountering a congested path. The DTE receiving frames with the BECN bit set can request that higher-level protocols take flow control action as appropriate.

bandwidth-on-demand (BOD)   The ability to increase the available bandwidth when required. BOD usually deploys technology such as dialup or ISDN, which can be brought online only when required, thus minimizing the associated expense.

basic rate interface   See BRI.

B_c See committed burst (B_c).

B_e See excess burst (B_e).

bearer channel (B channel)   In ISDN, a full-duplex, 64-kbps channel used to send user data.

BECN   See Backward Explicit Congestion Notification.

binding   In DHCP, the association of a Layer 3 IP address with a Layer 2 MAC address. The DHCP client requests the Layer 3 information from the DHCP server, which then associates the client's MAC address with the supplied Layer 3 address.

bit-oriented   A class of data link layer communication protocols that can transmit frames regardless of frame content. Compared with byte-oriented protocols, bit-oriented protocols provide full-duplex operation and are more efficient and reliable.

bit rate   The speed at which bits are transmitted, usually expressed in bits per second (bps).

BOOTP   A protocol used by a network node to determine the IP address of its Ethernet interfaces to affect network booting.

BRI   Basic Rate Interface. An ISDN interface composed of two B channels and one D channel for circuit-switched communication of voice, video, and data.

byte-oriented   A class of data-link communication protocols that use a specific character from the user character set to delimit frames. These protocols have largely been replaced by bit-oriented protocols.

C

cable   Internet access provided by CATV service providers by multiplexing the Internet signal with the television signal. The ITU approved the Data Over Cable Service Interface Specification (DOCSIS) in March 1998. It defines interface standards for cable modems and supporting equipment.

callback client   A device that initiates a communication session with a callback server and then disconnects, allowing the callback server to call the client. This provides increased security, bill aggregation, and cost reduction.

callback server   A server that accepts connections from a callback client and then disconnects the client and calls back at a predetermined number. This provides increased security, bill aggregation, and cost reduction.

campus LAN   An interconnection of LANs within a limited geographic area, such as a military base or large corporation.

cell   The basic unit for ATM switching and multiplexing. Cells contain identifiers that specify the data stream to which they belong. Each cell consists of a 5-byte header and 48 bytes of payload.

central office (CO)   The local telephone company office to which all local loops in a given area connect and in which circuit switching of subscriber lines occurs.

challenge   A random string sent during the CHAP authentication process. The remote machine encrypts the challenge using information stored locally and then returns a response to the machine that issued the challenge. The challenge frequency can be controlled.

Challenge Handshake Authentication Protocol   See CHAP.

channelized   A channelized T1 is an access link operating at 1.544 Mbps that is subdivided into 24 channels (23 B channels and one D channel) of 64 Kbps each. The individual channels or groups of channels connect to different destinations and support dial-on-demand routing (DDR), Frame Relay, and X.25. Also called fractional T1. A channelized E1 is an access link operating at 2.048 Mbps that is subdivided into 30 B channels and one D channel. It supports DDR, Frame Relay, and X.25.

channel number   A number that identifies a logical channel in a physical trunk.

channel service unit (CSU)   A digital interface device that connects end-user equipment to the local digital telephone loop. Often referred to together with DSU as CSU/DSU.

channel service unit/data service unit (CSU/DSU)   A single physical device that combines the functionality of a CSU and DSU.

CHAP   Challenge Handshake Authentication Protocol. A security feature supported on lines using PPP encapsulation that prevents unauthorized access. CHAP does not itself prevent unauthorized access; it merely identifies the remote end. The router or access server then determines whether that user is allowed access.

character-oriented   A character-oriented protocol uses a particular code set for transmission, with some of the characters in the code set reserved for control functions. Asynchronous and binary synchronous protocols are examples of this protocol.

CIR   Committed Information Rate. The rate at which a Frame Relay network agrees to transfer information under normal conditions, averaged over a minimum increment of time. CIR, measured in bits per second, is one of the key negotiated tariff metrics.

circuit-switched   Traffic that is moved through a network by following a dedicated physical path that is established by forming an end-to-end connection through the network.

circuit-switching   A switching system in which a dedicated physical circuit path must exist between sender and receiver for the "call's" duration. Used heavily in the telephone company network. Circuit switching can be contrasted with contention and token passing as a channel-access method, and with message switching and packet switching as a switching technique.

classful   A system of IP addressing that relies on predefined class boundaries. This system often results in the wasting of large numbers of IP addresses.

classless   A system of IP addressing that assigns bits to the network and host without regard for class boundaries. Allows the optimal distribution of address space.

client   A node or software program (front-end device) that requests services from a server.

client/server   Describes distributed computing (processing) network systems in which transaction responsibilities are divided into two parts: client (front end) and server (back end). Both terms (client and server) can be applied to software programs or actual computing devices. Also called distributed computing (processing).

CO   See central office (CO).

committed burst (B_c)   A negotiated tariff metric in Frame Relay internetworks. The maximum amount of data (in bits) that a Frame Relay internetwork is committed to accept and transmit at the CIR.

Committed Information Rate   See CIR.

committed rate measurement interval (T_c)   The time interval during which the user can send only B_c (a committed amount of data) and B_e (an excess amount of data). In general, the duration of T_c is proportional to the traffic's burstiness. T_c is computed (from the subscription parameters of CIR and B_c) with the formula $T_c = B_c \div CIR$. T_c is not a periodic time interval. Instead, it is used only to measure incoming data, during which time it acts like a sliding window. Incoming data triggers the T_c interval, which continues until it completes its commuted duration. See also CIR and committed burst size (B_c).

Compressed SLIP (CSLIP)   A SLIP extension that, when appropriate, allows just header information to be sent across a SLIP connection, reducing overhead and increasing packet throughput on SLIP lines.

compression   Applying an algorithm to data to remove redundancy to increase a transfer's efficiency. Compression occurs at the sending end, and decompression occurs at the receiving end.

congestion   Traffic in excess of the network's capacity.

connectionless   Describes data transfer without the existence of a virtual circuit.

connection-oriented   Describes data transfer that requires the establishment of a virtual circuit. See also connectionless.

Consultative Committee on International Telephone and Telegraph (CCITT)   An international organization responsible for the development of communications standards. Now called the ITU-T.

Consumer DSL (CDSL)   A version of DSL, trademarked by Rockwell Corp., that is somewhat slower than ADSL (1 Mbps downstream, probably less upstream). Has the advantage that a splitter does not need to be installed at the user's end.

Control field   In an HDLC frame, identifies the frame's function. Can be Information (I), Supervisory (S), or Unnumbered (U).

core layer   The layer in hierarchical network design that is concerned with the high-speed reliable transfer of data between core devices.

core link   A link, usually a trunk, between core layer devices.

CPE   See customer premises equipment (CPE).

CPU   Central Processing Unit. The part of a computer that controls all the other parts. It fetches instructions from memory and decodes them. This may cause it to transfer data to or from memory or to activate peripherals to perform input or output.

cyclic redundancy check (CRC)   An error-checking technique in which the frame recipient calculates a remainder by dividing frame contents by a prime binary divisor. The calculated remainder is then compared to a value stored in the frame by the sending node. If the values match, the frame is assumed to have been transmitted without the introduction of errors.

CSU/DSU   See channel service unit/data service unit (CSU/DSU).

customer premises equipment (CPE)   Terminating equipment, such as terminals, telephones, and modems, usually supplied by the telephone company and installed at customer sites. CPE is usually connected to the telephone company network.

D

data circuit-terminating equipment (DCE)   See data communications equipment (DCE).

data communications equipment (DCE)   Data communications equipment (EIA expansion) or data circuit-terminating equipment (ITU-T expansion). The devices and connections of a communications network that comprise the network end of the user-to-network interface. The DCE provides a physical connection to the network, forwards traffic, and provides a clocking signal used to synchronize data transmission between DCE and DTE devices. Modems and interface cards are examples of DCE.

Data-Link Connection Identifier (DLCI)   A value that specifies a PVC or SVC in a Frame Relay network. In the basic Frame Relay specification, DLCIs are locally significant (connected devices might use different values to specify the same connection). In the LMI extended specification, DLCIs are globally significant (DLCIs specify individual end devices).

data service unit (DSU)   A device used in digital transmission that adapts the physical interface on a DTE device to a transmission facility such as T1 or E1. The DSU is also responsible for such functions as signal timing.

data terminal equipment (DTE)   A device at the user end of a user-network interface that serves as a data source, destination, or both. DTE connects to a data network through a DCE device (for example, a modem) and typically uses clocking signals generated by the DCE. DTE includes such devices as computers, protocol translators, and multiplexers.

delay   How long frames are held up by processing in the network.

delta channel (D channel)   A full-duplex, 16-kbps (BRI) or 64-kbps (PRI) ISDN channel usually used for out-of-band signaling.

demarc   The demarcation point between carrier equipment and CPE. The point at which the customer turns over control to the WAN service provider.

demarcation point   See demarc.

destination address   The address of a network device that is receiving data.

DHCPACK   A unicast message produced by the DHCP server, notifying the DHCP client that it may use the requested resources.

DHCPDECLINE   A message issued by the DHCP client, refusing the network configuration information being offered by the DHCP server.

DHCPDISCOVER   A broadcast message sent by a host to locate a DHCP server.

DHCPNAK   A unicast message from the DHCP server to the DHCP client, informing it that the network configuration information previously offered is no longer available.

DHCPOFFER   An offer of network configuration information to a client.

DHCP Pool   The address space allocated for DHCP to assign to hosts.

DHCP Relay   A router's ability to accept the DHCP broadcasts on one segment and forward them to another segment as a unicast. This allows DHCP servers to be located on a segment different from the host.

DHCPRELEASE   A message from the DHCP client that it no longer requires the supplied network configuration information and that the resources may be reallocated.

DHCPREQUEST   A request by a DHCP client for permission to use the network configuration previously offered by the DHCP server.

dialer interface   A virtual interface that can be configured to use one or more physical interfaces.

dialer pool   A collection of ISDN BRI physical interfaces that can be used by a dialer interface.

dialer profile   Separating the logical configuration information from the physical configuration for dialup (ISDN) connections. Allows optimal use of physical interfaces.

dial-on-demand routing (DDR)   A configuration that allows an ISDN interface to be brought up only under predefined conditions. Often used for ISDN backup of primary packet-switched connectivity.

directed broadcast   A directed broadcast address for a physical network has all 1s in the host ID part of the address. The network ID and the subnet ID must be valid network and subnet values. When a packet is sent to a network's broadcast address, a single copy travels to the network, and then the packet is sent to every host on that network or subnetwork.

Discard Eligibility (DE)   The DE bit is set to on in Frame Relay traffic that exceeds the CIR. This traffic is the first to be discarded if required to reduce congestion.

diskless workstation   A workstation without disk drives. This is often deployed in secure environments to prevent the unauthorized removal of data or the uploading of potentially dangerous files.

distributed processing   The sharing of processing tasks between clients and servers on a network.

distribution layer   An intermediary between the core and access layers. Is usually where the routing functions on a well-designed network are found. The distribution layer is also where policies are usually implemented using access lists.

distribution link   Normally a Frame Relay or ATM connection found in the distribution layer of the three-layer hierarchical network design model.

docking station   A device to allow laptop computers to function easily with monitors and other devices. These are designed so that desktop components can be cabled to the docking station and then the laptop dropped into place when required.

Domain Name System (DNS)   A system used in the Internet to translate names of network nodes into addresses.

DSL   Digital Subscriber Line. A technology for bringing high-bandwidth information to homes and small businesses over ordinary copper telephone lines. xDSL refers to different variations of DSL, such as ADSL, HDSL, and RADSL.

DSL Access Multiplexer (DSLAM)   A mechanism at the phone company's central location that links many customer DSL lines to a single ATM line. A splitter separates the voice and sends it to the PSTN and sends the data to a DSLAM.

Dynamic Host Configuration Protocol (DHCP)   A method of automatically assigning network configurations to hosts.

dynamic NAT   The rewriting of source address information as a packet moves between the inside and outside networks.

dynamic route   A route that adjusts automatically to network topology or traffic changes.

E

EIA   Electronic Industries Association. A group that specifies electrical transmission standards. The EIA and TIA have developed numerous well-known communications standards, including EIA/TIA-232 and EIA/TIA-449.

EIA/TIA-232   A common physical layer interface standard developed by EIA and TIA that supports unbalanced circuits at signal speeds up to 64 kbps. Formally known as RS-232.

EIA/TIA-449   A popular physical layer interface developed by EIA and TIA. Essentially, a faster (up to 2 Mbps) version of EIA/TIA-232 that is capable of longer cable runs. Formerly called RS-449.

EIA/TIA-530   Two electrical implementations of EIA/TIA-449: RS-422 (for balanced transmission) and RS-423 (for unbalanced transmission).

EIGRP   Enhanced Interior Gateway Routing Protocol. An advanced version of IGRP developed by Cisco. EIGRP provides superior convergence properties and operating efficiency and combines the advantages of link-state protocols with those of distance vector protocols.

EIR   Excess Information Rate. Traffic in excess of the guaranteed rate for a given connection. Specifically, the excess rate equals the maximum rate minus the guaranteed rate. Excess traffic is delivered only if network resources are available and can be discarded during periods of congestion.

Electronic Industries Association   See EIA.

encapsulation   The wrapping of data in a particular protocol header, trailer, or both. For example, Ethernet data is wrapped in a specific Ethernet header before network transit. Also, when bridging dissimilar networks, the entire frame from one network is simply placed in the header used by the other network's data link layer protocol.

encrypt   The application of a specific algorithm to data to alter the data's appearance, making it incomprehensible to those who are not authorized to see the information.

Enhanced Interior Gateway Routing Protocol   See EIGRP.

error recovery   The ability to detect and recover from errors that have been introduced into the data stream.

excess burst (B_e) A negotiated tariff metric in Frame Relay internetworks. The number of bits that a Frame Relay internetwork attempts to transmit after B_c is accommodated. B_e data is, in general, delivered with a lower probability than B_c data because the network can mark B_e data as DE.

Excess Information Rate See EIR.

F

failure The unsuccessful completion of a planned event such as authentication. Authentication failure occurs when supplied credentials do not match those stored in the database.

fast-switched A Cisco feature whereby a route cache is used to expedite packet switching through a router.

fault-tolerant A system's ability to respond gracefully to a system or component failure.

FCS Frame Check Sequence. The extra characters added to a frame for error-control purposes. Used in HDLC, Frame Relay, and other data link layer protocols.

FECN Forward Explicit Congestion Notification. This bit is set by a Frame Relay network to inform the DTE receiving the frame that congestion was experienced in the path from source to destination. DTE receiving frames with the FECN bit set can request that higher-level protocols take flow-control action as appropriate.

file services A server's ability to provide files and storage to remote clients.

File Transfer Protocol See FTP.

firewall A router or access server, or several routers or access servers, can be designated as a buffer between any connected public networks and a private network. A firewall router uses access lists and other methods to ensure

the private network's security by allowing only specified traffic to pass through.

flag 1. A special mark indicating that a packet is unusual in some manner, such as an error flag. 2. To mark an object to indicate that a certain event has occurred. 3. A special code that indicates a frame's beginning and end.

floating static route A static route that has been configured with a higher metric than those learned by dynamic processes. The route becomes active only when the dynamic route disappears from the routing table.

flow control A technique for ensuring that a transmitting entity, such as a modem, does not overwhelm a receiving entity with data. When the buffers on the receiving device are full, a message is sent to the sending device to suspend the transmission until the data in the buffers has been processed. In IBM networks, this technique is called pacing.

form factor The physical size and shape of a system or system component, such as a motherboard.

Forward Explicit Congestion Notification See FECN.

FRAD Any network device that provides a connection between a LAN and a Frame Relay WAN.

frame check sequence See FCS.

Frame Relay An industry-standard, switched data link layer protocol that handles multiple virtual circuits using HDLC encapsulation between connected devices. Frame Relay is more efficient than X.25, the protocol for which it is generally considered a replacement.

Frame Relay access device See FRAD.

Frame Relay assembler/disassembler See FRAD.

FTP File Transfer Protocol. An application protocol that is part of the TCP/IP protocol stack. FTP is used to transfer files between network nodes and is defined in RFC 959.

full mesh   A network topology in which every device directly connects to every other device.

G–H

global address   In NAT, the address of a packet on the inside network as it appears to devices on the outside network.

HDLC   High-level Data Link Control. A bit-oriented synchronous data link layer protocol developed by the ISO. Derived from SDLC, HDLC specifies a data encapsulation method on synchronous serial links using frame characters and checksums.

helper address   An address configured on an interface to which broadcasts received on that interface are sent.

hierarchical network design   A Cisco model that defines how networks should be designed in layers. Each layer has its own roles and responsibilities and produces a network that delivers high performance and is both manageable and scalable.

High Bit Rate DSL (HDSL)   One of the earliest forms of DSL. Used for wideband digital transmission within a corporate site and between the telephone company and a customer. The main characteristic of HDSL is that it is symmetrical, providing an equal amount of bandwidth in both directions.

High-Density Binary 3 (HDB3)   A European digital network transmission protocol that allows information and control data to be embedded in the transmission bit stream. HDB3 code is a bipolar signaling technique and is based on Alternate Mark Inversion (AMI). HDB3 extends AMI by inserting violation codes whenever there is a run of four or more 0s.

High-level Data Link Control   See HDLC.

hijack   When a connection's integrity is compromised, allowing an unauthenticated host to move traffic across the link. A session is stolen from an authorized host by someone who pretends to be that authorized host.

hot-swappable   When you can replace a component or device without first having to power down the system. This minimizes downtime.

HTTP   The protocol used to transfer data over the World Wide Web.

hub-and-spoke   A networking topology commonly deployed in Frame Relay networks. All traffic from remote sites is sent to a central site, thus minimizing the number of PVCs that must be purchased and maintained.

hunt group   An arrangement of a group of telephone lines such that a single telephone number is listed in the directory. A person dialing that listed number is automatically connected by the telephone switching equipment to an available line in the group.

Hypertext Transfer Protocol   See HTTP.

I

idle timeout   How long a connection remains active while not moving data.

IETF   Internet Engineering Task Force. A task force consisting of more than 80 working groups responsible for developing Internet standards. The IETF operates under the auspices of the Internet Society (ISOC).

IMAP   Internet Messaging Access Protocol. The protocol that is gradually replacing POP as the main protocol used by e-mail clients to communicate with e-mail servers. Using IMAP, an e-mail client program can retrieve e-mail and can manipulate messages stored on the server without having to actually retrieve the message.

in-band signaling   Transmission within a frequency range normally used for information transmission.

information frame (I-frame)   A type of HDLC frame that contains the Send Sequence Number, which is the number of the next frame to be sent, and the Receive Sequence.

inside global address   See global address.

inside interface   In NAT, this is usually a router's LAN interface. The inside interface network often uses private address space, which must be translated to a routable address before being placed on the outside network.

inside local address   The address by which a host on the inside network sees another host on the same network.

inside network   In NAT, the network on one side of the router is designated as the inside network, and the network on the other side of the router is designated as the outside network. The inside network usually deploys private address space. These addresses must be mapped to routable addresses before moving to the outside network. Typically, a company maps its local inside network addresses to one or more global outside IP addresses. It also unmaps the global IP addresses on incoming packets back into local IP addresses.

Integrated Services Digital Network   See ISDN.

interesting traffic   Traffic defined as being able to invoke a dialup connection such as an ISDN link.

internal network   In NAT, this is usually the LAN network that uses private address space.

International Telecommunication Union Telecommunication Standardization Sector   See ITU-T.

Internet Engineering Task Force   See IETF.

Internet Messaging Access Protocol   See IMAP.

Inverse ARP   Inverse Address Resolution Protocol. Describes the method of building dynamic routes in a network. Allows an access server to discover the network address of a device associated with a virtual circuit.

IPv4   Internet Protocol Version 4. The version of IP that is still in use on the Internet and in most environments. It uses a 32-bit addressing scheme, represented by four 8-bit (0 to 255) numbers separated by periods, such as 123.3.12.255. This addressing scheme allows for a maximum of about 4.3 billion numbers.

IPv6   Internet Protocol Version 6. The next generation of IP. Started in 1991, this specification was completed in 1997 by the IETF. IPv6 is backward-compatible with IPv4 and is designed to fix its shortcomings, such as data security and maximum number of user addresses.

ISDN   Integrated Services Digital Network. A communication protocol, offered by telephone companies, that permits telephone networks to carry data, voice, and other source traffic.

ISDN (like) DSL (IDSL)   IDSL (ISDN DSL) is somewhat of a misnomer, because it is closer to ISDN data rates and service at 128 Kbps than to the much higher rates of ADSL.

ITU-T   International Telecommunications Union Telecommunication Standardization Sector (formerly the Consultative Committee for International Telegraph and Telephone [CCITT]). An international organization that develops communication standards.

J–L

jitter   Analog communication line distortion caused by the variation of a signal from its reference timing positions. Jitter can cause data loss, particularly at high speeds.

LAN Local-area network. A high-speed, low-error data network covering a relatively small geographic area, up to a few thousand meters. LANs connect workstations, peripherals, terminals, and other devices in a single building or other geographically limited area. LAN standards specify cabling and signaling at the physical and data link layers of the OSI model. Ethernet, FDDI, and Token Ring are widely used LAN technologies.

LAPB Link Access Procedure, Balanced. The data link layer protocol in the X.25 protocol stack. LAPB is a bit-oriented protocol derived from HDLC.

LAPD Link Access Procedure on the D channel. The ISDN data link layer protocol for the D channel. LAPD was derived from the LAPB protocol and is designed primarily to satisfy the signaling requirements of ISDN basic access. Defined by ITU-T Recommendations Q.920 and Q.921.

LAPF Link Access Procedure for Frame Relay. The data link layer protocol used by Frame Relay as defined in ITU-T Recommendation Q9.222 and ANSI T1.618.

LAPM Link Access Procedure for Modems. An automatic repeat request (ARQ) used by modems implementing the V.42 protocol for error correction.

laptop A small, lightweight, battery-powered, mobile computing device. Laptop computers rival the power of the desktop environment while providing mobility to the user.

last mile 1. The telecommunications technology that connects the customer's home directly to the cable or telephone company. 2. The portion of the cable or telephone company that is wired directly into the customer's home.

latency 1. The delay between the time when a device requests access to a network and the time it is granted permission to transmit. 2. The delay between the time when a device receives a frame and the time that frame is forwarded out the destination port.

LCP Link Control Protocol. Establishes, configures, and tests data-link connections for use by PPP.

lease In DHCP, how long a client can use the supplied network configuration without having to ask permission from the DHCP server.

leased line A transmission line reserved by a communications carrier for a customer's private use. A leased line is a type of dedicated line.

legacy DDR When the configuration information is applied directly to the physical interface. Legacy DDR severely limits the flexibility of dial-on-demand connections and has been widely replaced by dialer profiles.

Link Access Procedure, Balanced See LAPB.

Link Access Procedure for Frame Mode Services See LAPF.

Link Access Procedure for Frame Relay See LAPF.

Link Access Procedure for Modems See LAPM.

Link Access Procedure on the D channel See LAPD.

Link Control Protocol See LCP.

link-establishment frame A type of LCP frame used to establish and configure a PPP link.

link-maintenance frame A type of LCP frame used to manage and debug a PPP link.

Link Quality Monitoring (LQM) A feature in the PPP suite that allows devices to analyze the quality of the link between them.

Link Quality Report (LQR) A type of PPP link monitoring that works by having a device request that its peer (the other device on the link) keep track of statistics about the link and send them in reports on a regular basis.

link-termination frame   A type of LCP frame used to terminate a PPP link.

LMI   Local management interface. A set of enhancements to the basic Frame Relay specification. LMI includes support for a keepalive mechanism, which verifies that data is flowing; a multicast mechanism, which provides the network server with its local DLCI and the multicast DLCI; global addressing, which gives DLCIs global rather than local significance in Frame Relay networks; and a status mechanism, which provides an ongoing status report on the DLCIs known to the switch. Known as LMT in ANSI terminology.

load balancing   In routing, a router's ability to distribute traffic over all its network ports that are the same distance from the destination address. Good load-balancing algorithms use both line speed and reliability information. Load balancing increases the utilization of network segments, thus increasing effective network bandwidth.

local access rate   The connection rate between a Frame Relay site and the Frame Relay provider.

local address   The address of a host as seen by another host on the same network.

local-area network   See LAN.

local dial number (LDN)   Also called local directory number. Used for call routing. The LDN is associated with a SPID and therefore with North American BRI interfaces. It is necessary for receiving incoming calls on the second B channel.

local loop   A line from the premises of a telephone subscriber to the telephone company CO.

local management interface   See LMI.

logical broadcast   Some protocol types have a logical broadcast address. When an address space is subnetted, the last address typically is reserved for broadcasts. All hosts on a specific network hear these broadcasts.

M

mainframe   A large computer that supports many users and has the storage and computing capacity needed for large data sets. It generally stores data on large reel-to-reel magnetic tapes that require extensive physical storage space.

MD5   Message Digest 5. An algorithm used for message authentication in SNMP v.2. MD5 verifies the communication's integrity, authenticates the origin, and checks for timeliness.

Message Digest 5   See MD5.

modem   A modulator-demodulator device that converts digital and analog signals. At the source, a modem converts digital signals to a form suitable for transmission over analog communication facilities. At the destination, the analog signals are returned to their digital form. Modems allow data to be transmitted over voice-grade telephone lines.

multicast   A single packet copied by the network and sent to a specific subset of network addresses. These addresses are specified in the destination address field.

multilink   The simultaneous use of multiple links to transmit different segments of the same message.

Multi-Link Protocol (MLP)   An extension of PPP that allows the two ISDN B channels available on a BRI to be used as a single transmission line.

multiplexing   A scheme that allows multiple logical signals to be transmitted simultaneously across a single physical channel.

multipoint   A communications line that has multiple endpoints.

N

NAT   Network Address Translation. A technique that allows a network to use one set of addresses for internal traffic and another set for traffic that must leave the network.

NAT pool   A group of IP addresses that the NAT process uses to translate an internal address to before moving the packet to the external network.

NBMA   Nonbroadcast multiaccess. A multiaccess network that either does not support broadcasting (such as X.25) or in which broadcasting is not feasible (for example, a Switched Multimegabit Data Service [SMDS] broadcast group or an extended Ethernet that is too large).

NCP   Network Control Protocol. A protocol that establishes and configures different network layer protocols, such as for AppleTalk over PPP.

Network Address Translation   See NAT.

Network Control Protocol   See NCP.

Network File System   See NFS.

network management   A generic term used to describe systems or actions that help maintain, characterize, or troubleshoot a network.

network operating system   See NOS.

network terminating unit (NTU)   Equipment at the customer premises that terminates a network access point.

Network Termination device type 1 (NT1)   A device that is required to connect ISDN terminal equipment to an ISDN line. The NT1 connects to the two-wire line (twisted-pair copper wiring) that your telephone company has assigned for your ISDN service.

Network Termination device type 2 (NT2)   An intelligent customer premises device that can perform switching and concentration, such as a digital PBX. It typically terminates primary rate access lines from the local ISDN switch.

NFS   Network File System. A commonly used distributed file system protocol suite developed by Sun Microsystems that allows remote file access across a network. In actuality, NFS is simply one protocol in the suite. NFS protocols include NFS, RPC, External Data Representation (XDR), and others. These protocols are part of a larger architecture that Sun calls Open Network Computing (ONC).

nonbroadcast multiaccess   See NBMA.

Nonreturn to Zero Level   See NRZ-L.

NOS   Network operating system. A generic term that refers to what are really distributed file systems. Examples of NOSs include LAN Manager, NetWare, NFS, and VINES.

NRZ-L   Nonreturn to Zero Level. An encoding scheme in which signals maintain constant voltage levels with no signal transitions (no return to a zero-voltage level) during a bit interval.

NT frame format   An ISDN frame format for traffic traveling from the network to the terminal.

null-modem cable   A cable used to join computing devices directly through the serial ports, rather than over a network.

O

one-layer design   A modification of the hierarchical network design model that places the functionality of all layers (core, distribution, and access) into a single layer. It is often used for extremely small networks.

one-way hash   A method of transforming data that cannot be undone. One common form of a one-way hash is Message Digest 5 (MD5).

Open Shortest Path First   See OSPF.

operating system   See OS.

OS   Operating system. A collection of software designed to provide control over the local hardware and a user interface. The OS controls hardware functionality based on user commands passed through the user interface or shell.

OSPF   Open Shortest Path First. A link-state, hierarchical Interior Gateway Protocol (IGP) routing algorithm proposed as a successor to Routing Information Protocol (RIP) in the Internet community. OSPF features include least-cost routing, multipath routing, and load balancing. OSPF was derived from an early version of the Intermediate System-to-Intermediate System (IS-IS) protocol.

out-of-band signaling   A transmission that uses frequencies or channels outside the frequencies or channels normally used for information transfer. Out-of-band signaling is often used for error reporting in situations in which in-band signaling can be affected by whatever problems the network might be experiencing.

outside interface   In NAT, this is usually the interface that connects to the Internet or WAN.

outside network   In NAT, this is usually the WAN or Internet, and it uses routable IP addresses. The outside network is connected to the outside interface.

overhead   The consumption of bandwidth by the movement of frames used for network management and that do not contain data.

overloaded NAT   See PAT.

P

packet switching   A networking method in which nodes share bandwidth with each other by sending packets.

PAP   Password Authentication Protocol. An authentication protocol that allows PPP peers to authenticate one another. The remote router attempting to connect to the local router is required to send an authentication request. Unlike CHAP, PAP passes the password and hostname or username in the clear (unencrypted). PAP does not prevent unauthorized access; it merely identifies the remote end. The router or access server then determines if that user is allowed access. PAP is supported only on PPP lines.

partial mesh   A network in which devices are organized in a mesh topology, with some network nodes organized in a full mesh and with others connected to only one or two other nodes in the network. A partial mesh does not provide the level of redundancy of a full-mesh topology, but it is less expensive to implement. Partial-mesh topologies are generally used in the peripheral networks that connect to a fully meshed backbone.

Password Authentication Protocol   See PAP.

PAT   Port address translation. A many-to-one translation of IP addresses as packets move between inside and outside networks. Usually, many private internal addresses are translated to a single routable outside IP address by assigning each translation a different port number.

peer   A computer of equal importance in a peer-to-peer networking arrangement.

peer-to-peer   Peer-to-peer computing calls for each network device to run both client and server portions of an application. Also describes communication between implementations of the same OSI model layer in two different network devices.

performance   A measurement of the efficiency of a network or computer system.

Permanent Virtual Circuit   See PVC.

Personal Computer Memory Card Industry Association (PCMCIA)   An association that produced a standardized interface for interface cards used in laptop computers. The 16-bit PCMCIA interface has been widely replaced by the 32-bit cardbus interface.

physical broadcast   A Layer 2 event whereby all bits in the Layer 2 address are set to on. This broadcast is heard by all devices at Layer 2.

physical interface   A tangible interface that can have cables connected, as opposed to a logical interface, which is a collection of configuration settings that must be applied to a physical interface for use.

Plain Old Telephone Service (POTS)   See PSTN.

playback   A type of attack in which packets are recorded from a physical medium and then are replayed later to gain access to a restricted network or device.

point of presence   See POP.

point-to-point   A type of physical connection in which one physical device is directly connected to another physical device.

Point-to-Point Protocol   See PPP.

POP   Point of presence. The point of interconnection between the communication facilities provided by the telephone company and the building's main distribution facility.

Port Address Translation   See PAT.

port replicator   A device, similar to a docking station, that allows a laptop user to permanently connect peripherals. The peripherals are connected to the port replicator, and then a laptop computer is connected when access to the devices is required.

Post Office Protocol (POP)   A protocol used by an e-mail client to retrieve e-mail from a mail server. This protocol has been widely replaced by IMAP.

PPP   Point-to-Point Protocol. A successor to SLIP, PPP provides router-to-router and host-to-network connections over synchronous and asynchronous circuits.

Predictor   An algorithm used to compress data over a PPP link.

PRI   Primary Rate Interface. An ISDN interface to primary rate access. Primary rate access consists of a single 64-Kbps D channel plus 23 (T1) or 30 (E1) B channels for voice or data.

Primary Rate Interface   See PRI.

print services   The ability of a networked computer system to field, manage, and execute print requests from other network devices.

private addresses   A collection of IP addresses that have been reserved for use on private networks only. Private addresses are specified by RFC 1918.

process-switched   An operation that provides full route evaluation and per-packet load balancing across parallel WAN links. This involves transmitting entire frames to the router CPU, where they are repackaged for delivery to or from a WAN interface. The router selects the route for each packet. Process switching is the most resource-intensive switching operation the CPU can perform.

Protocol field   A PPP frame field that identifies the protocol encapsulated in the frame's Information field.

PSTN   Public Switched Telephone Network. A general term that refers to the variety of telephone networks and services in place worldwide. Sometimes called Plain Old Telephone Service (POTS).

Public Switched Telephone Network   See PSTN.

PVC   Permanent virtual circuit. A virtual circuit that is permanently established. PVCs save bandwidth associated with circuit establishment and teardown in situations in which certain virtual circuits must exist all the time. Called a permanent virtual connection in ATM terminology.

Q–R

Q.920/Q.921   ITU-T specifications for the ISDN User-Network Interface (UNI) data link layer.

Q.931   An ITU-T specification for signaling to establish, maintain, and clear ISDN network connections.

quality of service (QoS)   A measure of performance for a transmission system that reflects its transmission quality and service availability.

RAM   The volatile memory that can be read and written by a microprocessor.

random-access memory   See RAM.

read-only memory   See ROM.

redirector   Software that intercepts requests for resources within a computer and analyzes them for remote-access requirements. If remote access is required to satisfy the request, the redirector forms a remote procedure call (RPC). It sends the RPC to lower-layer protocol software for transmission through the network to the node that can satisfy the request.

redundancy   1. In internetworking, the duplication of devices, services, or connections so that, in the event of a failure, the redundant devices, services, or connections can perform the work of those that failed. 2. In telephony, the portion of the total information contained in a message that can be eliminated without loss of essential information or meaning.

region   In a three-layer hierarchical design, individual LANs are interconnected in a star topology through access links to form an area. These areas are then connected through distribution links to form regions.

Response   The reply to a request or packet.

RFC 951   Describes the BOOTP process.

RFC 1055   Defines SLIP, which is currently a de facto standard commonly used for point-to-point serial connections running TCP/IP. It is not an Internet standard.

RFC 1334   Defines two protocols for authentication: PAP and CHAP.

RFC 1542   Provides additional information on the BOOTP process.

RFC 1631   Presents a preliminary design for NAT and discusses its pros and cons.

RFC 1661   Describes PPP, a standard method of transporting multiprotocol datagrams over point-to-point links.

RFC 1918   Describes the requirements for allocating IP address space for private networks.

RFC 1994   Describes PPP CHAP.

RFC 2131   Describes the DHCP process.

robustness   The ability of a network or device to survive failures in one or more components or processes.

ROM   Nonvolatile memory that can be read, but not written, by the microprocessor.

routable   A packet that controls an IP address that does not belong to RFC 1918 and is transported through a network.

routable address   An IP address that is not defined as part of the RFC 1918 address space for private networks.

routing loop   A network problem in which packets are routed in an endless circle.

R reference point   References the point (connection) that is between a non-ISDN-compatible device and a terminal adapter.

S

scalability   The ability of a network to easily grow to accept the addition of new servers and/or clients.

Serial Line Internet Protocol   See SLIP.

server   A node or software program that provides services to clients.

server farm   A collection of servers offering services to clients that have been collected into a single area. Duplicate servers provide for redundancy and load balancing.

Server Message Block   See SMB.

Service Access Point Identifier (SAPI)   Layer 2 information that specifies which Layer 2 data-link entity will process a Layer 2 frame, and the Layer 3 entity that will receive that information.

service profile identifier   See SPID.

service provider   A company or organization that provides subscribed-to services to another group or organization.

services   An application or process provided by a server to a client in a client/server relationship.

Signaling System 7   See SS7.

Simple Mail Transfer Protocol   See SMTP.

SLIP   Serial Line Internet Protocol. A standard protocol for point-to-point serial connections using a variation of TCP/IP.

smart serial cable   The Cisco compact, high-density Smart Serial connector supports a wide variety of electrical interfaces when used with the appropriate transition cable—the smart serial cable.

SMB   Server Message Block. A file-system protocol used in LAN Manager and similar NOSs to package data and exchange information with other systems.

SMTP   Simple Mail Transfer Protocol. An Internet protocol that provides e-mail services.

source address   The address of a network device that is sending the data.

source port   The calling port's number.

SPID   Service profile identifier. A number that some service providers use to define the services to which an ISDN device subscribes. The ISDN device uses the SPID when accessing the switch that initializes the connection to a service provider.

split horizon   A routing technique in which information about routes is prevented from exiting the router interface through which that information was received.

S reference point   References the points that connect into the NT2, or customer switching device. It is the interface that enables calls between the various customer premises equipment.

SS7   Signaling System 7. A standard common channel signaling (CCS) system used with Broadband ISDN (BISDN) and ISDN.

Stacker   A compression algorithm used to compress packets moved across a serial link.

star   A LAN topology in which endpoints on a network are connected to a common central switch by point-to-point links. A ring topology that is organized as a star implements a unidirectional closed-loop star instead of point-to-point links.

static map   A mapping of Layer 2 to Layer 3 information. An example is mapping DLCI to IP addresses in Frame Relay.

static NAT   A form of NAT that allows the network administrator to specify a mapping between inside and outside addresses. This is usually used to allow internal servers to be accessed from the outside world.

static route   A route that is explicitly configured and entered into the routing table. Static routes take precedence over routes chosen by dynamic routing protocols.

statistical multiplexing   A technique whereby information from multiple logical channels can be transmitted across a single physical channel. Statistical multiplexing dynamically allocates bandwidth only to active input channels, which makes better use of available bandwidth and allows more devices to be connected than with other multiplexing techniques. Also called statistical time-division multiplexing, or stat mux.

status-inquiry message   In Frame Relay, allows a user device to inquire about the network's status.

status message   In Frame Relay, a response to the status-inquiry message. Status messages include keepalives and PVC status messages.

subinterface   One of a number of virtual interfaces on a single physical interface.

success   Completing a task as planned with the desired results.

supervisory frame (S-frame)   Used to acknowledge frames, request retransmissions, or ask for suspension of transmission. The Supervisory code denotes the type of supervisory frame being sent.

SVC   Switched virtual circuit. A virtual circuit that is dynamically established on demand and is torn down when transmission is complete. SVCs are used in situations in which data transmission is sporadic. Called a switched virtual connection in ATM terminology.

switched virtual circuit   See SVC.

Symmetric DSL (SDSL)   Similar to HDSL, with a single twisted-pair line, carrying 1.544 Mbps (U.S. and Canada) or 2.048 Mbps (Europe) each direction on a duplex line. It's symmetric because the data rate is the same in both directions.

synchronous   A term that describes digital signals that are transmitted with precise clocking. Such signals have the same frequency, with individual characters encapsulated in control bits (called start bits and stop bits) that designate the beginning and end of each character.

T

T_c See committed rate measurement interval (T_c).

TCP/IP   A common name for the suite of protocols developed by the U.S. Department of Defense (DoD) in the 1970s to support the construction of worldwide internetworks. TCP and IP are the two best-known protocols in the suite. TCP functions at Layer 4 of the OSI model, and IP functions at Layer 3.

TDM   Time-division multiplexing. A technique in which information from multiple channels can be allocated bandwidth on a single wire based on preassigned time slots. Bandwidth is allocated to each channel regardless of whether the station has data to transmit.

TE frame format   The ISDN frame format that travels from the terminal to the network.

telco   An abbreviation for telephone company.

terminal   A simple device at which data can be entered into or retrieved from a network. Generally, terminals have a monitor and a keyboard, but no processor or local disk drive.

Terminal Adapter (TA)   A device used to connect ISDN BRI connections to existing interfaces such as EIA/TIA-232. Essentially, an ISDN modem.

Terminal Endpoint Identifier (TEI)   A field in the LAPD address that identifies a device on an ISDN interface.

Terminal Equipment type 1 (TE1)   Uses an interface that complies with the ISDN User-Network Interface (UNI) recommendations. This device can connect to and work with ISDN.

Terminal Equipment type 2 (TE2)   Uses an interface that complies with interface recommendations other than the ISDN interface recommendation. This device requires a terminal adapter to connect to and work with ISDN.

three-layer hierarchical design   The Cisco hierarchical design model that defines how networks should be designed in layers. Each layer has its own roles and responsibilities and produces a network that delivers high performance and is both manageable and scalable. The three layers are core, distribution, and access.

three-way handshake   The procedure used during CHAP authentication. A challenge is sent to the computer trying to authenticate. This challenge is a random string that is then hashed using information stored locally. The resulting hash is sent back to the device that offered the challenge. The challenging machine also performs the same hash locally. The two hashes are compared. If they are the same, a message is sent to the remote device, saying it can gain access. If the hashes are not the same, the remote machine is denied access.

TIA   Telecommunications Industry Association. A trade association representing providers of communications and information technology.

time-division multiplexing (TDM)   A technique in which information from multiple channels can be allocated bandwidth on a single wire based on preassigned time slots. Bandwidth is allocated to each channel regardless of whether the station has data to transmit.

timeout value   A timeout is an event that occurs when one network device expects to hear from another network device within a specified period of time, but does not. The timeout that results usually prompts a retransmission of information or the elimination of the session between the two devices. The specified length of time is the timeout value.

topology   A map of the physical arrangement of network nodes and media within an enterprise networking structure.

translation   In NAT, the rewriting of the source header information in an IP packet as it moves between the inside and outside networks.

translation table   The table that maintains a record of the NAT translations that are currently active.

T reference point   In ISDN, the T reference point is electrically identical to the S interface. It references the outbound connection from the NT2 to the ISDN network.

trial-and-error attack   A form of network attack in which the perpetrator continually tries to gain entry into the network by trying different passwords or techniques.

trunk line   A physical and logical connection between two ATM switches across which traffic in an ATM network travels. An ATM backbone is composed of a number of trunks.

two-layer design   A streamlined version of the three-layer hierarchical model that condenses the functions of the core, distribution, and access layers into two layers.

two-way handshake   The procedure used by PAP authentication. A device that wants to authenticate sends a username/password pair in clear text to the device. The device compares this information to the information stored locally and then either allows or denies access.

U

Uniform Resource Locator (URL)   A standardized addressing scheme to access hypertext documents and other services that use a World Wide Web (WWW) browser.

unnumbered frame (U-frame)   An HDLC frame used for various control and management purposes, including link startup and shutdown and mode specification.

U reference point   Defines the two-wire interface between the NT1 and the ISDN network owned by the phone company.

USB   Universal Serial Bus. A standard for connecting peripherals to computers, including low-bandwidth digital still and video cameras. USB supports low- and medium-bandwidth peripherals. The USB standard has at least two versions: USB 1.0 and USB 2.0. USB is managed by the Universal Serial Bus Implementers Forum, Inc. (USB-IF), a nonprofit corporation founded by the group of corporations that developed the USB specification. See http://www.usb.org/.

V

V.35   An ITU-T standard that describes a synchronous, physical layer protocol used for communications between a network access device and a packet network. V.35 is most commonly used in the U.S. and Europe and is recommended for speeds up to 48 Kbps.

Variable-Length Subnet Mask   See VLSM.

VC   Virtual circuit. A logical circuit created to ensure reliable communication between two network devices. A VC is defined by a virtual path identifier/virtual channel identifier (VPI/VCI) pair. It can be either a PVC or SVC. Virtual circuits are used in Frame Relay and X.25. In ATM, a virtual circuit is called a virtual channel.

version control   Ensuring that all users are working with the same version of data files. This is one of the benefits of client/server technology, in which files are stored on the server and shared between the clients when requested.

virtual circuit   See VC.

virus   A program designed to spread itself by first infecting executable files or the system areas of hard and floppy disks and then making copies of itself. Viruses usually operate without the knowledge or desire of the computer user.

VLSM   Variable-Length Subnet Mask(ing). The ability to specify a different subnet mask for the same network number on different subnets. VLSM can help optimize available address space.

W

WAN   Wide-area network. A data communications network that serves users across a broad geographic area and often uses transmission devices provided by common carriers. Frame Relay, SMDS, and X.25 are examples of WANs.

web browser   A GUI-based hypertext client application, such as Mosaic, used to access hypertext documents and other services located on innumerable remote servers throughout the WWW and the Internet.

wide-area network   See WAN.

wireless NIC   A network interface card designed to connect a workstation to a wireless network. A number of standards currently exist, including IEEE 802.11 a/b/g.

workstation   A powerful, single-user computer system usually used for scientific and technical applications.

World Wide Web   See WWW.

WWW   World Wide Web. A large network of Internet servers that provide hypertext and other services to terminals that run client applications, such as a WWW browser.

X

X.21   An ITU-T standard for serial communications over synchronous digital lines. The X.21 protocol is used primarily in Europe and Japan.

X.25   An ITU-T standard that defines how connections between DTE and DCE are maintained for remote terminal access and computer communications in public data networks (PDNs). X.25 specifies LAPB, a data link layer protocol, and packet-level protocol (PLP), a network layer protocol. Frame Relay has, to some degree, superseded X.25.

xDSL   A term referring to all forms of DSL technology.

Index

Notes

Notes

Notes

Notes

Notes

Notes

Notes

Notes

Notes

Notes

Register this Book for
Exclusive Content

Gain access to the following benefits when you register *WAN Technologies CCNA 4 Companion Guide* on ciscopress.com.

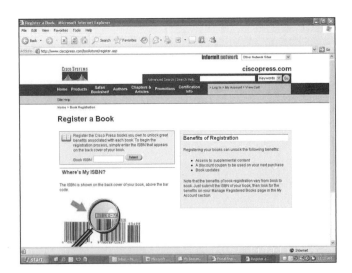

- **Packet Tracer** configuration files for activities described in the book

- PDF of chapter 5, "RIP, IGRP, and Static Route Concepts and Configuration", from *CCNA ICND Exam Certification*

- PDF of Part II, chapter 5, "Frame Relay", from *CCNA Flash Cards and Exam Practice Pack*, Second Ed.

- Coupon code for **35% off** most Cisco Press titles

To register this book, go to **www.ciscopress.com/bookstore/register.asp** and enter the book's ISBN located on the back cover. You'll then be prompted to log in or join ciscopress.com to continue registration.

After you register the book, a link to the supplemental content will be listed on your My Registered Books page.

ciscopress.com

Learning is serious business.   **Invest wisely.**